THE POLITICAL ECONOMY OF THE SPECTACLE
AND POSTMODERN CASTE

Studies in Critical Social Sciences Book Series

Haymarket Books is proud to be working with Brill Academic Publishers (www.brill.nl) to republish the *Studies in Critical Social Sciences* book series in paperback editions. This peer-reviewed book series offers insights into our current reality by exploring the content and consequences of power relationships under capitalism, and by considering the spaces of opposition and resistance to these changes that have been defining our new age. Our full catalog of *SCSS* volumes can be viewed at https://www.haymarketbooks.org/series_collections/4-studies-in-critical-social-sciences.

Series Editor
David Fasenfest (Wayne State University)

Editorial Board
Eduardo Bonilla-Silva (Duke University)
Chris Chase-Dunn (University of California–Riverside)
William Carroll (University of Victoria)
Raewyn Connell (University of Sydney)
Kimberlé W. Crenshaw (University of California–LA and Columbia University)
Heidi Gottfried (Wayne State University)
Karin Gottschall (University of Bremen)
Alfredo Saad Filho (King's College London)
Chizuko Ueno (University of Tokyo)
Sylvia Walby (Lancaster University)
Raju Das (York University)

The Political Economy of the Spectacle and Postmodern Caste

John Asimakopoulos

Haymarket Books
Chicago, IL

First published in 2019 by Brill Academic Publishers, The Netherlands.
© 2019 Koninklijke Brill NV, Leiden, The Netherlands

Published in paperback in 2020 by
Haymarket Books
P.O. Box 180165
Chicago, IL 60618
773-583-7884
www.haymarketbooks.org

ISBN: 978-1-64259-352-5

Distributed to the trade in the US through Consortium Book Sales and Distribution (www.cbsd.com) and internationally through Ingram Publisher Services International (www.ingramcontent.com).

This book was published with the generous support of Lannan Foundation and Wallace Action Fund.

Special discounts are available for bulk purchases by organizations and institutions. Please call 773-583-7884 or email info@haymarketbooks.org for more information.

Cover design by Jamie Kerry and Ragina Johnson.

Printed in United States.

10 9 8 7 6 5 4 3 2 1

Library of Congress Cataloging-in-Publication Data is available.

To the departed: academic freedom and tenure

Contents

About *The Political Economy of the Spectacle and Postmodern Caste*   IX
Foreword   X
    Greg Palast
Acknowledgements   XIV
List of Illustrations   XV

Introduction: Busting out of Plato's Cave   1

1 The Symbolic Institution of Society   3
   1 Symbolic Interactionism   5
   2 Interaction Exchange and Collective Norms   7
   3 Critical Theory and Post-Structuralism/Postmodernism   14
      3.1 *Cornelius Castoriadis*   17
      3.2 *Michel Foucault*   21
      3.3 *Guy Debord*   23
      3.4 *Jean Baudrillard*   26
   4 Beyond Post-Structuralism/Postmodernism   29

2 The Spectacle   33
   1 Audience Segmentation   33
      1.1 *Sociocultural and Spatial Segmentation*   37
      1.2 *Educational Segmentation*   40
      1.3 *Economic Segmentation*   44
      1.4 *Political Segmentation*   46
   2 Total Propaganda   47
   3 Symbolic Institutions   54
      3.1 *Educational Institutions*   55
      3.2 *Economic Institutions*   58
      3.3 *Political Institutions*   61
      3.4 *Legal Institutions*   67
      3.5 *Protective Institutions*   68

3 It's All Spectacular   73
   1 Spectacular History   73
   2 Postmodern Spectacles   79
      2.1 *Doubleplusgood: Spectacular Capitalism*   81
      2.2 *Plusgood: Spectacular Socialism/Communism*   88

    3   Spectacular Class   90
    4   The Quantum Mechanics of Value and Capital   99
        4.1   *The Relativity of Value*   99
        4.2   *There Is No Spoon: Capital(ism)*   102

4 **The Monetization of Everything**   108
    1   Life, Flesh, and Death   109
    2   Food, Water, and the Environment   120
    3   Cities, Nations, and Culture   124
    4   Time and Space   127
    5   The Global Spectacle   130
        5.1   *Finance*   131
        5.2   *Trade*   134
        5.3   *Segmented Labor*   136

5 **The Structure of Postmodern Caste**   138
    1   Social Order   138
        1.1   *Privileges and Disabilities Based on Ascription*   139
        1.2   *Who Pays the Piper?*   143
        1.3   *Extreme Structural Inequality*   146
    2   Caste Groups   157
        2.1   *Ruling Caste*   159
        2.2   *Nobles*   162
        2.3   *Privileged Labor*   164
        2.4   *Required Labor*   167
        2.5   *Precarious Labor*   169
        2.6   *Institutional Slaves*   172
    3   Legitimizing Twenty-First-Century Serfdom   177
        3.1   *Mr. Baptist Has Been Too Harsh on the Slavers*   177
        3.2   *Teaching the Right Lessons*   179

Conclusion: Bakunin's Conundrum   184

Bibliography   189
Index   217

About *The Political Economy of the Spectacle and Postmodern Caste*

"People have to engage in autonomous extra-institutional action to change social relations." Asimakopoulos's important concluding point captures the vital agenda which motivated the arguments of his new book. In accessible, straightforward and jargon-free prose, and elaborating upon Castoriadis's, Foucault's, Debord's and Baudrillard's insights, he raises fundamental and challenging questions for radical theory and praxis, and concurrently, he draws out the social and political implications of his analysis of the political economy of the society of the spectacle. Asimakopoulos's passion and commitment are remarkable.

> *Christos Memos*
> Author of *Castoriadis and Critical Theory*; Lecturer, University of Abertay Dundee, Scotland

Busting out of Plato's cave: the title of the introduction tells us what the book is about. How do we get out of here, out of this cave of lies and oppression? This is the only question worth asking. John Asimakopoulos explores the cave to its horrible depths in lively detail. And leaves us with the question of whether there is any way out other than stringing the rich up from the nearest lamppost.

> *John Holloway*
> Author of many books; Professor, Autonomous University of Puebla, Mexico

Foreword

Greg Palast

John Asimakopoulos begins by telling us we are all slaves. Hey, *thanks for that!* Now, a guy with a sensitive ego like me says, "But *I'm* not a slave." Forget it. Asimakopoulos says all us slaves are brainwashed into *believing* we are free so we don't rebel. And it's true, I haven't rebelled. Who are "They" who enslave us? You know, "Them." They are the rulers, the landlords of the planet. They own it; They suck out our resources and They suck out our soul. The soul part is what sets Asimakopoulos apart from Karl Marx.

Marx gave us "class" – stratification of We the People into *economic* groups: capitalists, bourgeois functionaries, proles (most of us) and lumpens (the under- or often-unemployed). Asimakopoulos says Marx deceived himself, ignoring the social and psychological *castes* we are locked into. And castes have been around a very long time, well before the Industrial Revolution and the Bolshevik revolution, neither of which were revolutions at all, says Asimakopoulos. Because after all the production of cars built and blood spilt, we are still divided into slave and master.

There is nothing new under the sun, Asimakopoulos says, except the "spectacle" – the social tools and images that are imposed (or dangled as temptation) for us slaves. Old slaves had Heaven and Hell to keep their noses to the rulers' grindstones. The new slaves have Facebook pages. And since we can't get no satisfaction, we grope for *status*. It's only after reading Asimakopoulos that I understood why several of my readers were absolutely indignant that I would not let them join my Facebook "friends" page (which had reached the allowed limit of 5,000 "friends.") Instead, they had to address me through my "fan" page. They didn't like the demotion: a "fan" is, after all, a subordinate, a supplicant. A "friend" is at eye level. But I really don't have 5,000 "friends." None were at my wedding – nor my divorce. It's just *spectacle*, a con, a show, my "friend."

And I am damn pleased that I have "friends" and "fans." Hundreds of thousands of them. And I have fans and friends because *I follow the Algorithm*. If I don't follow the Algorithm (or, more correctly, pay experts to pretend to be Me in the Algorithm), I will lose friends and fans. I am a slave to the Algorithm. I am a good cyber-slave on the Facebook Plantation. And like the slaves in *Gone with the Wind*, I love my master, The Algorithm. Though the status high it delivers is ridiculously short-lived. I need another fix, and another and another. Last month, my social net guru told me, I had a "reach" on Facebook and Twitter exceeding 10 million. And I want more! – Although I have no idea what "reach" means. And to Asimakopoulos, this is the key to Their Control: Addiction.

I'm an investigative reporter. (Asimakopoulos is likely amused by the claim. He'd say I play an investigative reporter on television and in newspapers. Anyway....) I had discovered that in the American state of Georgia, the election for Governor was rigged by the rulers of the state who removed 340,134 citizens from the voter rolls. So these voters could not cast ballots. They had been erased, disappeared. Vanished. And therefore, while the winner was chosen well before Election Day, the spectacle of an election marched on, with televised debates, pundits predicting a "close race," and over two million lined up to cast ballots in this mockery of democracy. The voters who were disappeared were removed from the rolls because supposedly, they'd left the state. But they hadn't. They were right there. I know. I hired experts in "address list hygiene" (the folks who know where every American was last Tuesday) to state, categorically, these voters had not moved, not disappeared, but lived in the exact addresses in Georgia where they'd always lived. But the pundits said on television: *These are the rules. They may not be fair, but this is a Democracy, so you can always vote to change the rules.* If you can vote. So we are enthralled in what Asimakopoulos calls "simulated democracy." But to expose our democracy as a spectacle, merely a shadow on the wall, is to let the hoi polloi in on the secret that they do not choose their leaders. And if you're led by those you don't choose, well, you're a slave. So the rulers must maintain what Asimakopoulos labels, "the Illusion of choices."

In such a system, I had no reason to believe I could get my revelations, my sad little rags of fact, onto the big TV shows. But my video director told me, "Don't worry, you were at the top of 'Reddit' three times!" I didn't know about this Reddit thing, but I was assured that appearing on Reddit made me temporary King of the Internet—for minutes, maybe *several* minutes. So I asked if there were a way we could get our next story on Reddit again. One day I had no idea what Reddit was, the next I would do nearly anything to get into the center ring of the Reddit Circus. Because I had found a corner of spectacle screen that surrounds us that will justify my fact-mining toils. I now need my Reddit fix. I am addicted to my new role in the Spectacle.

There are two things we do as modern slaves: we *obey* and we *pretend*. Indeed, we would not obey unless we pretended that one day, we or our children will become one of the rulers, one of Them. Because *class* mobility is difficult but not inconceivable (via luck, education, assassination leading to change of leadership, and so on), the rulers have hardened the borders of *caste*, making entry into their circle that much harder. That is, says Asimakopoulos, "The rich are endogamous." The ruling rich have intercourse with the ruling rich. "Intercourse" as in meeting, conversing, exchanging ideas and children—all in a tight iron-enclosed corral exemplified by The Jockey Club, Skull and Bones, New Orleans Mardi Gras *crewes*, the Republican National Committee, the

Clinton Foundation, the Comintern, the front table at Cipriani in the basement of the New York Stock Exchange, the Federal Reserve Board, the red carpet at the seasonal opening of the Met, the poker table at the Petroleum Club, the Vatican, Bohemian Grove, the annual dinner party in the Hamptons honoring Michael Milken's prostate (there is such a thing. I know, because, undercover, I worked my way in among a bevy of nine dining billionaires).

It's a mating ritual too. Their daughters fuck their sons while their fathers fuck the rest of us. The mothers look gorgeously sculpted, take yoga and downers. (They are chemical concubine slaves, but we cry not for those warming in the master's house.) In other words, They are real good at remaining Them. Notes Asimakopoulos:

> Pierre-Louis La Rochefoucauld, duc d'Estissac, a well-known postmodern [French] noble, is the ninth generation grandson of François Alexandre Frédéric de La Rochefoucauld,

And, as his forebears, he remains richer than God. And, in the USA, the measure of inequality,

> the income Gini in postmodern 2016 was 0.481—higher than the feudal thirteen colonies at 0.437 in 1774.

Revolutionary change? Feh! China's inequity Gini matches the US almost exactly.

It seems there has been no real change since that pre-historic time, described by Rousseau, when Thug said to Ugh, "Here is a line I've drawn around the best dirt and if you step over the line, I'll hit you on the head with this big rock." And so Ugh accepted the legitimacy of private property and Thug's authority. Same as it ever was. But now, it's more entertaining, more enchanting. "Enchanting" as in "under a spell." (I'm proud that I get more mentions in this book than Rousseau—There's that false status thing again.) In *The Wizard of Oz*, Toto, that little rascal of a dog, chases the Wizard out from behind a curtain and the man behind the spectacle was exposed. Exposure eliminated his power which was all based on the *imagery* of power, fear and legitimate authority. The curtain was pulled back. Simple. But how do you pull back the curtain when it surrounds you? Asimakopoulos quotes Baudrillard:

> *Disneyland is presented as imaginary in order to make us believe that the rest is real, whereas all of Los Angeles and the America that surrounds it are no longer real.*

Writing from LA, I feel it directly. It's kind of scary. I go on television here in Los Angeles—and think I'm leaving reality to perform. But in fact, I may be just switching screens. I was allowed one fleeting moment on the MSNBC screen. This was my chance to shout, "The emperor has no clothes! – America has no elections! It's all fixed." But my message comes out: "Obey your television! It will tell you the newest truth!" Because a bit of dissent simply legitimizes the spectacle, very much like the shitting monk in the corner of a crèche legitimizes the fantasy that the baby boy in the straw was born of a virgin. If you pretend, you will obey. We are like that guy at the end of the film *2001* in a museum created by extraterrestrials. We can do what we want—as long as we don't leave the museum. We *are* the spectacle.

So, are we screwed? Well, yes, says Asimakopoulos. And so, he concludes, we are justified in picking up the gun against the 3,000-year-old aristocracy and their Slaves-R-Us system:

> "[R]esistance by the oppressed in a caste-war, declared by elites, is not terrorism but self-defense through guerrilla warfare"

...even though he has already told us there have been no successful revolutions, because the guys with the guns simply want to join the circle of self-reproducing monsters. Ah, well, happy endings are for chumps. For slaves.

Journalist Greg Palast is the author of The Best Democracy Money Can Buy *and co-director of the film of the same name.*

Acknowledgements

I am deeply indebted and grateful for the works and guidance of my friend and colleague Richard Gilman-Opalsky, my mentor in postmodern philosophy. My colleague and wife Karen Márquez-Aponte helped me reflect on many ideas in this work and contributed as an exemplary research assistant. She has my deepest gratitude. Special recognition is due to David Fasenfest, editor of this series (Studies in Critical Social Sciences) and the journal *Critical Sociology*, for his lifetime work and support of progressive scholarship. He is one of the many unsung heroes of academia who help work like this see the light of day. I thank my parents, George and Georgia, for society's thankless job of raising a postmodern working-class family and for their love. I am also indebted to professional copyeditors, especially Chris Dodge. His meticulous copyediting has saved me from much embarrassment. Although I am not a gambler, I also thank Lady Luck for being employed as a tenured professor, which makes my academic production possible. It might have been otherwise. Countless potential discoveries, innovations, and advancements are never made because most faculty and intellectuals have been discarded, living as coffee baristas and wait staff versus the alternative of a homeless existence in a McDonaldized contingent academia. Last but not least, I thank my colleagues Joel Nathan Rosen and "brother" Ali Shehzad Zaidi, for helping edit parts of this manuscript; the job was torturous at best.

Illustrations

Figure

5.1 Annual two-parent, two-child family budgets in 10 largest family budget areas, 2014   166

Tables

2.1 Wealth distribution in 2013 for the bottom 90%, top 10% and 1% of households   59
5.1 Wealth shares in percentages and Gini for six countries   148, 149
5.2 Income shares in percentages and Gini for six countries   150, 151
5.3 Feudal caste groups and land/wealth distribution in percentages for five countries   152, 153

Introduction: Busting out of Plato's Cave

Morpheus: Can you tell me, Neo, why are you here? ... Do you believe in fate, Neo?
Neo: No.
Morpheus: Why not?
Neo: Because I don't like the idea that I'm not in control of my life.
Morpheus: Let me tell you why you are here. You have come because you know something. What you know you can't explain but you feel it. You've felt it your whole life, felt that something is wrong with the world. You don't know what, but it's there like a splinter in your mind, driving you mad. It is this feeling that brought you to me. Do you know what I'm talking about?
Neo: The Matrix?
Morpheus: Do you want to know what it is? The Matrix is everywhere, it's all around us, here even in this room. You can see it out your window or on your television. You feel it when you go to work or go to church or pay your taxes. It is the world that has been pulled over your eyes to blind you from the truth.
Neo: What truth?
Morpheus: That you are a slave, Neo. Like everyone else, you were born into bondage, kept inside a prison that you cannot smell, taste, or touch. A prison for your mind.

–*The Matrix*

What better way to enslave people than to convince them that they are free because anyone can see physical chains but few can perceive mental shackles. You too are a slave. You probably do not know it, and that is because you are not supposed to. You were intended for a life of servitude before you were born. You think you live in a class system in which anyone can achieve fame, fortune, and power. That opportunity is everywhere, and all you have to do is grab your piece of the pie. Yet somehow, deep down, beyond the media propaganda celebrating you and your nation, you have a feeling that something is just not right with the world as it is presented to you. You are correct.

David Graeber concluded his 2011 book *Debt: The First 5,000 Years* with a chapter titled "1971: The Beginning of Something Yet to Be Determined"—referring to the neoliberal transformation begun in the 1970s.[1] In my own

---

[1] Graeber, 2011.

research I started with the hypothesis that neoliberalism was a break from capitalism and reintroduced caste relations from past epochs. However, my findings were clear: there has been no change when it comes to caste. There have been no new epochs, no new modes of production. Rather, caste has been the only constant. The only change is its dress that theorists perceived as distinct economic systems or epochs. What we have today is a caste system, and the odds are that you are at the bottom of it.

This position resolves the contradiction of free and wage labor coexisting alongside slave and indentured labor including financial systems, merchant trade, industry, and more found throughout history—not just during capitalism. Marxists may disagree, saying that at least the legal system under capitalism is not based on feudal privileges. But it is. Slavery was codified in the United States up to 1864 and has been legally practiced thereafter in various reincarnations, through Jim Crow and segregation up to 1964 but continuing to this day through prison Jim Crow.[2] In fact, the legal code forming the basis of many modern legal systems is inherited from the Corpus Juris Civilis of AD 529, when Byzantine emperor Justinian I codified ancient Roman law going back to the Twelve Tables of 449 BC.

Orthodox ideology is a 'spectacular' version of reality and therefore false upon conception. There are no historical inevitabilities. That idea was propaganda by Marx and Engels to sell their ideas as scientific in order to discredit Bakunin (an anarchist) during the First International. Economic determinism was mostly based on Engels's effort to develop what he coined "scientific socialism," although he considered the base–superstructure relationship to be reciprocal. Ironically, there is ample evidence that Marx was not as deterministic as others paint him, and many theorists since have rejected such determinism. Another problem for us with Marx is that he lived long and was a prolific writer, and so there are countless contradictions and unclear meanings, as well as evolution of thought from the twenty-year-old student Marx to the sixty-three-year-old Marx. His theories of value, exploitation, history, and more should be seen for what they are: analytical tools rather than scientific laws. Modern thinkers need to move beyond the 'sacred' writings of dead nineteenth-century white men and focus on what remains constant: unequal distribution of material resources, power, and authority.

---

2 Alexander, 2012.

CHAPTER 1

The Symbolic Institution of Society

In hierarchical orders, elites control the social structure and cultural production. Every society has a structure comprising statuses and roles within groups, networks, and institutions. Statuses are socially defined positions within a group or society—work status, for example. Statuses can be achieved or ascribed, but overall one has a dominant master status.[1] Achieved status is something that one has to work for, to obtain through one's own efforts—becoming a licensed plumber, for example. Ascribed statuses are those we are born into without our consent and over which we have no power to change—one's skin color, for example, or whether or not one is born into a royal family. A master status is the status that dominates all others in determining an individual's overall position in society. Hierarchical orders rank ascribed statuses, such as white skin and black skin, and achieved statuses, such as being a plumber versus being a lawyer. These status rankings are derived by power relations reflecting the interests of the dominant group. Elites imbed these rankings in society's structure to maintain their privileges and pass them to their descendants. Consequently, all status rankings are caste-based and therefore ascribed to one degree or another. Thus, every hierarchical order is either an established caste system or one in the making. In horizontal (egalitarian) orders, there are no rankings of status, but the reality is that there will be differences in achieved status. For example, someone will earn a reputation as an exceptional computer programmer. What would be lacking in an egalitarian order is a quantitative ranking linked to differential remuneration, power, or authority.

Social roles are a set of expectations that are attached to a specific status. For example, the status of mother carries with it social roles including that of caregiver, educator, et cetera.[2] In hierarchical orders people relate to each other through a narrow set of roles delimited by dominant relations. In postmodern society, it is market relations mediated through images that shape how we relate to others. These are social relations between alienated individuals. For example, a marriage is exalted as a partnership between two individuals, with benefits such as combined finances. In horizontal orders people relate as individuals based on egalitarian social relations that cut across a variety of social roles and statuses. At work, for example, a woman may be an employee,

---

1 See Merton, 1968: 422–438.
2 Ibid.

a mother whose parental needs are respected, and a citizen with equal resources, power, and authority as her supervisor or governmental administrator.

Groups are formed by people who share similar values and beliefs and who interact regularly. We belong to numerous groups and so have multiple affiliations. Unfortunately, in hierarchical structures multiple group affiliations tend not to cut across social strata. If they do, there will typically be an internal social hierarchy reflecting the hierarchy of groups in society. Thus, people's social networks are limited to their social strata, and their opportunities are limited accordingly. Further limiting, in postmodern societies many groups are not real but virtual, existing in cyberspace. Therefore, social interactions in cyberspace are not real but simulations of real world interactions.

Social institutions formalize power relations that shape the organizing principles of a society. These reproduce and reinforce dominant relations through socialization. For example, Gramsci wrote that cultural hegemony in advanced capitalist societies uses compulsory schooling, the mass media, and popular culture to indoctrinate people in the dominant ideology.[3] Key institutions include political, economic, religious, and educational bodies, as well as the military, the family, and news media. If people spend most of their time interacting within hierarchical spaces, including at work, school, church, and home, are they living in a democratic society? Can equality be checked at the door from nine to five and resume thereafter? In horizontal orders, institutions reflect the common good derived by a demos with equal resources, power, and authority. These principles are ideally incorporated into the institution of the family, which is the foundation of society. Overall, institutions function as administrative bureaucracies facilitating and implementing decisions by the citizenry. Essentially these are public utilities.

Social interaction creates culture. In hierarchical orders, the general culture (as opposed, for example, to subcultures) is always that of the dominant group. It is a set of beliefs and practices that maintain and reproduce social relations based on unequal distribution of resources, power, and authority. Major cultural elements include values, norms, sanctions, and language. Values are collective conceptions of what is considered good, desirable, and proper, or bad, undesirable, and improper in a culture. These are elite values in hierarchical orders and values of the demos in horizontal orders. Values are reflected in norms, which are expected patterns of behavior backed by sanctions. Every society requires common norms for social integration. In hierarchical orders, norms are determined and imposed top-down by elites, therefore these are alienated norms for everyone else. In horizontal orders, norms are derived

---

3 Gramsci, 1971.

through natural interactions of the demos that are repeated and institutionalized. Sanctions are penalties and rewards for conduct concerning a social norm. Conformity to norms is rewarded with positive sanctions, whereas nonconformity is punished with negative sanctions. In hierarchical orders, elites use sanctions to maintain their rule. In horizontal orders, sanctions are used to maintain norms commonly agreed upon for the good of the individual and society.

The foundation of every culture, however, is language, defined as an abstract system of word meanings and symbols. Language is a powerful tool of socialization, and according to the Sapir-Whorf hypothesis it shapes how we perceive the world. In hierarchical orders, elites possess linguistic dominance. Linguistic structures shape our cognitive scheme and therefore, as conceptualized by Foucault, the framework of the overall discourse of society. Language is used as a delivery device for propaganda to maintain the conformity and complacency of the population. In horizontal orders, language is a medium of communication between sovereigns. It shapes our cognition and enables discourse through collective egalitarian values and the equal distribution of resources, power, and authority.

The only material elements of society are people and things they construct or manufacture, such as buildings, infrastructure, and objects such as staplers. All other elements constituting society—statuses, roles, groups, institutions (as concepts), values, norms, sanctions, and language—are nonmaterial, mental constructs with symbolic meanings created through repeated social interaction.

1   Symbolic Interactionism

Society is constructed out of symbolic meanings. Auguste Comte (1798–1857), founder of Western sociology, argued (in contrast to the argument of political economists) that the basic unit of society is not the individual but the family, broken down in its simplest form to the couple.[4] Thus, society is based on a symbolic blood union of two peoples. Families across cultures and time have also included adopted members, and people away from their blood families sometimes create new ones, as, for example, incarcerated women who assume roles as mothers, daughters, wives, and husbands. This reflects human nature: people are social animals with an innate need for human interaction. Peter

---

4   Coser, 2003.

Blau referred to this need as "social attraction," the building block of society.⁵ This is why even the most hardened prisoners break down at the idea of solitary confinement.

George Herbert Mead (1863–1951) and Charles Horton Cooley (1864–1929) founded symbolic interactionism, one of three major sociological perspectives focusing on microsociology and social psychology. Symbolic interactionism is derived from the American philosophy of pragmatism. The term itself was coined by Mead's student Herbert Blumer (1900–1987). Blumer argued that people act toward things based on the meaning they ascribe to them.⁶ These meanings are derived from social interaction that is modified through interpretation and inner reflection, mediated through rituals, symbols, and language that create meaning. For interactionists, the environment in which the interaction takes place is also important in creating meaning or the "definition of the situation."⁷ In *Social Organization*, Cooley developed the concept of "primary groups."⁸ These are among the most powerful agents of socialization, and from these we obtain our values, beliefs, and overall sense of morality. Using the concept of the "looking-glass self," Cooley further established the link between an individual's conceptualization of self through social interaction and the dual relationship between an individual and society.⁹

For symbolic interactionists, all social reality—including stratification—is entirely constructed, based on shared ascribed meanings placed on symbols, objects, people, and places. Classical sociologist Émile Durkheim believed that a "moral sentiment" of the "conscious collective" is needed to maintain social cohesion.¹⁰ This moral sentiment regulates our behavior by means of internalized and commonly held values and beliefs. For Mead too, social interaction

---

5   Blau, 1992.
6   Blumer, 1986.
7   William Isaac Thomas developed the concept of "definition of the situation": "Preliminary to any self-determined act of behavior there is always a stage of examination and deliberation which we may call the 'definition of the situation'. And actually not only concrete acts are dependent on the definition of the situation, but gradually a whole life-policy and the personality of the individual himself follow from a series of such definitions" (Thomas, 1923: 42).
8   A primary group is a small group characterized by intimate, face-to-face association and cooperation. Primary groups are powerful agents of socialization and impact the development of roles and statuses. See Cooley, 1909.
9   *Looking-glass self* refers to the process of obtaining a sense of self (the unique identity that distinguishes a person from others) through interactions with others. This includes how we present ourselves to others and how others evaluate us. Cooley, 1909.
10 The conscious collective is a set of shared beliefs, ideas, and moral attitudes that operate as a unifying force in society. See Durkheim, 1984.

leads to commonly agreed upon rules and norms of behavior.[11] Over time, through repeated interactions, these meanings and values become institutionalized, assuring continued reproduction of existing social relations. This demonstrates, as Blumer believed, that the creation of social reality is a continuous process, a praxis driven by human agency. However, under capitalism, market relations have encroached on our time. Thus, most people interact through a narrow set of social roles delimited by a market logic, to the detriment of all other social roles. The implication is that moral sentiment, commonly agreed norms, institutionalized meanings, and social reality in postmodern society are derived from market-based interactions.

Contemporary analytical conflict theorist Randall Collins identifies the roots of social stratification in symbolic interaction, through what he terms "interaction ritual chains."[12] Rituals produce and reproduce symbols (and therefore meaning) that people incorporate in their social interactions. However, symbols and meanings are stratified, some valued more than others. Therefore, stratification is constructed at the microsociological level through social rituals and interactions.

Rituals play an important role in socialization. These include national celebrations like Memorial Day, pledging allegiance to a flag, or the deference shown to people of high status or authority. Rituals are intended to habituate the demos into irrational allegiances, identifications, and beliefs. These also serve to alter, create, shape, and institutionalize memory. On Thanksgiving, Native American genocide is not mentioned. On Memorial Day, fallen soldiers are remembered but not the real reasons they were sent to war, beyond the formal national narrative that is propaganda.

2 Interaction Exchange and Collective Norms

Critical sociologist Peter Blau (1918–2002) connected symbolic meanings, values, and social stratification through social exchange theory, a variant of rational choice theory combining economics and behavioral psychology.[13] Irrespective of Blau's own conceptualizations, a fundamental premise of social exchange theory is that all human interactions involve forms of exchange. These exchanges are not limited to market or monetary transactions or even to tangible things. Rather these can include anything from social obligations

---

11   Coser, 2003.
12   Collins, 2004.
13   Blau, 1992.

to emotional exchanges, as with a personal relationship. Thus, the concept of exchange (fiercely resisted by communists and anarchists) is not the exclusive purview of capitalism or economics. Another point of exchange theory is that people will exchange what they value. In this sense, conceptually, value originates from a social relationship, based on social interaction (exchange). It is social interaction that determines the value of what is being exchanged within a broader cultural context. Yet the context in which an exchange takes place is itself a product of a society's collective social interactions. Even more important, exchange is not static but an ongoing process. It is through the continuous process of exchange that norms of fair value emerge. This is the relationship basis of exchange and value. An exchange (relationship) is an ongoing process that reproduces itself in a dialectical manner. Value is not something natural but rather something imagined, for without a society there can be no value.

Accordingly, Weber identified four types of "social action" based on different rationalities and values. These include goal-oriented rational action (*zweckrational*), typically based on logical or scientific (measurable) calculations. This type is associated with classical economics that assumes people are rational actors seeking to maximize their utility. Value-oriented action (*wertrational*), occurs when individuals use rational means to achieve subjective goals defined by subjective meaning. For example, in many traditional societies an honor killing may be valued as a goal even if that entails a long prison sentence or execution. Emotional or affective action combines means and ends, making it emotional and impulsive. Here the means themselves are emotionally fulfilling and become ends in themselves. For example, a person catching one's spouse in the act of intercourse with someone else may find it appropriate to stab the spouse multiple times, as police reports sometimes document. Traditional action occurs when the means and ends are determined by custom and tradition. An example would be the succession of monarchs.

For Blau, social attraction leads to social relations and exchange, through which we obtain social integration, the establishment of friendship bonds but also of domination.[14] Social integration is achieved with small exchanges that eventually lead to trust and expanded exchange. The series of exchanges leads to the establishment of general norms such as reciprocity. Exchange also leads to the differentiation of society. Blau observes that people value social approval and seek it, as George Caspar Homans argued.[15] Social approval is based on conformity to general norms such as reciprocity. Therefore, there is a voluntary aspect to the acceptance of stratification.

---

14 Ibid.
15 Homans, 1974.

If people seeking social approval internalize social norms and values favoring inequality, they will be socialized into hierarchies and the reproduction of inequalities. As Max Stirner argued prior to symbolic interactionism—and contemporary non-sociologist thinkers John Zerzan and Hakim Bey have afterward—ultimately inequality has its origins in the internalization of symbols and therefore culture itself.[16] Zerzan argues, similarly to Foucault, that internalization of symbols is a form of domination through culture. Thus, those who control the production of symbols, meanings, and language (Debord's spectacle) shape the social order. These are elements of the dominant ideology reflecting the culture of the group in power. For example, the expression 'time is money' demonstrates activity for profit to be a valued social norm in a market society. This is why Debord, Zerzan, and Bey, among others, believe that disrupting dominant meanings, symbols, and so on through various forms of cultural *détournement* is the best and most effective form of resistance in postmodern spectacular society.

The process of exchange can be equitable, with equal rewards moving from one party to another, but power differentials are created if there is an unequal exchange. You have power if you can offer what others need but they have nothing to offer that you value. Those who have nothing valuable will offer their conformity in exchange for what they need. Peoples' acceptance of power over them is rooted in generalized norms of conforming if the benefits outweigh the cost.[17] However, by choosing to do without certain goods and services, we can end power over us.[18] This is one thing when it comes to designer clothing or iPhones, which are unnecessary and have plenty of substitutes available, but it is another thing when real material needs like food, water, and shelter are monopolized.

Unlike Homans, it is these general norms of exchange that Blau uses to explain the greater structure of society. These common norms and values make indirect exchange possible. In this regard, Blau discusses universalistic values as media of differentiation and exchange. These values give rise to differentiation because all in society accept them but not all have them. Second, by becoming an indirect form of exchange, these values give rise to money, as Georg Simmel posited.[19] Money is a medium of exchange that can be measured, evaluated, and offered in indirect exchanges because of its general acceptability.

---

16 Bey, 2003; Stirner, 2004; Zerzan, 1999.
17 Blau, 1992.
18 Ibid.: 118–119.
19 Simmel, 2011.

Blau demonstrates that institutions (upon which social structures rest) are created by a series of micro-social exchanges that abide by societal norms and values. Blau says that three conditions must be met for aspects of social structures to become institutionalized. Patterns of organized community life must become formalized and part of the historical conditions that persist through time; social values that legitimate these patterns must be transmitted in the process of socialization; and society's dominant groups must be interested in the reproduction of these patterns. These reflect the historical dimensions of social life, the impact of the past on the present. Institutions constrain the social structure just as they constrain the behavior of individuals. However, over time people can change the institutions that confine them.

The cultural heritage of a society contains a counter-institutional component consisting of unrealized values and ideals. The cognitive dissonance between unrealized but culturally expected ideals results in people opposing existing institutions, and thus change. Social mobility and conflict contribute to structural change of population structures.[20] When power is not exercised fairly—for example, when it is exploitative—it leads to collective rationalization not to obey. This gives birth to opposition ideologies and movements, identical to Homans's aggression-approval proposition.[21] Power differences create pressure toward change, since it can be assumed that people experience submission to power as a hardship from which they would prefer to escape. Alternatively, advantages that people may derive from their ruler or government may outweigh the hardships of submitting, thus neutralizing the power imbalance. The significance of power imbalances for social change depends therefore on the reactions of the governed to the exercise of power. Social norms define what power demands are fair or just and which ones are excessive in relationship to the advantages. Although legitimate authority rests on social norms and sanctions collectively agreed upon by subordinates, this does not mean that all groups in a society support institutionalized authority or even that a majority do, as Merton pointed out.[22]

Structural conflict is linked to status group inequality, group size, social mobility between groups, and the probability of intergroup social contact. For Blau and Simmel, multi-group affiliations and intersections lead to a reduction in the intensity and occurrences of conflict. Group and especially individual mobility reduce conflict. But if unequal distribution of power and authority cut across multi-group affiliations and intersections of consequence, increasing

---

20   Blau, 1992.
21   Homans, 1974.
22   Merton, 1968.

these would only reveal the general inequality structurally produced along caste lines void of substantive mobility. To use Weber's terminology, a person will realize that one's class, status, and power rankings are consistently low, which sociologists term "status consistency."

Max Weber (1864–1920) was an analytical critical theorist associated with the Frankfurt School and classical sociology. His work also provided the foundations for the development of symbolic interactionism. For him, symbolic meanings are the basis of social structures. Unlike Marx, who focused on relations in production, Weber identified two structural forms of stratification derived from power and honor that condition the economic and social orders. He did not privilege one over the other, arguing that the two orders are interconnected.

"Economic order" refers to production from which stratification based on Marxian concepts of class or "market situation" stem. For Weber, class situation ("class position" or "class location" in Marxist terms) is synonymous with "class," "life chances," and "market situation":

> (1) a number of people have in common a specific causal component of their life chances, in so far as (2) this component is represented exclusively by economic interests in the possession of goods and opportunities for income, and (3) is represented under the conditions of the commodity or labor markets. [These points refer to 'class situation,' which we may express more briefly as the typical chance for a supply of goods, external living conditions, and personal life experiences, in so far as this chance is determined by the amount and kind of power, or the lack of such, to dispose of goods or skills for the sake of income in a given economic order. The term 'class' refers to any group of people that is found in the same class situation.][23]

Weber believes that class position does not necessarily lead to class-based economic or political action unless it results from an understanding of the causes of that position and its consequences. Here he echoes Marx's conceptualization of class consciousness. Therefore, "class" as an economic category or social relation is not exclusive to the capitalist epoch any more than stratification by status is exclusive to feudalism.

"Social order" refers to society generally, in what is more commonly known contemporarily as the social sphere (as distinguished from the economic sphere). The major components of the social order, especially consumption

---

23 Quoted in Gerth and Mills, 1946: 181. Brackets in original.

patterns, are cultural. Accordingly, people form "status groups" that are stratified by honor. Weber writes: "'Classes' are stratified according to their relations to the production and acquisition of goods; whereas 'status groups' are stratified according to the principles of their *consumption* of goods as represented by special 'styles of life.' . . . The differences between classes and status groups frequently overlap."[24]

Status group membership determines one's "status situation"—in Weber's words, "every typical component of the life fate of men that is determined by specific, positive or negative, social estimation of *honor*."[25] Honor, in turn, is based on lifestyles that are themselves symbolic, a point made by Thorstein Veblen.[26] Lifestyles include consumption of certain goods, status distinctions based on rituals, restrictions on social intercourse, marriage, and dress (and against performing physical labor), and more. Weber writes: "In content, status honor is normally expressed by the fact that above all else a specific *style of life* can be expected from all those who wish to belong to the circle. Linked with this expectation are restrictions on 'social' intercourse (that is, intercourse which is not subservient to economic or any other of business's functional purpose). These restrictions may confine normal marriages to within the status circle and may lead to complete endogamous closure."[27] For Weber, the deferential distribution of honor and status upon which the social order rests are illegitimately obtained: "The members of almost inaccessible sects and all sorts of circles setting themselves apart by means of any other characteristics and badges . . . usurp 'status' honor. The development of status is essentially a question of stratification resting upon usurpation. Such usurpation is the normal origin of almost all status honor. . . . For all practical purposes, stratification by status goes hand in hand with a monopolization of ideal and material goods or opportunities, in a manner we have come to know as typical."[28] Therefore, the social structure determines the distribution of power—beyond economic resources: "The structure of every legal order directly influences the distribution of power, economic or otherwise. . . . 'Economically conditioned' power is not, of course, identical with 'power' as such. On the contrary, the emergence of economic power may be the consequence of power existing on other grounds."[29]

---

24 Weber, quoted in Gerth and Mills, 1946: 193.
25 Ibid.: 187.
26 Veblen, 2012.
27 Weber, quoted in Gerth and Mills, 1946: 187–188.
28 Ibid.: 188, 190.
29 Ibid.: 180.

Weber argues that periods of technological or economic transformation disrupt existing social orders, implying a power struggle between competing elites. The ongoing exchange of power elites during the transition period gives the impression of structural mobility. However, over time, new estimations of group honor are established, along with positive and negative privileges. Therefore, Weber concludes that stratified social orders evolve into caste systems by structurally embedding predetermined opportunities for the life chances of each status group (e.g., in legal code):

> Every technological repercussion and economic transformation threatens stratification by status and pushes the class situation into the foreground. Epochs and countries in which the naked class situation is of predominant significance are regularly the periods of technical and economic transformations. And every slowing down of the shifting of economic stratifications [mobility] leads, in due course, to the growth of status structures and makes for a resuscitation of the important role of social honor.... But the road from this purely conventional situation to legal privilege, positive, or negative, is easily traveled as soon as a certain stratification of the social order has in fact been 'lived in' and has achieved stability by virtue of a stable distribution of economic power.... Where the consequences have been realized to their full extent, the status group evolves into a closed 'caste.'[30]

Dahrendorf points out: "In translating Weber's term *Stand*, most translators have used the word 'status.' This—though not false—is misleading in that it does not convey the double meaning of the German Stand as 'status' and 'estate.' In the passage quoted here, Weber undoubtedly meant to describe status in an estate context (rather than, for example, prestige status). This is only one example of the exigencies of translations—and of their creativity. By the very fact of misleading they can create terms that acquire a life of their own."[31] Castoriadis too considers hierarchical orders to be castes derived from unequal distribution of resources among families.[32]

In addition, Weber pointed out that when "there are underlying differences which are held to be 'ethnic' . . . these people form communities, acquire specific occupational traditions of handicrafts or of other arts, and cultivate a belief in their ethnic community. They live in a 'diaspora' strictly segregated

---

30 Ibid.: 188, 194.
31 Dahrendorf, 1959: 7, footnote 5.
32 Castoriadis 1993: 223.

from all personal intercourse, except that of an unavoidable sort, and their situation is legally precarious."[33] When these differences solidify into 'status segregation', extreme caste orders emerge. The various ethnicities and social groups that formerly lived in a horizontal order become stratified into a hierarchical system. These caste groups are tolerated because they serve certain functions for the social order—for example, to serve as soldiers. Although Weber used the Jewish diaspora as an example, the same is true of groups in the United States like blacks. They are an African diaspora, structurally segregated, perform work reserved for them (e.g., in low-wage fast-food jobs), and their situation is precarious both economically and existentially as the epidemic of killings by police demonstrate. This community also serves a number of systemic functions—for example, they are overrepresented in the low ranks of soldiers and provide a source of profit under the new prison Jim Crow.[34]

Thus, for Weber, status is social esteem derived from estates (the double meaning of the German *Stand*). This is logical since status is an expression of a lifestyle. But estates are castes. The term "estate" is designated for European caste systems to distinguish them from those of other regions (based, for example, on Hinduism).

3   Critical Theory and Post-Structuralism/Postmodernism

To this day, critical theory in the social sciences (especially sociology) is dominated by the works of two nineteenth-century white men. One is Marx, a critical conflict theorist, while the other is Weber, an analytical conflict theorist. Contemporary conflict theory within the sociological perspective has been stalled in Marxist critical theory, with revivals in analytical conflict theory. The most important theoretical developments have been by autonomists delving into sociology but still rooted in the Marxist tradition and philosophy. Their strength and insights are primarily due to their combining of Marxism with anarchist theory. Anarchist theory is a broader approach than Marxism (often refuting Marx). It is social critical theory with many variants representing a more fruitful and evolving approach.

Some of the most important social critical thinkers of the twentieth century have been post-structuralists or postmodernists, with the terms "post-structuralism" and "postmodernism" contested. Meanings vary according to discipline—for example, psychology, art, or the social sciences. These theorists

---

33 Gerth and Mills, 1946: 189.
34 See Alexander on the new Jim Crow (2012).

represent an evolution from Marxist theory and a break from it. This is true of Debord, Castoriadis, and Baudrillard, who began as Marxists but broke from Marxism in their later writings. For some critical scholars, postmodernism is not a significant intellectual development.[35] According to Alex Callinicos it was born in the aftermath of the 1960s uprisings out of the political frustration and social mobility of disillusioned revolutionaries who were assimilated into the professional and managerial classes.

Post-structuralism and postmodernism emerged from continental structuralism. The later was derived from philosophy and linguistics largely in response to French humanism and existentialism by intellectuals such as Jean-Paul Sartre. In contrast to sociological structuralism, which focuses on macro-social structures (and is associated with the functionalist sociological perspective), continental structuralism is a micro-social approach centered on linguistics—the study of the structure and meaning of language and signs. According to linguistics (e.g., the Sapir-Whorf hypothesis), we conceptualize the world through language. Meanings, the mind, and social world are shaped by linguistic structures. Ferdinand de Saussure (1857–1913), considered the founder of linguistics and a noted semiotician, influenced postmodern theorists including Jacques Derrida (1930–2004), Roland Barthes (1915–1980), and Jean Baudrillard. Charles W. Morris (1901–1979) was another important figure; as a behaviorist he had broken with his mentor, George Herbert Mead. However, sociologists (e.g., critical theorist and philosopher Jürgen Habermas) have increasingly been drawn to continental structuralism and linguistics.

Philosopher and linguist Barthes, considered to be the founder of semiotics, has been influential in structuralism, post-structuralism, social theory, and anthropology. Semiotics, originally distinct from sociology, takes a broader view than linguistics, although remaining a micro approach. It goes beyond linguistic structures, examining all communication, including meaning-making and structures of sign and symbol systems. Semiotics is generally divided into three branches: semantics (the relation between signs and the things to which they refer; i.e., their meaning), syntactics (the relation among or between signs in formal structures), and pragmatics (the relation between signs and sign-using agents or interpreters).

Continental structuralism is often associated with the French "Gang of Four" that included Foucault, Barthes, Claude Levi-Strauss (1908–2009), an anthropologist and ethnologist widely regarded as the father of structural anthropology, and Jacques Lacan (1901–1981), a psychoanalyst and psychiatrist

---

35 See, for example, Alex Callinicos, 1990.

who influenced linguistics, critical and literary theory, French philosophy, sociology, feminist theory, and film theory.

Jacques Derrida (1930–2004), a philosopher who influenced anthropology, historiography, sociolinguistics, psychoanalysis, and political theory, is considered the starting point of post-structuralism. Postmodern theory, popular in sociology, is often seen to either have no demarcation point with post-structuralism or to be a hyperbolic extension of it. In fact, there is much ambiguity as to what exactly "postmodernism" means, often depending on the disciplinary context. Within sociology, C. W. Mills (who used the term to describe the post-Enlightenment era) and Georg Simmel are considered early postmodernists.[36] In addition to the Gang of Four, major post-structuralists and postmodernists include Jacques Derrida; Gilles Deleuze (1925–1995), a philosopher influential in literature, film, and fine art; Judith Butler, an American philosopher and gender theorist who has had an impact on political philosophy, ethics, and feminist, queer, and literary theory; and Julia Kristeva, a philosopher, literary critic, psychoanalyst, sociologist, and feminist influential in critical analysis, cultural theory, feminism, and semiotics.

Symbolic interactionism and postmodernism share the same foundations and theorists. They see social structure ordered by meanings through rituals, symbols, and language. Many symbolic interactionists were also psychologists and clinicians (e.g., George Mead and Erving Goffman), tying them to the branch of sociology known as phenomenology. Phenomenological theory is rooted in European philosophy. The term "phenomenology" was first used by Edmund Husserl (1859–1938), a German philosopher who defined it as the study of what can be directly observed by our senses. A central tenet of this approach is that whatever cannot be observed through our senses is pure speculation. Alfred Schütz (1899–1959), also a German philosopher and sociologist, is considered one of the most influential figures in phenomenology. He adapted the work of Husserl to sociology, combining it with Weber's concept of *verstehen*, emphasizing the individual's definition of the situation.[37] Overall, the phenomenological approach assumes that in order to understand the world around us we have to forget all our preconceived notions of reality, referred to as "bracketing." Phenomenologists see people as active subjects with free will, basing this view on the fact that meanings are constructed in the mind. In this regard, language is of central importance because it creates meaning.

---

36   Mills, 2000b [1959]. See for example Weinstein and Weinstein, (1993) on Simmel.
37   *Verstehen* is a German word meaning "understanding." To fully comprehend behavior, we must learn the subjective meanings people attach to their actions—how they themselves view and explain their behavior.

Accordingly, there are abstract meanings that are independent of concrete situations, what Schütz termed "constructs of the second degree" and associated with positivists. Situated meanings (involving an actual situation) are based on a subject's interpretation of one's own behavior, what Schütz termed "constructs of the first degree."

For this work, the ideas of Castoriadis, Foucault, Debord, and Baudrillard are of particular importance.

3.1 *Cornelius Castoriadis*

Cornelius Castoriadis was an economist, philosopher, critical theorist, Autonomist-Marxist, semiotician, and pre-Situationist. His work represents both a break with Marx and a continuation of Marxism. Castoriadis studied Weber's theories of bureaucracy and rationalization, which influenced his views of history and modernity.[38]

According to Castoriadis, modern societies (as with most societies throughout history) are based on hierarchical organization, which is synonymous with bureaucracy and stratification of authority and income.[39] He observes that bureaucratic hierarchical societies, including self-proclaimed socialist nations such as the USSR, were based on capitalist production.[40] He refers to these so-called socialist states as comprising "state capitalism" (bureaucratic capitalism governed by a concentrated spectacle, according to Debord) in comparison to the Western free-market capitalism of the United States (governed by a diffuse-turned-integrated spectacle, according to Debord). Castoriadis concurs with Weber that hierarchical societies are either caste systems or caste systems in the making. A key factor for this is the family. Those with power will incorporate their privileges into the social structure and legal code to solidify their privileged position and secure it for their offspring:

> Thus, in large part the strata occupying the higher levels of the hierarchical pyramid perpetuate themselves by heredity. And that does not occur by chance. A social system always tends to reproduce itself. If some social strata have privileges, the members thereof will do everything they can—and their privileges signify precisely that they are capable of doing so to a large extent—to transmit these privileges to their descendants. To the extent that, in such a system, these strata have need of "new men"—because the managerial apparatuses are expanding and proliferating—they select,

---

38 Memos, 2014.
39 Castoriadis, 1993: 216–217.
40 Castoriadis, 1988.

among the offspring of "lower" strata, those deemed most "apt" in order to coopt them within their own strata. To this extent, it may appear that the "work" and the "abilities" of those who have been coopted have played a role in their career, and that their "merits" are being rewarded. Once again, however, "abilities" and "merits" here signify essentially the ability to adapt oneself to the reigning system, the better to serve it.[41]

Autonomy and heteronomy are central to Castoriadis's thought. In moral and political philosophy, autonomy is the capacity of an individual to make informed, un-coerced decisions. It is the basis for determining moral responsibility and accountability for one's actions. For Kant, morality presupposes autonomy in moral agents. Heteronomy is the state of being under the rule of another person or external constraints—the antithesis of autonomy.

In Castoriadis's *The Imaginary Institution of Society* he combines autonomy and heteronomy with Jacques Lacan's concept of the "imaginary."[42] Castoriadis posits that societies and their legal structures are founded on basic ideas regarding the world's nature and people's relationship to it. The imaginary of traditional societies made sense of the world through creation myths. These were heteronomous societies (from the Greek *hetero*, meaning "other"). Their imaginary identifies the origins, and thus legitimacy, of institutions (including laws, traditions, and behaviors) to be based on extra-social authority such as God, ancestors, or historical necessity. Power, authority, and material resources are concentrated, leading to relations between oppressors and the oppressed (those who govern and those who are governed).

Castoriadis defines autonomous societies (from the Greek $\alpha u\tau o$, meaning "by itself," and $\nu \acute{o} \mu o \varsigma$, meaning "law") as those whose imaginaries entail awareness that institutions (including laws, traditions, and behaviors) are created by people.[43] Societies based on autonomous imaginaries are self-governed ($\alpha u\tau o\nu o\mu o\acute{u}\nu\tau\alpha\iota$) by their demos. Economic, political, educational, and cultural institutions are based on widely accepted norms and values constructed through social interactions. Power, authority, and material resources are dispersed. This is a direct democracy, which is synonymous with theoretical anarchy (the lack of a central ruler) and communism (communal governance). Castoriadis presents as an example the ancient Athenians, who developed a system of continuous autonomy through direct democracy. Athenian citizens voted constantly in their general assembly of the city-state on various

---

41   Castoriadis, 1993: 223.
42   Castoriadis, 1997.
43   Castoriadis, 1991.

government matters and legislation. Athenian democracy included the idea of mandatory political participation as a structural process compared to passive forms of participation in representative democracies today.

Castoriadis's view of democracy as continuous praxis (through doing) is tied to the ancient Greek concept of *paideia* (pedagogy). Greek thinkers such as Plato and Aristotle considered paideia the basis of society's political system.[44] Education in this sense was understood in a broader context than in modern times. For one thing, paideia meant the training of a citizen's moral character, one's *constitution*. This sort of democracy is a way of life, with personal decisions and actions that have consequences. As understood by ancient Greeks, it meant participation in the commons through politics. In this regard, Castoriadis clarifies that "constitution" as used by the ancient Greeks, including Aristotle, literally meant the constitution, nature, or disposition of a people tying politics as a process to paideia, incorporating training in governance. "Constitution," Castoriadis writes, "means both the political institution/constitution and the way people go about common affairs. It is a scandal of modern philology that the title of Aristotle's treatise, Athenaion Politeia, is everywhere translated "The Constitution of Athens," both a straightforward linguistic error and the inexplicable sign of ignorance or incomprehension on the part of very erudite men. Aristotle wrote The Constitution of the Athenians."[45]

Education and political participation morph into one continuous culturally bound process. As Castoriadis explains, "This paideia is not primarily a matter of books and academic credits. First and foremost, it involves becoming conscious that the polis is also oneself and that its fate also depends upon one's mind, behavior, and decisions; in other words, it is participation in political life."[46] Democratic pedagogy socializes people to identify the interests of the commons with their own, fusing (in Marxist terms) private with public interests. Aristotle further argued that since education is designed to produce critical citizens who can govern, the curriculum becomes a public concern.[47] As such, public education was traditionally designed to promote cultural unity and social integration—the opposite of the alienating effects of postmodern educational systems.

Castoriadis points out that both capitalist and socialist societies claim to be based on reason and calculable science. Therefore, they share the same imaginary derived from the Industrial Revolution. This includes the assumption that

---

44   Ibid.: 161–162.
45   Ibid.: 109.
46   Ibid.: 161–162.
47   Aristotle, 1981: 452.

society is rational and that progress is defined through limitless material development as conceived by political economists such as Adam Smith and Karl Marx. In this regard, Marx considered capitalist organization—what Castoriadis refers to as technique (e.g., production based on factories) to be neutral, detached from the exploitation of the masses by capitalists. To the contrary, Castoriadis considers technique as an expression of a society's imaginary, which is why it too would have to change if the goal is self-managed communities: "Marx did not and could not develop such a technique. The reason is profoundly bound to his conception of history. Like the Hegelian Reason or Spirit of the world, in Marx it is the 'rationality' incarnated by technique (the development of productive forces) which makes history advance. This explains why Marx and Marxism could only be massive obstacles to a movement aiming at self-management, autonomy, self-government."[48]

For Castoriadis, real historical change requires a radical discontinuity from the prevalent imaginary. Such change is contingent, in contrast to ideological Marxism's determinist view of historical materialism unfolding into predictable epochs. For Marx, history followed rational laws of evolution independent of human praxis. Social movements were determined by technological history, rather than the other way around. For Castoriadis, history is contingent upon human agency as the driver of real change. There are no historical laws. Furthermore, radical change can only be implemented as a process of continuous revolution. Radical change is not something static or what follows a specific event, such as a popular revolution or exchange of elites such as Marx's dictatorship of the proletariat. In the anarchist tradition, going back at least to Pierre-Joseph Proudhon, education was an integral part of social and political transformation. For example, Proudhon (and other anarchists, including Charlotte Wilson and Errico Malatesta) preferred the idea of social revolution to the idea of political revolution, which meant a transformation in the social body instead of in the political institutions of the state. Ultimately Castoriadis came to see history as an antagonism between autonomous and heteronymous imaginaries—between horizontal and vertical structures, equality and inequality.

His conceptualization of history also had implications on the nature of crises, leading to another break with Marx. Ideological Marxism postulates that structural contradictions cause crises that will inevitably result in a systemic collapse. The collapse is guaranteed by the laws of history. This can be summed up by Marx's famous expression that capitalism contains the seeds of its own destruction. However, Castoriadis observed, as others did, that there was

---

[48] Castoriadis, 1984: 122–124.

nothing inevitable following crises. He and Debord believed that capitalism could limp along indefinitely in a state of perpetual crisis. It could even absorb crises in a continual process of rebirth, as the historical record has borne out. The implication is that change is not dependent on crisis, per se, but on people's response to it.

3.2 Michel Foucault

Michel Foucault (1926–1984) was a critical social theorist, philosopher, and historian of ideas. His early work was influenced by structuralism, but he went beyond structuralism in later life. He observed that power in societies has been historically transferred symbolically, moving from external to internal, mental regulation—self-policing.

Foucault argues that societies are organized by power and knowledge structures that strive toward normalization, defined as a system of judgment derived from power.[49] He identifies three aspects of power, which he calls instruments of power.[50] These are 1) hierarchical observation, where those in power can observe everything; 2) the power to make normative judgments and to punish those who do not comply with those norms; and 3) examination that combines the other two, the ability to identify and punish all those who violate elite norms. A system of normalization structures society around elite values that everyone must accept. The power to control norm creation serves as a mechanism for social control. Control is reinforced by social institutions that are constructed as self-sustaining systems for the reproduction of the dominant values and norms.

Language is an example of a power and knowledge system and control through normalization.[51] Accordingly, we are born into a society in which language and meaning are determined by those with linguistic dominance. Therefore, preexisting linguistic structures constitute our cognitive schema or framework. As such, they constitute a mental cage (echoing Weber's "iron cage," although Foucault believed that escape is possible) that constrains our thinking.[52] This is borne out in Foucault's famous metaphor in *Discipline and Punish* of the unstaffed prison tower based on Jeremy Bentham's Panopticon.[53] Inmates cannot tell if the tower has anyone inside it at any given time and thus know whether they are being observed, so they assume someone is always

---

49 Foucault, 1980.
50 Foucault, 1977.
51 Foucault, 1980.
52 Weber's concept of the "iron cage" appears in *The Protestant Ethic and the Spirit of Capitalism* (1992).
53 Foucault, 1977.

watching. Control in postmodern societies is internalized through social institutions, rendering the need of an actual guard unnecessary. Therefore, the Panopticon does not maintain control through the threat of punishment alone. It also establishes control without punishment. This represents a new form of technological power, which Foucault argued can be found in many institutions other than prisons (e.g., schools and hospitals).

Postmodern normalization of surveillance begins prior to conception, with potential parents monitoring their bodies for the optimal time to conceive and then testing for pregnancy. Humans are surveilled even before birth through technology such as ultrasound scans. At birth, surveillance of the body continues through medical exams, lab tests, and video monitors. Parents often place video or voice monitors in their infant's room. They also monitor caregivers (e.g., babysitters) with hidden cameras. As children grow, parents continue to track them through location apps on their cell phones, GPS chips in children's pockets, software monitoring online activity, and more. From age six to eighteen, children are conditioned to accept institutional monitoring performed by schools. Upon their graduation from these indoctrination camps, they experience surveillance at work, with employers monitoring keyboard strokes and online browsing, reading workers' email, listening in on their phone conversations, and watching them via security cameras. Corporations gathering personal information, with or without our knowledge, legally and illegally monitor our private lives almost constantly.[54] Mobile technology and apps ubiquitously track our location, web searches, purchasing habits, and more.[55] We tacitly comply every time we click "agree" on a non-negotiable multipage contract just to create an email account, use social media, or buy things.[56]

Foucault presented his conceptualization of history through the terms "archaeology" and "archaeological method." He argued that each historical period has been based on subconscious systems of thought and knowledge and that established boundaries of thought and language are specific to each period. This is similar to Castoriadis's concept of imaginaries characterizing different societies. Common notions of history are interpretations based on current thought and knowledge rather than contextualization using the prevailing perspectives of earlier times. History is not an unfolding series of events in a continuous narrative. Instead, change occurs through complex factors that shape discourses that can represent both continuities and breaks from the

---

54 Greenwald, 2014.
55 Ibid.
56 Hoback, 2013.

past. There is no Marxist historical necessity. Rather, history could easily have taken different paths.

3.3 Guy Debord

Guy Debord (1931–1994) was an Autonomist-Marxist semiotician, founding member of the Situationist International, member of Castoriadis's Socialisme ou Barbarie, and filmmaker. His work represents both a break with Marx and an attempt to save Marxist analysis. He was disillusioned by the failed uprisings of the 1960s, concluding that there was no possibility of revolution in the foreseeable future. One reason was that he saw people under technological capitalism becoming content with their lives, based on preselected choices of consumption parading as democracy. In this sense, Debord saw a Huxleyian dystopia pacified by *soma* rather than overt coercion. This led him to conceptualize modern means of resistance through *détournement*.[57] A similar rearrangement of meaning and symbols was conceived by Hakim Bey.[58] Debord hoped that exposing the contradictions and lies of the spectacle through *détournement* by an avant-garde, would lead to cognitive dissonance among the population. As Blau postulated, this would prompt people to question what is presented by the spectacle as truth and thus engage in resistance.[59]

Unfortunately, Debord lacked sociological training to describe the political economy of his concept of the spectacle. Rather, he emphasized the power of images and signs in postmodern society: "Images detached from every aspect of life merge into a common stream, and the former unity of life is lost forever. Apprehended in a *partial* way, reality unfolds in a new generality as a pseudo-world apart, solely as an object of contemplation. The tendency toward the specialization of images-of-the-world finds its highest expression in the world of the autonomous image, where deceit deceives itself."[60] However, this system "is not a collection of images; rather, it is a social relationship between people that is mediated by images."[61] Debord stresses the role of modern technology

---

[57] *Détournement*, originally developed in the 1950s by the Letterist International, is the turning of expressions of the capitalist system against itself, like turning slogans and logos against the advertisers or the political status quo. A contemporary example is the British street artist Banksy. "Minor *détournements*" take elements that in themselves are of no real importance—such as snapshots, press clippings, and everyday objects—and place them in a new context. "Deceptive *détournements*" take significant elements, such as major political or philosophical texts, great artwork, or works of literature, and place them in a new context that challenges the status quo.

[58] Bey, 2003.
[59] Blau, 1992.
[60] Debord, 1990: 12.
[61] Debord, 2012: 12.

for increased social control using images produced and presented as truth to the masses. Here he echoes symbolic interactionists in their emphasis on meanings shaping the social order. He also reflects Foucault in that control becomes internalized through socialization to accept these constructed meanings.[62]

The spectacle can take three different forms: concentrated, diffuse, and integrated. The concentrated spectacle entails what Debord referred to as bureaucratic capitalism. These bureaucratic societies are exemplified by what are commonly referred to in popular culture as socialist, like the Soviet Union. These societies are headed by dictators and based on overt control. However, the concentrated spectacle can also manifest as fascism in advanced capitalist societies, typically in times of crisis. It relies on violence and police terror. Those who benefit are the bureaucratic class.

> The concentrated form of the spectacle normally characterizes bureaucratic capitalism, though it may on occasion be borrowed as a technique for buttressing state power over more backward mixed economies, and even the most advanced capitalism may call on it in moments of crisis. Bureaucratic property is itself concentrated, in that the individual bureaucrat's relation to the ownership of the economy as a whole is invariably mediated by the community of bureaucrats, by his membership in that community. And commodity production, less well developed in bureaucratic systems, is also concentrated in form: the commodity the bureaucracy appropriates is the totality of social labor, and what it sells back to society—*en bloc*—is society's survival. The dictatorship of the bureaucratic economy cannot leave the exploited masses any significant margin of choice because it has had to make *all* the choices itself, and because any choice made independently of it, even the most trivial—concerning food, say, or music amounts to a declaration of war to the death on the bureaucracy. This dictatorship must therefore be attended by permanent violence. Its spectacle imposes an image of the good which is a resume of everything that exists officially, and this is usually concentrated in a single individual, the guarantor of the system's totalitarian cohesiveness. Everyone must identify magically with this absolute celebrity or disappear.[63]

---

62 Debord, 1990: 27–28.
63 Debord, 2012: 41–42.

The diffuse spectacle is associated with industrial capitalism. In contrast to the concentrated form, the diffuse spectacle sustains itself mostly through seduction, not violence, making it a more efficient system of control. The integrated spectacle is a synthesis of its two earliest manifestations and, as such, is the most advanced type. Its features include incessant technological renewal, merging of state and economy, secrecy, forgeries of the real, and a perpetual present. Debord traced the birth of this form to the liberal democracies of France and Italy. It represents the globalization of the hegemony of the commodity:

> The integrated spectacle shows itself to be simultaneously concentrated and diffuse, and ever since the fruitful union of the two has learnt to employ both these qualities on a grander scale. Their former mode of application has changed considerably. As regards concentration, the controlling centre has now become occult never to be occupied by a known leader, or clear ideology. And on the diffuse side, the spectacle has never before put its mark to such a degree on almost the full range of socially produced behaviour and objects. For the final sense of the integrated spectacle is this—that it has integrated itself into reality to the same extent as it was describing it, and that it was reconstructing it as it was describing it. As a result, this reality no longer confronts the integrated spectacle as something alien. When the spectacle was concentrated, the greater part of surrounding society escaped it; when diffuse, a small part; today, no part. The spectacle has spread itself to the point where it now permeates all reality.[64]

Like Castoriadis, Debord sees no difference in postmodern spectacular variations of capitalism such as socialism. China's embrace of Disney, a dominant symbol of capitalist culture, lays bare that Disney resorts, McDonald's, and Starbucks are ubiquitous across the globe because there is no variation in social orders or ideologies.

Aided by technology, governments rewrite history to manipulate public memory.[65] This enables elites to erase from memory inconvenient truths, replacing them with false "facts" that are unverifiable. Like Castoriadis and Baudrillard, Debord posited that history has ceased, in that there are no new events that radically or structurally alter social relations. This is exemplified by

---

64 Debord, 1990: 8–11.
65 Ibid.: 10–16.

Debord's belief that the society of the spectacle is a constant present with no past or future, a constant stream of images, symbols, and signs.

Debord argues that laws, which reflect values and norms, are also constructed by elites to control the demos. Therefore, he identifies a break in the historical process of norm formation from the interactions of the demos to those constructed by elites.[66] For him there is a real social structure that is not hidden by illusion because the illusion *is* reality. The illusion (dominant ideology) is built into the physical world—for example, through urban planning and architecture. The spectacle is presented by dominant social institutions as the only possible, thus *pragmatic*, option for social organization. The problem for Debord is that "society is imposed onto people, not created by them.... The society of the spectacle cannot be torn down so that we can see what is behind it.... *The problem is not that our reality is unreal, or hyperreal, as Baudrillard argued, but rather, that it is not of our own making*."[67] Last, Debord, like Baudrillard, believed that the spectacle is autonomous, with a life of its own.

3.4 *Jean Baudrillard*

Jean Baudrillard (1929–2007) was a Marxist sociologist (in his early writings), Situationist, semiotician, postmodernist, and significant poststructuralist, although he rejected the latter label.[68] He also contributed to psychoanalysis. Baudrillard was influenced by Lefebvre, Barthes, and other French thinkers. He was one of the first to use semiology for the analysis of objects and their encoding with a system of signs and meanings. Baudrillard argues that the transition from the early stage of competitive market capitalism to the stage of monopoly capitalism significantly expanded production capacity through new production methods and technologies. This prompted elites to create new needs based on the consumption of commodities for their signification of status (sign-values). He accepts that commodities have use and exchange values, as Marx postulated. However, in a departure from Marxism, he adds sign-values in a differential system indicating prestige, status, identity, et cetera. Sign-values are based on Veblen's concepts of conspicuous consumption and conspicuous leisure.[69] Baudrillard, though, goes further than Veblen, stating that symbolic consumption has become wider and deeper, engulfing all that is social. Accordingly, an object has functional (use) value (e.g., an automobile is a mode of transportation), exchange value (what it is worth relative

---

66   Ibid.: 70.
67   Gilman-Opalsky, 2011: 74.
68   Ibid.: 59.
69   Veblen, 2012 [1899].

to other things; e.g., ten automobiles may be worth one house), and symbolic value that people attach to the commodity (e.g., a dozen red roses on Valentine's Day symbolize romantic love). An object according to Baudrillard also has a sign-value within a system of objects. For example, an economy automobile will transport someone from point A to point B the same as a luxury automobile. But the economy car will convey symbolically a lower position or status in a stratified system than the luxury automobile that symbolizes a high status ranking.

Baudrillard's work on simulacra and simulations is related to that of Friedrich Nietzsche and Georg Lukács on reification, Guy Debord, Raoul Vaneigem, Jean-Paul Sartre, and the semioticians.[70] Simulacra are imitations of original things, while simulations imitate real processes or structures. Baudrillard identifies three types of simulacra corresponding to specific historical periods. Premodern society gave rise to first-order simulacra. These are obvious copies of real things that make no pretense of their nature and thus can be identified as such. Second-order simulacra correspond to the Industrial Revolution. These are mass-produced copies that are indistinguishable from the original, making them commodities. Because the copy is identical to the original, each copy is "real" or "original," and thus representation and reality break down.

Postmodernism (late capitalism) corresponds to third-order simulacra that precede the original or never had a prototype. Therefore, they can obtain any meaning, even disconnected from that of any possible original. The distinction between reality and representation disappears. These simulacra have saturated society to the point where all meaning becomes infinitely mutable, therefore meaningless, in what Baudrillard termed the "precession of simulacra." Reality and meaning have been replaced with perceived reality constructed by symbols and signs that are simulacra creating a new hyperreality:

> The simulacrum is never what hides the truth—it is the truth that hides the fact that there is none. The simulacrum is true.... Thus, everywhere in Disneyland the objective profile of America ... is drawn. All its values are exhaled.... embalmed and pacified.... But this masks something else and this "ideological" blanket functions as a cover for a *simulation of the third order*: Disneyland exists in order to hide that it is the "real" country, all of "real" America that is Disneyland. ... Disneyland is presented as imaginary in order to make us believe that the rest is real, whereas all of Los Angeles and the America that surrounds it are no longer real, but belong to the hyperreal order and to the order of simulation. It is no longer

---

70 Gilman-Opalsky, 2011: 35.

a question of a false representation of reality (ideology) but of concealing the fact that the real is no longer real.[71]

In addition, Baudrillard argues that reality is unknowable—if not constructed outright—because we only see fragments of it from our subjective perspective—as argued by phenomenology.

Baudrillard also writes about the "phantom" of capital that is able to stage its own death and come back again as a "simulacrum of value."[72] In effect, he claims that this is no longer a capitalist system in a traditional or real sense but a representation of it, an advanced spectacle beyond that described by the Situationists.

Neoconservative Francis Fukuyama scandalized academia when he argued that history ended in the post–Cold War era:

> What we may be witnessing is not just the end of the Cold War, or the passing of a particular period of postwar history, but the end of history as such: that is, the end point of mankind's ideological evolution and the universalization of Western liberal democracy as the final form of human government. This is not to say that there will no longer be events to fill the pages of Foreign Affair's yearly summaries of international relations, for the victory of liberalism has occurred primarily in the realm of ideas or consciousness and is as yet incomplete in the real or material world. But there are powerful reasons for believing that it is the ideal that will govern the material world in the long run.[73]

Debord and Baudrillard would agree with Fukuyama's thesis and appreciate the irony of "communist" China opening Shanghai Disney Park Resort in 2016, the first on the mainland, after the Hong Kong Disneyland Resort. For Baudrillard, however, history ended after the bourgeois/French revolution—much earlier than Fukuyama realized. According to Baudrillard, events must meet two conditions in order to be historic: "First, they must be unprecedented in some way, either phenomenologically or in terms of the problems they pose (or resolve). And second, they must be world-historical in scale, which is to say, they must clearly transform relationships between large subsets of peoples, politically, regionally, nationally, internationally, etc. Historic events, in other words, reframe debates and self-understandings, and change relations of

---

71 Baudrillard, 1994: 1, 12–13.
72 Ibid.: 152–153.
73 Fukuyama, 1989: 3.

power.... History consists only of new antagonisms, not old events reoccurring in different ways and places."[74]

4 Beyond Post-Structuralism/Postmodernism

Baudrillard's work is useful but borders on metaphysical philosophy flirting with nihilistic ideology. Baudrillard believed that there are no facts and that reality is unknowable. I believe that social facts exist, can be observed, and understood in the sense of expanding our knowledge of the subject. Facts can be understood with quantitative methods, qualitative measures, or both. For example, if we wish to evaluate the spread of Ebola, a quantitative approach would be appropriate. It is not necessary in this case to be absolutely accurate with figures in order to understand how much it is spreading. However, if we want to know what it means to have Ebola, quantitative methods are useless. Here knowledge is enhanced by qualitative methods such as ethnography or interviews with those carrying the disease. We might learn from those who are infected that this means being socially isolated, fearing almost certain death in a short period, or being handled as an object rather than a person.

In contrast to Baudrillard's phenomenological perspective and to the social sciences' pretenses of value neutrality (implying "objective" research), I believe that the subjective position (and thus morality) of the researcher matters and is not an impediment to the pursuit of knowledge. As McLaren stipulates, critical thinking presupposes a critical pedagogy that incorporates philosophy with education.[75] Critical pedagogy, in turn, presupposes praxis based on ethical choices. I take the moral position that the social should dominate the economic and that equality is preferable to inequality. In *Social Structures of Direct Democracy* I argue additionally that equality is also more efficient, based on both economic and social measures.[76]

Contrary to Debord and Baudrillard, I think that the true illusion lies in believing that the illusion is real. There is a *real* social structure that has not merged with the spectacle but is hidden behind it. No matter how much the spectacle imbeds itself in reality, reality remains independent of it. This explains why the spectacle relies heavily on security forces. Debord and Baudrillard believe the spectacle is autonomous, with a life of its own. I see it as an

---

74 Gilman-Opalsky, 2011: 48–49.
75 McLaren, 2015.
76 Asimakopoulos, 2016.

instrument of deception. It does not live a virtual existence on a dead planet. It is operated by people who program and maintain the technology and systems with the purpose of amassing power, authority, and material resources.

As with anarchist theory, this book goes beyond class-based analyses. Class corresponds to production and is therefore conceptually limited for the critical analysis of social structures. Class-based analysis would identify the domination of capitalists over workers but miss that of men over women in patriarchal societies. More so, it is not even clear what class is. I share Weber's contention that social classes are castes in the process of solidification during periods of anomie (radical change or flux). Ultimately, therefore, all hierarchical social structures are castes. Thus, the dynamic analysis of Marxist class conflict is reconceptualized more broadly between oppressors and the oppressed.

It is here that the poverty of disciplines is revealed, exposing the value of the intersectionality that is central to autonomist and anarchist analyses. As we have seen, all major figures and founders of symbolic interactionism were not sociologists, economists, psychologists, historians, critical theorists, or from any other singular discipline or approach. Nor were they all or exclusively semioticians, linguists, phenomenologists, et cetera. To the contrary, they have all been interdisciplinary, often contributing to many subfields of micro and macro analysis. This work is intersectional because all oppression intersects in complex ways.

Conflict permeates all social orders and is the engine of change. History is not linear, determined by technological development or scientific laws. Castoriadis, Foucault, Debord, and Baudrillard correctly consider real historical change to be transformative. It occurs when social relations are structurally altered relative to resources, power, and authority. Therefore, history is contingent upon collective action in a seesaw (continuous praxis) between the oppressed and oppressors battling over the distribution of resources, power, and authority. Although conflict is situated in the discourse of the time and place, the only constant is opposition groups where a few have more than, and or dominate, the majority.

Every hegemonic order throughout history has shared the same structure with varying spectacular expressions that are falsely perceived as history. Production techniques, technology, forms of finance and banking, et cetera, are part of an overall social structure but do not determine it. What is perceived as historical change is the evolution of technology. For example, during the feudal era, churches were adorned with images of a hellish afterlife if one did not submit to God's will (meaning the king's). In postmodern society, a different sort of scary images are transmitted electronically on phones or TVs with threats that limits will be placed on one's consumption if one does not attend to one's credit score—and none of the credit agencies disclose the formulas (algorithms) according to which they calculate these fictitious scores.

When Debord identified the emergence of the integrated spectacle, it was in its infancy. It has now matured into its true form, a caste system, as theorized by Weber. As the integrated spectacle matured, so did elites of nations governed by concentrated spectacles—for example, the Soviet Union and China. The collapse of the USSR taught Russian elites that overt control by a concentrated spectacle can reach a point of implosion. Now China and the former Soviet states are adopting models of governance from Western industrial democracies based on the integrated spectacle. This also demonstrates, as postmodernists predicted, the expanding colonization of national social structures into an integrated global structure. International conflicts are not between peoples, nations, or opposing ideologies. They are between super and subordinate global elites. These are intra-elite conflicts within the same system, not inter-elite conflicts between substantively different systems.

Like Castoriadis, I posit that historically there have been only two distinct eras—'epochs' in Marxist terminology. One was egalitarian and based on horizontal social structures. The second has been unequal and based on hierarchical (vertical) social structures. In horizontal orders, power and authority are shared by all. The structures are based on autonomous imaginaries and derived from the interactions of an autonomous demos in a continuous process (praxis) of direct democracy. Control is maintained by the demos based on common values that merge private with public interests. The only examples of horizontal orders are perhaps prehistoric hunting and gathering communities.[77] The direct democracy of ancient Athens is another example of a horizontal order among citizens because it was still a society based on slavery and patriarchy.

Hierarchical orders are based on heteronymous imaginaries. These are established through violence by elites to expropriate authority and material resources from the demos. Control is primarily maintained by propaganda to insure internalization of dominant values. These alien(ating) values, norms, symbols, et cetera, are imposed top-down, transforming the demos into a heteronomous audience. Therefore, postmodern societies are not constructed from the bottom up by an autonomous demos through organic interactions and shared norms. In addition, distinctions are often made based on whether power is based on wealth, politics, military capabilities, or something else entirely. In reality, it is all power. In the language of international relations, power

---

77 Harrison, 2017.

is "fungible," from the Greek *plastikos*, meaning able to take different forms (e.g., military, political, economic, cultural, and more). Similarly, social scientists see capital as fungible power in social relations. Sociologists, however, distinguish between legitimate and illegitimate authority. Legitimate authority is institutionalized power recognized by those over whom it is exercised. Illegitimate authority is not institutional but is raw power not recognized by those over whom it is exercised. I postulate that all power and authority are illegitimate in hierarchical societies—a position shared by Weber and Dahrendorf.[78]

---

[78] Dahrendorf, 1959; Weber in Gerth and Mills, 1946.

CHAPTER 2

The Spectacle

Every spectacle has three components: audience segmentation, propaganda, and symbolic institutions.

∴

1 Audience Segmentation

Baudrillard writes:

> Throughout the 'civilized' world the construction of stockpiles of objects has brought with it the complementary process of stockpiles of people.... That is 'mass production,' not in the sense of a massive production or for use by the masses, but the production of the *masses*. The masses are the final product of all sociality, and at the same time, as putting an end to sociality, because these masses that one wants to believe *are* the social, are on the contrary the site of the implosion of the social. *The masses are the increasingly dense sphere in which the whole social comes to be imploded, and to be devoured in an uninterrupted process of simulation.*[1]

Hierarchical orders transform the demos into segmented audiences targeted by propaganda. The extent of segmentation is determined by available technology and propaganda sophistication.[2] Segmentation in hierarchical societies is based on primary castes and their sub-castes. India, for example, has a traditional caste system, divided into six primary castes with thousands of sub-castes. Traditional castes and their subdivisions are primarily based on occupation, regional location, and physical attributes (e.g., skin color, with lighter-skinned people ranked higher). Due to rudimentary technology and unsophisticated propaganda, segment variation in traditional caste systems was limited to the above categories. However, there was a real community organized around organic social interaction (as elaborated in Chapter 1).

---

1 Baudrillard, 1994: 68.
2 Foer, 2017; Maheshwari and Stevenson, 2017.

Segmentation in postmodern hierarchical systems continues to be caste-based but with endless categories targeted by sophisticated propaganda and advanced technology, especially algorithms. In addition to traditional caste segments based on skin color, occupation, region, age, gender, height and weight, modern segments can be based on sleep patterns, sexual preferences and practices, brand preferences, consumption patterns, places visited, medical conditions, and much more. The dominant segment category is market-based. Market segments divide the world down to the individual level: personalized advertising targets you on Amazon and countless other websites thanks to computer cookies.[3] The spectacle even co-opts its most ardent opponents into global market segments and sub-segments. This includes jihadists who consume various Western services and goods such as cell phones and high-fashion burkas from Europe's "avant-guard" designer houses.[4]

Some audience segments (e.g., based on age or gender) cut across castes while others do not. Some, such as party affiliation, are voluntary. Others consist of captive audiences, such as prison inmates, employees, and students. My concept of audiance segmentation is similar to that of "multiple affiliations" described by Simmel and Blau. Some audience segments reside in the real world and entail people with face-to-face association (e.g., a local Rotary Club), as with Simmel and Blau's concept. Postmodern audience segmentation can also include virtual affiliations such as online communities based on disembodied virtual interactions. Simmel and Blau argue that multiple affiliations reduce conflict when cutting across power and authority relations.[5] But that is rarely the case. Multiple affiliations tend to be between the sub-segments of primary castes (inter-segment overlapping affiliations) that have similar social rankings. Therefore, neither material resources nor power nor authority cut across differentially ranked primary audience segments. Rather these multiple affiliations are between people who share similar material resources, authority, power, and opportunities. The authority of a factory worker who is president of a social club composed of other workers is purely nominal and

---

3   Computer cookies are files created by websites and stored in one's computer to track preferences, typically for target marketing.
4   Asher, 2016.
5   Simmel observed that people in preindustrial times interacted with a small number of groups consisting of similar people. As a result, a person did not have an individual sense of self, personality, but "was wholly absorbed by, and remained oriented toward, the group" (1955: 151). Advances in transportation and communication technology made it possible for multiple independent diverse groups to overlap in "an infinite range of individualizing combinations" (1955: 155). This allowed individuals to become more unique than in the past and to develop an individual sense of self.

does not extend to the social order. These affiliations hide the reality that the 99 percent of the population have only nominal power and authority across all of their affiliations.

The audience is not a crowd, although many, including Debord, use the terms "audience" and "crowd" interchangeably. Sociologically, a crowd is a random gathering, an aggregate of individuals who do not share common norms or values or interact regularly. Sociologically, the audience is a group, because it has been socialized into accepting the spectacle's norms and values, regularly interacting within predetermined scripts. Crowds are not desired by the spectacle because, unlike audiences, they are not controlled, and thus they are unpredictable and may act outside of accepted scripts. A crowd may dissipate after a street protest over a youth's death at the hands of police, or it may turn into an insurrection, as in Greece. Crowds have the potential to spark rebellion, as with the 1960s ghetto revolts in many US cities.[6] Crowds often represent autonomous collective action that can shatter the illusion of the simulated social order.

Postmodern caste systems render the demos into an audience of alienated consumers. Nothing is left to chance; all audience interactions are scripted/simulated, inorganic. Take, for example, when a store employee or neighbor asks, "How are you today?" In traditional societies based on organic interaction, one may answer "Not well," and it then would be normal to discuss: "Oh, tell me about it." When someone in a postmodern society asks how you are, the expected and scripted response is "good, thank you." But, if the response is off-script (e.g., "Terrible, I am getting divorced and my mortgage is past due"), then the simulated interaction is broken and the fakery revealed.

George Ritzer, using Erving Goffman's *dramaturgical approach*, shows how a simple interaction like buying a cup of coffee has become a scripted performance written by a corporation.[7] Ritzer writes:

> While people's performances at Starbucks show individual variation and vary from one visit to another, Goffman makes the point that performances, and the fronts associated with them, tend to become institutionalized. This is certainly true for employees, whose fronts and performances are institutionalized by the company that employs them, but it is also true

---

6 See Asimakopoulos (2011) for a detailed analysis.
7 According to Goffman's dramaturgical approach (1959), people engage in social interaction like actors performing on the stage of life. In public, people act as if they are on their "front stage," performing for their audience based on how they wish to be perceived, typically according to prevailing norms, values, and expectations of behavior. In private, people are "back stage," behaving as themselves because there is no audience for which to perform.

for customers whose fronts and performances become more informally institutionalized over time. The point is that people tend to *select* and *not create* their fronts and performance. They enter established fronts and select the pre-established, acceptable performances for such settings. This is clearly true for Starbucks' employees, but it also happens with customers, although for them it is much more informal and they are much less conscious of the pre-established character of both the front and performance. *Indeed, they may think they are spontaneously creating both front and performance, when in fact the company has played a powerful role in pre-structuring and pre-determining both* [emphasis added].[8]

Because social interactions could deviate from the script, they are eliminated whenever possible by the spectacle. For example, in past eras people conducted their banking in person, but today, thanks to digitization, payments and deposits are now made electronically from anywhere in the world, without face-to-face interaction. Digitized online retail is the epitome of alienating commodity fetishization, fulfilling all (and none) of your wants—needs, according to propaganda—free from autonomous human interaction. Today's automated "customer service" is another example in which interaction is limited to a machine giving you the options of which buttons to push on the phone rather than talking with a person. Amazon does not even have a phone number for customer service, only email accounts, and heaven help you if you get stiffed big-time by an Amazon third-party seller.

To be part of an audience today means to be an alienated individual in an alienated community, what Debord referred to as "the lonely crowd."[9] This leads one to seek a "segment" with which to achieve a fellow feeling—a sense of belonging, of community:

> [With] the advent of long-distance mass communications, the isolation of the population has become a much more effective means of control. But the general trend toward isolation ... must also embody a controlled reintegration of the workers based on the planned needs of production and consumption. Such an integration into the system must recapture isolated individuals as individuals *isolated together*. Factories and cultural centers, holiday camps and housing developments—all are expressly oriented to the goals of a pseudo-community of this kind. These imperatives pursue the isolated individual right into the *family cell*, where the

---

8   Ritzer, 2008: 221.
9   Debord, 2012: 22.

generalized use of receivers of the spectacle's message ensures that his isolation is filled with the dominant images—images that indeed attain their full force only by virtue of this isolation.[10]

Technology corporations claim that communications technology such as the internet empowers individuals to find others to form virtual versus real communities. These virtual communities are not communities where everyone knows each other but often consist of anonymous individuals hiding behind a screen name or avatar. Although social media ostensibly allow one to increase one's social contact, psychologists find that teenagers who use social media in fact have *less* social contact and experience greater alienation, depression, and suicide.[11] One study based on 1,095 adults found that those who stopped using Facebook for a week felt happier than those who continued using it.[12]

It is indicative that public opinion polls are not based on an actual demos engaged in collective assessment in any associational sense or in the tradition of Habermas's discursive democracy. Rather, these are opinions of individuals based on preselected topics, often with preselected answers to choose from. This is a simulation of public opinion. As Gilman-Opalsky writes:

> Opinion polls claim to present what the public thinks, when in fact they actually *construct* the public using calculations that add up privately held opinions, processed with expedience, through surveys. But public opinion is not the sum total of private opinion. Private opinion reflects the interests of private persons thinking and speaking as individuals, whereas public opinion expresses and embodies a collective interest, collectively assessed. For public opinion, there must actually be *a cohesive public sphere* that can consider the issues in a public forum of some kind, and can formulate a collective perspective that is distinguished from the perspective of individuals as such.... In fact, the social 'science' of polling has managed a remarkable trick—it can present us with public opinion in the absence of an actually existing public![13]

1.1   *Sociocultural and Spatial Segmentation*

Housing under hierarchical orders is structurally segregated. In India, lower castes like the Untouchables, known as the Dalit (the repressed), are forced to

---

10   Ibid.: 122.
11   Twenge, 2017.
12   Happiness Research Institute, 2015.
13   Gilman-Opalsky, 2011: 46–47.

live in ghettos in or outside of major cities. The Dalit are forbidden from entering temples and sacred places. US blacks were segregated in ghettos and were denied entrance to some public spaces and businesses such as restaurants. Housing remains segregated in the United States, limiting access to quality schools, food, employment, health care, and public services. An ethnographic study by critical human geographers is indicative:

> [The researchers] investigated a southwestern middle school located in an urban neighborhood, the Dead Ends. This local sociocultural marker of place is an intentional double entendre: it is at once one of hundreds of communities of color that lack connection to interstates and roadways due to intentional city planning and one lacking in opportunities for a life outside of its confines. Mobility within the community was also limited, a lack of possibilities made more stark in contrast to the major metropolitan area in which it was embedded, replete with public transportation, suburbia and major roadways. As but one example of how the Dead Ends was theoretically and practically bounded, a freeway both divided this community from predominantly White, middle-upper class suburbs, and there was no local access to the freeway in spite of its overwhelming presence.[14]

Many ghettos such as Newark, New Jersey, did not even have a movie theater for over thirty years after the ghetto revolts in the 1960s. A middle school student from the Dead Ends urban ghetto in 2017 is succinct: "It's not like there is anything to do here. All there is to do is walk around with your friends. We don't have a skating rink or a movie theater. We don't have grocery store or a bank... nothing".[15] Data from 1970 to 2000 show that in addition to race-based separation there has been an increase in economic segregation.[16] This is not a result of self-segregation alone but also of policies.[17] Poor people live where rents are cheap, away from the affluent. Moreover, homeownership usually requires a mortgage, which exacerbates segregation. In 2000, US homeownership reached 67.4 percent, but for blacks and Hispanics it was less than half.[18] Researchers reanalyzed loan approval and performance data from a 1996 Boston Fed study.[19] They found that loan-approval disparities between whites and

---

14   Boske et al., 2019: 5.
15   Boske et al., 2019: 16.
16   Massey et al., 2009.
17   Ibid.; Reeves, 2017.
18   Ross and Yinger, 2002.
19   Ibid.

minorities were not a result of new underwriting standards. Rather, the fair-lending enforcement regulations failed to identify discrimination in terms of disparate impact (structural discrimination) and disparate treatment (overt discrimination). Perversely, these regulations shield discriminating lenders from investigation.

Spatial segmentation is accompanied by restrictions on social intercourse and physical contact between upper and lower castes, as in India. Social intercourse between castes is limited to hierarchical employment relations. Elites never have to interact with the bottom 99 percent. McDonald and Robinson write:

> When Lehman's CEO arrived by limousine in the morning at a VIP entrance at the back of the building, his driver had already called ahead alerting the front desk in the lobby of his majesty's imminent arrival. The front-desk attendant then hit a button programming one of the elevators in the rear bank to go directly to the thirty-first floor. A security guard would then hold the elevator until Fuld's arrival. This was Fuld's private transport to the heavens, the one that preserved his godlike existence. Into this rarefied capsule he slipped silently, and was, in a way, beamed up to his somber mahogany-paneled office, far from the madding crowd. He left the building the same way, which was not, I thought naively, much of a way to keep your finger on the pulse.[20]

Castes are endogamous. This reproduces and intensifies social and spatial segregation, skill sets, occupations, and resources. Marriage restrictions are often codified. In the slaver United States, interracial marriages were banned well into the twentieth century. Although interracial marriages are now legal, they remain stigmatized. Regardless of codification, caste intra-marriage is structurally reinforced. Typically people court, date, and marry those who are geographically and socially proximate for various reasons, ranging from social acceptance to simple availability. For example, who are the available men in a ghetto community?

A lack of social interaction prevents elites from seeing the oppressed as human beings, resulting in a lack of empathy. The poor become undeserving "others." This dehumanization makes it psychologically easier to pass policies that harm poor people, such as slashing food stamps. Dehumanization serves to justify brutality, epitomized by the Nazis who deemed Jews to be rats worthy of gas chambers.

---

20   McDonald and Robinson, 2009: 90.

Social and spatial isolation of castes leads to the development of subcultures, which are also reinforced by endogamous marriage. Distinctions include customs, traditions, practices, and rituals in addition to cultural signifiers such as attire, accent and vocabulary, gestures, and so on. Subcultures have their own informal rules and regulations (e.g., wealthy people consider talking about money vulgar).

The masses are exposed to mindless entertainment such as Hollywood films like *Dumb and Dumber* and *Dumb and Dumber To* [sic], starring Jim Carrey. They are distracted by sports like football, basketball, and baseball, debating such matters as who is the best pitcher rather than social problems. They consume music glorifying violence against women, gays, and drug-dealer competitors. They rely on social media and the occasional tabloid for information, rendering them poorly informed on everything of substance. Most cannot identify major countries on a map. Lower castes dress differently and speak devalued dialects with distinct accents. Blacks in the United States developed Ebonics, which elites brand as bad English, whereas poor people in England speak Cockney. Poor people's attire and grooming are distinct from that of upper castes.

Elites attend charity balls and high-society functions. They prefer to play sports that are socioeconomically segregated (e.g., tennis and lacrosse). In fact, Ivy League sports were explicitly established so that affluent students would not have to compete against superior working-class counterparts from public universities. As spectators of popular sports, they self-segregate in luxury skyboxes to maintain spatial and social distance from lower castes. They discuss "problems" like how to control the political system and how to discipline labor and break unions. Elites (with exceptions, such as President Trump) read the *New York Times* or the *Wall Street Journal*. They are well informed regarding economic, political, and international events and issues. Many can quickly find a country on the map and are likely to have been there. Elites speak formal English with distinct accents, wear expensive clothing, and sport costly haircuts.

1.2 *Educational Segmentation*

Aldous Huxley writes in *Brave New World Revisited*: "Under a scientific dictator education will really work—with the result that most men and women will grow up to love their servitude and will never dream of revolution. There seems to be no good reason why a thoroughly scientific dictatorship should ever be overthrown."[21] Whether or not they learned to love their work, lower castes historically did not have access to education beyond learning the skills

---

21 Huxley, 2004 [1958]: 340.

required to perform their parents' jobs. With the advent of industrialization and increasing bureaucratization of society, the labor force had to operate machinery, requiring literacy. This forced elites to introduce education for industrial serfs. Public education, however, lead to a militant demos, culminating in the 1960s social justice movements. Elites responded with caste war, beginning with attacks on public education to suppress critical thinking. This required the simplification of most tasks, which twenty-first-century technology made possible, permitting the postmodern spectacle to function with an uneducated population. For example, McDonald's developed cash registers with pictures of menu items. The cashier touches the picture of what is being ordered, the register totals the order, the cashier enters the amount of money given by the customer, and the register then instructs the employee how much change is due. If payment is rendered with a credit card, the last two steps become unnecessary. Automation has eliminated the need for serfs entirely in some cases, as brick-and-mortar retailers have been replaced by online sellers. Even traditional retailers are shedding serfs. For example, Amazon's new brick-and-mortar supermarkets (Go Stores) operate without cashiers or checkout lines.[22]

Robert Putnam observes that deepening and hardening educational inequality is "leading us down the road toward a—frankly, a caste society."[23] Poor districts are designed to fail. Educational segmentation in the United States is structural, based on local financing.[24] Lower-caste children are raised in ghettos where poor people lack the means to finance their own education. Impoverished communities with a low tax base cannot afford to build more schools, resulting in chronic overcrowding in dilapidated buildings that may lack heating in winter and air conditioning in the summer.[25] Books are outdated or insufficient. Computers and other equipment are outdated, insufficient, or broken. Windows are repaired with cardboard and tape. Many teachers are from the bottom of the barrel because high-performing educators avoid these dismal environments and are attracted by affluent school districts with better working conditions and salaries. Advanced courses are not typically offered in ghetto schools, and neither are many basic ones. Art, music, and foreign languages are the first to go because of budget shortfalls. Toilets back up, flooding classrooms with feces.[26] Rapes and murders occur on school grounds.[27] Many students drop out, ending up in prison or the military, on welfare, or getting

---

22 Johnston, 2018.
23 PBS NewsHour, 2015. See also Rosiek and Kinslow, 2016.
24 Reeves, 2017.
25 Kozol, 1991; Kozol, 2005.
26 Kozol, 1991.
27 Ibid.

by as drug dealers, prostitutes, or fast-food workers—just like the few who did graduate. Consequently they die in the ghettos where they were born.

Rich people live in communities with far higher property tax revenues.[28] These districts can afford schools resembling high-end college campuses, ones with outstanding facilities—athletic fields, theaters, computer rooms, heated swimming pools, recording studios and television stations, et cetera.[29] Classrooms are climate-controlled. Teacher-student ratios are low. Many teachers hold doctorates. Advanced placement courses and student clubs of all sorts abound. Almost all students graduate and enter Ivy Leagues thanks to rigged admissions policies.[30]

Upon graduation, armed with the proper signaling mechanism (an Ivy League degree), upper-caste children are offered fast-track career paths with high income, power, and authority.[31] Therefore, they can afford to live in the same sort of affluent communities they came from. Educational attainment legitimizes structurally rigged outcomes against poor people in favor of the affluent, reproducing the social order. Richard Reeves argues that the top 20 percent of the population (what he considers the upper middle class) is inoculating itself by rigging the educational system through school zoning, resulting in the growing disparities discussed here.[32] He concurs that upper-middle-class children become upper-middle-class adults, arguing that class separation becomes class perpetuation. This generational transmission of material resources, status, and power is the very basis of a caste system.

What passes for college education for the masses is virtual—and virtually worthless. This online education consists of endless standardized form-filling tests requiring mnemonic answers, algorithm-based machine scoring, and almost no handwriting. For-profit educational or technology corporations such as Pearson and Apple enter into collaborative programs with public universities to create Massive Open Online Courses (MOOCs). These are first-order simulacrums of college courses. The student is placed in an isolated relationship with an algorithm—between Googled information and context for that information. Face-to-face interaction between students and teachers is

---

28 Kozol, 1991; Kozol, 2005; Massey et al., 2009; Putnum, 2015.
29 Ibid.
30 Golden, 2006; Reeves, 2017.
31 In economics, *signaling* occurs when one sends information about oneself to another party. For example, job applicants signal their ability to employers through educational credentials (e.g., a bachelor's degree). Here upper-class applicants signal their class membership to prospective employers by obtaining degrees from elite educational institutions. See Domhoff, 2010: 51–54; Mills, 2000a [1956]: 62–68, 106–107.
32 Reeves, 2017.

digitized into a distant image, an online simulacrum of a real classroom with simulacrum instructors. For example, a professor of computer and cognitive science developed an algorithm named Jill as a component of online courses. Jill is an artificial intelligence teaching assistant that answers students' questions.[33] This is part of an online master's degree(!) at Georgia Tech, a traditional university. In the meantime, brick-and-mortar university education with human faculty is increasingly reserved for elites able to pay the higher tuition, including at Georgia Tech.

Higher college enrollment rates for the lower castes are not necessarily all good news.[34] Poor students are more likely to enroll in community colleges (14 percent of all poor people in 1972 but 32 percent in 2004) than at selective four-year universities where structural opportunities stem from.[35] Of those who attend community colleges, only 12 percent go on to obtain a bachelor's degree. Admissions rates for students from the bottom economic quartile at selective universities were 4 percent in 1972 and rose to 5 percent recently, compared to 26 percent (1972) and 36 percent for the top quartile. At the most selective institutions, the ratio between the students from top and bottom economic quartiles was 14 to 1. Worse, much of the recent growth in college enrollment by poor students has been at for-profit institutions such as the University of Phoenix and Kaplan University (acquired by Purdue University in 2017). This sector accounted for 13 percent of all full-time undergraduate enrollment in 2013, compared to 2 percent in 1991. These corporations are enrollment mills that milk federal student loan money, a major example being the now defunct Corinthian Colleges.[36] Students would either drop out at extraordinary rates or obtain worthless degrees from unaccredited programs. In the end, they were saddled with historic levels of student loans at taxpayers' expense for private profit. However, to reap the rewards of a college degree, one must graduate. College graduation rates are quite different between socioeconomic groups. In 2010, the graduation rate for the bottom economic quartile was the same as in the 1970s, at around 10 percent.[37] In contrast, the graduation rate for the top economic quartile in the 1970s was 40 percent, and this rose to 70–80 percent by 2010.[38] In addition, high-scoring poor children are less likely to obtain a college degree than their low-scoring rich counterparts. A family's socioeconomic status has always been the biggest predictor of educational success.

33 PBS NewsHour, 2017.
34 Putnam, 2015.
35 Ibid.
36 Allen, 2015; Putnam, 2015.
37 Putnam, 2015: 187.
38 Ibid.

Educational segmentation also reproduces unequal cultural capital. For example, educated affluent white parents have more close friends and broader social networks, and their children have a wider range of informal mentors.[39]

1.3   Economic Segmentation

Spatial segmentation intensifies caste-based employment because jobs are geographically segmented. Poor communities have few employers, most being fast-food corporations and small shops providing poverty wages. Major employers are typically located near affluent communities. Many poor people do not have cars to commute to better jobs, and, if they do have cars, they are unreliable. In addition, increasingly privatized mass transit is expensive and inefficient, requiring long hours to travel relatively short distances.

Economic segmentation determines differential consumption. Affluent communities are targeted with sophisticated propaganda. Residents enjoy exotic vacations, luxury cars, jewelry, exclusive dining and shopping, health care at award-winning hospitals, et cetera. They shop at picturesque downtown commercial districts and high-end luxury malls with exclusive anchor stores like Neiman Marcus and Nordstrom. They choose from products that are high-end and safe at retailers that offer better-than-average customer service and return policies. The shopping malls and stores they frequent are beautifully decorated and furnished, with couches and massage chairs for shoppers. The spaces are large, to prevent crowding, because upper castes are uncomfortable if their three-foot bubble of personal space is violated. These shopping centers are clean, with impeccable bathrooms providing privacy and amenities.

Poor people have limited consumption opportunities. Their downtowns are dilapidated, adorned with discarded condoms, syringes, and other trash, where homeless people sleep on sidewalks. They are targeted with ads for liquor stores, pawnshops, predatory payday lenders, check-cashing services, and bail bond agents. They shop at bare-bones mini-malls if they are lucky to have any near their communities and small stores with high prices. The few shopping centers available to them are typically big-box stores such as Walmart, offering low-quality and even dangerous products. These stores are crowded and dirty, with small grimy bathrooms offering little privacy. Customer service and return policies are poor, and customers are monitored as potential shoplifters.

Product segregation includes food and water. Rich people enjoy organic and exotic foods with extravagant prices, often purchased from specialty stores. Poor people live in food deserts where the only available food is at fast-food chains and convenience stores. It is almost impossible to find fresh produce in

---

39   Ibid.

these food deserts.[40] Available food is processed, a simulacrum of real food. It is unhealthy, contributing to obesity, high cholesterol, and diabetes in adults and children. Caste-based food restrictions are often codified, as in India. In the United States, Missouri GOP congressman Rick Brattin introduced House Bill 813 according to which recipients of the supplemental nutrition assistance [food stamps] program would be prohibited from using the benefits to purchase seafood or steak. Because, as Brattin states, 'I have seen people purchasing filet mignons and crab legs with their EBT cards. When I can't afford it on my pay, I don't want people on the taxpayer's dime to afford those kinds of foods either.'[41] He does understand but does not care that the value of food stamps (Supplemental Nutrition Assistance Program—SNAP) is insufficient to purchase enough food to survive let alone to buy healthy or "luxury" food such as vegetables or meat.[42] Note that about one-third of US households receive food stamps.[43] In 2018, the Trump administration proposed changes in SNAP that would limit recipients' food choices: over 80 percent of SNAP recipients "would get about half of their benefits in the form of a 'USDA Foods package.' The package was described in the budget as consisting of 'shelf-stable milk, ready to eat cereals, pasta, peanut butter, beans and canned fruit and vegetables.' The boxes would not include fresh fruits or vegetables."[44] Given that food stamps are a government program for poor people, they represent codified caste-based food restrictions: a third of the country must be semi-starved, eating poor-quality food.

Elites drink bottled water delivered to their door. Lower castes draw polluted tap water, as in Flint, Michigan. State authorities concealed the lead poisoning of the city's water supply for months, affecting 8,657 children under the age of six.[45] The water situation was different for Flint elites and corporations:

> General Motors discovered that the water from the Flint River was causing their car parts to erode and negotiated with the state to have the water supply at the corporate offices switched back to the Detroit water system. Similarly, a Flint hospital noticed that the water was damaging its instruments and decided to set up its own private filtering system. A local university did the same thing. David Rosner and Gerald Markowitz observed that "10 months before the administration of Governor Snyder

---

40 *Nutrition Digest.*
41 Ferdman, 2015.
42 McMillan, 2016; *Nutrition Digest.*
43 McMillan, 2016.
44 NPR, 2018.
45 Tanner, 2016.

admitted that Flint's water was unsafe to drink, the state had already begun trucking water into that city and setting up water coolers next to drinking fountains in state buildings" in order for state workers to be able to drink a safe alternative to the Flint water.[46]

1.4 Political Segmentation

Voting machines in poor neighborhoods are unreliable and often lack replacement parts.[47] There are no funds to enable these communities to update their equipment. Their citizens must contend with multi-hour waiting lines at polling stations. Voting rosters are outdated, preventing many from casting ballots. State-sponsored disenfranchisement schemes are rampant.[48] Illegal tactics are used to reduce voter turnout—for example, spreading rumors that the police will be at polling stations to arrest people with outstanding warrants. Poor people are denied voting rights because of prior felonies. These circumstances suppress the political participation of poor people, whose votes may not be counted anyway. This is a continuation of Jim Crow. Rich people experience short waits at polling stations with new machines.[49] Get-out-the-vote drives are intense, with micro-targeting based on computerized algorithms. Voting rosters are up-to-date. Billionaires like the Koch brothers send conservatives perfectly prepared mail-in ballots using large voter databases while challenging ballots mailed from poor communities.[50]

An insidious form of disenfranchisement is economic hardship, such as that of poor people forced to work long hours to servive due to poverty wages. Voting takes place on a Tuesday, a workday, and they have little time and energy for political participation. But, as Aristotle pointed out, for democracy to function, citizens need time to become engaged and informed regarding public matters.[51] As Richard Wolff observes: "A functioning democracy would require that all people be provided with the time, information, counsel, and other supports needed to participate effectively in decision-making in the workplace and at the local, regional, and national levels of their residential communities. The economic realities of capitalism preclude that for the overwhelming majority."[52]

---

46   Giroux, 2017: 19.
47   Norden and Famighetti, 2015.
48   Palast, 2004, 2012a.
49   Norden and Famighetti, 2015.
50   Palast, 2004; Palast, 2012a.
51   Aristotle, 1981.
52   Wolff, 2012: 95.

Structural segmentation includes gerrymandering, establishing a political advantage for a party or candidate by manipulating district boundaries. It is telling that incumbents rarely lose. Gerrymandering is also used to help or hinder particular groups based on background factors like ethnicity, race, and religion. The results of this can be seen in the 2012 congressional elections. Democrats, who are in theory sympathetic to poor people, received 1.1 million more votes than Republicans but received fewer congressional seats, leaving Republicans in the majority due to rigged districts.[53]

Politicians are actors, often literally, giving speeches tailored for specific audience segments. Between 2001 and 2016, Hillary and Bill Clinton made over $120 million in Wall Street speeches. Hillary's rate was $225,000 per talk. As a presidential hopeful, she refused to disclose the contents of her speeches at Wall Street firms in which she supported unrestrained free trade and balancing the budget in a way that would require cuts in Social Security. She claimed Wall Street was not to blame for the collapse of 2008 and stated that her wealth made her "kind of far removed" from working people.[54] Her rhetoric contradicted that of her public speeches, a contradiction she did not justify except to state that it was necessary to have "both a public and a private position."[55]

2 Total Propaganda

In *Nineteen Eighty-Four*, obedience was not enough; one had to believe the lies.[56] Why? Because if people simply obey, at some point they may resist if they believe that the social order is unfair and they are being lied to.[57] Therefore, elites must constantly socialize people to internalize the dominant ideology that legitimizes the system.

All hierarchical systems are based on propaganda, the only difference being its extent and depth.[58] In early societies, simple or primitive propaganda formed an embryonic spectacle, which Debord failed to recognize.[59] These

---

53 Palmer and Cooper, 2012.
54 Chozick, et al., 2016.
55 Ibid.
56 Orwell, 1992 [1949].
57 Blau, 1992.
58 Propaganda is the spreading of a message with ideas and information that may or may not be true but is intended to persuade its targeted audience to think and behave in a certain manner.
59 Debord believed that the spectacle emerged in modern times with the advent of capitalism.

societies had primitive technological delivery systems for propaganda—for example, via town criers, postings of decrees in town squares, and messengers on horseback. As a result, the reach and depth of propaganda was limited. It manifested as the legal code, holidays, public statues of the emperor and gods, and elite patronage of favored art and scholarship. As Debord observed, architecture also represents propaganda and power relations. Medieval cathedrals were the tallest buildings, symbolizing the dominance of religious ideology. Now skyscrapers are the tallest buildings, representing the dominance of market ideology.

The twenty-first-century spectacle shifted from primarily external to internalized control facilitated by the agents of socialization.[60] These include language, schools, culture/media/technology (now all three have morphed into one), the workplace, religion, and the state, all of which shape our values, norms, behavior, and worldview. Constant socialization in all spheres of life transformed postmodern nations into Goffman's "total institutions" masquerading as capitalist or socialist democracies.[61]

Propaganda has become ubiquitous thanks to digital technology, modern telecommunications (especially the internet and mobile computing), and advances in psychology. This is *total propaganda*, based on signs without originals—third-order simulacra. Total propaganda uses algorithms in online advertising, electoral campaigning, and more, targeting audience segments with surgical precision. Algorithms made "versificators" (novel-writing machines) imagined in *Nineteen Eighty-Four* a reality. In the 2016 presidential campaign, both parties deployed *bots* (algorithms), also known as *zombies* in social media. Bots generated a third of pro-Trump and a fifth of pro-Clinton tweets.[62] This type of bots are "socialbots" that may actually replicate depending on the social networking platform (e.g., Facebook and Twitter). Socialbots attempt to convince media users that they are a real person so as to spread propaganda clandestinely, and often they are successful. "Social media bots can be scarily natural. A study showed that 30 percent of users can be deceived by a bot. Well made bots can even gain your trust. For example, meet Lajello, a fictitious member in a book lovers' network. He became the second most liked and appreciated person within this network."[63]

The consumption of total propaganda is assured in large part thanks to the addictive nature of technology. Industry engineers who became whistle-blowers

---

60 Foucault's Panopticism now has reached its zenith. See, for example, Ahmed, 2018.
61 Goffman, 1961.
62 Guilbeault and Woolley, 2016.
63 Finger, 2015.

say that smart phones, tablets, and their applications are addictive by design that is referred to in the industry as "persuasive technology design." The reason for this is that companies earn more ad revenue the more time people spend using them.[64] It is telling that the average person checks his or her phone about 150 times a day, or every six minutes.[65] Children and young people are especially vulnerable. The Pew Research Center found that people ages eighteen to twenty-four exchange an average of 110 texts per day. And MRI brain scans of children who play video games over twenty hours per week are similar to those of drug and alcohol addicts.[66]

Propaganda shapes our cognitive framework through language because of elite linguistic dominance. Advertisers changed "Merry Christmas" to "Happy Holidays" in search of the dollars of non-Christian shoppers. George W. Bush's administration voided the Constitution and Bill of Rights with what was euphemistically named the Patriot Act, emulating Orwell's "freedom is slavery."[67] Linguistic propaganda uses slogans like "we fight for freedom" and symbols such as the US flag that elicit emotional responses (e.g., through appeals to nationalism, family, and traditional values). The purpose is to make people act irrationally. This has been demonstrated by MRI brain scans of subjects who participated in Walter Mischel's "Stanford marshmallow test."[68] The test found that when our emotions light up our ventral striatumin (the back of the brain, linked to addictions), the prefrontal cortex that gives us the capacity to reason was unable to take control.[69] Poverty, fear, and anxiety increase the receptivity of propaganda as well. Aldous Huxley explains how an autonomous demos is transformed through the emotional appeals of propaganda into an audience, using quotes from Hitler:

> The masses are utterly contemptible. They are incapable of abstract thinking and uninterested in any fact outside the circle of their immediate experience. Their behavior is determined, not by knowledge and reason, but by feelings and unconscious drives. It is in these drives and

---

64 PBS NewsHour Extra, 2017
65 Ibid.
66 Ibid.
67 Orwell, 1992 [1949].
68 The Stanford marshmallow experiment by psychologist Walter Mischel studied delayed gratification in the 1960s and 1970s. A child was offered a choice between one small reward provided immediately or two small rewards (marshmallows, cookies, or pretzels) if one waited for approximately fifteen minutes. During the test, the children were left alone in the room. The majority chose immediate gratification after visible efforts to resist.
69 Casey et al., 2011.

feelings that 'the roots of their positive as well as their negative attitudes are implanted.' To be successful a propagandist must learn how to manipulate these instincts and emotions. 'The driving force which has brought about the most tremendous revolutions on this earth has never been a body of scientific teaching which has gained power over the masses, but always a devotion which has inspired them, and often a kind of hysteria which has urged them into action. Whoever wishes to win over the masses must know the key that will open the door of their hearts.' . . . In post-Freudian jargon, of their unconscious.[70]

Referring to a post-World War II British program to teach students in public schools how to identify propaganda, Huxley informs us that

there were many persons to whom its activities seemed profoundly objectionable. Certain educators, for example, disapproved of the teaching of propaganda analysis on the grounds that it would make adolescents unduly cynical. Nor was it welcomed by the military authorities, who were afraid that recruits might start to analyze the utterances of drill sergeants. And then there were the clergymen and the advertisers. The clergymen were against propaganda analysis as tending to undermine belief and diminish churchgoing; the advertisers objected on the grounds that it might undermine brand loyalty and reduce sales. . . . These fears and dislikes were not unfounded. Too searching a scrutiny by too many of the common folk of what is said by their pastors and masters might prove to be profoundly subversive. In its present form, the social order depends for its continued existence on the acceptance, without too many embarrassing questions, of the propaganda put forth by those in authority and the propaganda hallowed by the local traditions.[71]

Spectacles systematically attack science and facts, replacing them with pseudo-facts to increase the receptivity of propaganda. Throughout the twentieth century, the tobacco industry employed "merchants of doubt" who for years persuaded the masses against the dangers of smoking.[72] When the tobacco industry's lies were exposed, the same merchants of doubt went to work for fossil fuel companies promoting climate change denial. Their tactics

---

70 Huxley, 2004 [1958]: 272. Ellipses in original.
71 Ibid.: 329–330.
72 Oreskes and Conway, 2010.

included establishing nonprofit think tanks secretly financed by the industry, with names implying protection of public interests. Propaganda thrives by glorifying ignorance while vilifying intellect and critical thinking as per Orwell's "Ignorance Is Strength."[73]

Postmodern societies shifted from economies based on industrial production and consumption of tangible goods to production and consumption of images, as Debord and Baudrillard posited. Content production is concentrated in a few media companies. In addition to integrating, these corporations are merging with service providers. The latter own the "pipes" that deliver content—for example, cable, phone, and wireless companies. Control of cultural production and distribution suppresses the dissemination of art and news that challenge social relations. This is no different from past hierarchical systems in which elites determined through their patronage what constitutes art and culture.

The media merged with politics, the military, the economy, and entertainment. It has become *propagentertainment* for distraction, reminiscent of Huxley: "But even in Rome there was nothing like the non-stop distraction now provided by newspapers and magazines, by radio, television and the cinema. In *Brave New World* non-stop distractions of the most fascinating nature (the feelies, orgy-porgy, centrifugal bumble-puppy) are deliberately used as instruments of policy, for the purpose of preventing people from paying too much attention to the realities of the social and political situation."[74]

Propagentertainment often manifests as a Hollywood movie, product placement (e.g., James Bond driving a BMW), or promotional tie-ins (e.g., toys in "Happy Meals"). It can appear as apparel, talking heads, elections, or protests. It can appear in social media like Twitter, YouTube, and Facebook, in Google searches, and in the ads that target us. Five technology companies, worth 10 percent of the S&P 500—Google, Amazon, Microsoft, Apple, and Facebook—mold how we think, filter the world, and shape culture by monopolizing the distribution of information.[75] For example, they manipulate which content (e.g., among search results, news stories, advertisements, Facebook pages, and YouTube videos) is presented first—or not at all.[76] As Baudrillard observes, the medium has become one with the message surrounding us in a bubble of propaganda: "The medium itself is no longer identifiable as such, and the

---

73 Orwell, 1992 [1949].
74 Huxley, 2004 [1958]: 267.
75 Foer, 2017; Maheshwari and Stevenson, 2017.
76 Ibid.

confusion of the medium and the message ... is the first great formula of this new era."[77]

Propagentertainment presents a worldview that blurs the lines between real and fake (if such lines can be said to exist). Cultural, political, and economic celebrities play themselves in cameos or roles in movies and scripted "reality" shows. Real shows and news broadcasts are imbedded in movies to simulate reality. Mock commentary by real news shows and anchors is imbedded in movies. In turn, movies and shows imbed themselves in the real world. When another iteration of the *Star Wars* franchise was released in December 2015, White House Press Secretary Josh Earnest walked onto the pressroom stage flanked by two Stormtroopers in full garb.[78] Behind such theatrical displays lies the success of actors-turned-politicians like Ronald Reagan, Arnold Schwarzenegger, and billionaire reality show star Donald Trump.

The bureaucratic systems that control cultural production and the media censor information. China deploys a "cyber wall" constructed by Western technology companies such as Cisco Systems and Facebook in the name of market access—meaning profits.[79] In market-based systems such as the United States, information is controlled through the privatization and concentration of media. Private ownership maintains the illusion of free media (compared to state-owned media), enabling their acceptance by the demos as providers of objective news rather than propaganda.

Propaganda is hidden by an illusion of choices and perspectives. There are thousands of radio and TV stations, newspapers, magazines, and publishers, but in the United States six conglomerates own 90 percent of all media outlets.[80] The illusion is based on the logical fallacy that big numbers must mean many choices and therefore a plurality, a democracy of voices. However, Chomsky observed that "in the American mass media you cannot find a single journalist, not a single syndicated political commentator who is a socialist.... Here in the United States there is an astonishing degree of ideological uniformity for such a complex country."[81] Chomsky demonstrates how media propaganda, rather than overt control, shapes public opinion.[82] For example, a Harvard study asked five thousand Americans how they thought wealth is distributed in the United States. Most believed that it was distributed far more evenly than it actually is. Asked to choose their ideal distribution of wealth,

---

77   Baudrillard, 1994: 30.
78   BBC, December 18, 2015.
79   Isaacnov, 2016.
80   Lutz, 2012.
81   Quoted in Gilman-Opalsky, 2011: 71.
82   Chomsky, 1989, 1994, 2002.

92 percent picked one that was more equitable.[83] Another study found that Fox network viewers were far more likely than others to be ignorant of basic facts related to economics and foreign policy, their errant beliefs reflecting the network's conservative propaganda.[84] Now "fake news" proliferates, especially on Facebook, which often constitutes the primary source of news for its users.

Hierarchical societies also deploy propaganda to control memory, an obstacle to domination.[85] In the words of Debord:

> Spectacular government, which now possesses all the means necessary to falsify the whole of production and perception, is the absolute master of memories. . . . Spectacular domination's first priority was to eradicate historical knowledge in general; beginning with just about all rational information and commentary on the most recent past. . . . With consummate skill the spectacle organises ignorance of what is about to happen and, immediately afterwards, the forgetting of whatever has nonetheless been understood. The more important something is, the more it is hidden. . . . With the destruction of history, contemporary events themselves retreat into a remote and fabulous realm of unverifiable stories, uncheckable statistics, unlikely explanations and untenable reasoning.[86]

Historical memory exposes the ever-changing lies of propaganda, which endlessly alters the past with revisionist accounts—about which Debord was especially critical. An example is the deification of Ronald Reagan by conservatives, although the same conservatives would have branded his actual record "communist" today. China offers a socialist example of state-controlled collective memory. For example, most of the Chinese population is unaware of the government's Tiananmen Square massacre of 1989.[87] In Orwell's *Nineteen Eighty-Four* all inconvenient facts disappear.[88] He got the idea from the Soviet Union, where, for example, university students were told to tear out certain pages of textbooks because of references to anything or anyone declared an enemy of the "people." Ancient emperors would destroy monuments and public references to those they hated so that they would be forgotten. For example, the Persian king threatened to expunge the Spartan king Leonidas and his three hundred from historical memory if they did not surrender.

---

83 Norton and Ariely, 2011.
84 Greenwald, 2004.
85 Giroux, 2014.
86 Debord, 1990: 10, 13–14, 16.
87 PBS NewsHour, 2014.
88 Orwell, 1992 [1949].

3 Symbolic Institutions

Aldous Huxley writes:

> Under the relentless thrust of accelerating over-population and increasing over-organization, and by means of ever more effective methods of mind-manipulation, the democracies will change their nature; the quaint old forms—elections, parliaments, Supreme Courts and all the rest—will remain. The underlying substance will be a new kind of non-violent totalitarianism. All the traditional names, all the hallowed slogans will remain exactly what they were in the good old days. Democracy and freedom will be the theme of every broadcast and editorial—but Democracy and freedom in a strictly Pickwickian sense. Meanwhile the ruling oligarchy and its highly trained elite of soldiers, policemen, thought-manufacturers and mind-manipulators will quietly run the show as they see fit.[89]

Social institutions within hierarchical societies merely symbolize their "manifest function," which was never meant to be realized.[90] Therefore these are *symbolic institutions*, third-order simulacra detached from the original meanings of the values that they purportedly espouse. This leads to contradictions resulting in situations in which, for example, the demos considers institutional processes rigged or ineffective without rejecting the institutions. Americans have low voter participation rates, believing Congress and the presidency do not reflect popular interests.[91] Yet Americans will point to these institutions as proof that the United States is a democracy. These institutions represent democracy without being democratic.

Symbolic institutions serve a number of latent functions, producing, legitimizing, and disseminating the dominant ideology, upon which the social order is based and from which it us reproduced. They mask elites from scrutiny, maintain the appearance of public control, and mediate "malreported" facts and the cognitive dissonance generated by the contradictions between propaganda and experience.[92]

---

89 Huxley, 2004 [1958]: 333–334.
90 According to Robert Merton (1968) manifest functions are obvious, stated, expected, or intended and typically beneficial. Latent functions are not obvious, unstated, unexpected, or unintended and typically malevolent.
91 United States Elections Project, 2017.
92 Winston Smith in Orwell's *Nineteen Eighty-Four*, working at the Ministry of Truth, finds slips of paper with terse messages suggesting that "malreported" and "malquoted" issues of a newspaper were to be corrected (1992 [1948]).

3.1   *Educational Institutions*

Universities symbolize critical thinking and freedom of speech. In reality, they disseminate propaganda while quelling independent thought. Elites purchase academics, universities, and think tanks to draft bills that in turn are enacted by puppet politicians.[93] An undercover investigation by Greenpeace demonstrated how easy and cheap it is to purchase academics from prestigious universities—to get them to say anything. Posing as representatives of fossil fuel interests, undercover investigators made agreements with William Happer of Princeton and Frank Clemente of Penn State University to publish bogus papers in support of the fossil fuel industry. Harper's price was $8,000 and Clemente's was $15,000 for an eight-to-ten page paper and $6,000 for newspaper opinion pieces.[94] Another climate change denier, Willie Soon of the Harvard-Smithsonian Center, was financed almost entirely by the fossil fuel industry and the Koch brothers.[95]

These are not isolated cases of unethical academics. Entire disciplines have been corrupted, above all economics.[96] The reactionary Koch brothers donated over $68 million from 2005 to 2013 to 398 institutions of higher learning to influence academic departments and their curricula. The agreements stipulated that the money would be donated on the condition that the centers, departments, and faculty would be congruent with the Kochs' ideology, requiring the brothers' approval.[97] The *Tampa Bay Times* revealed that the Koch Charitable Foundation agreed to give Florida State University a large donation to fund programs in its Economics Department, provided that the foundation appoint the advisory committees that hire the professors and conduct their annual evaluations.[98] Professors at public universities make on average $50,000 to $100,000 annually. However, the foundation offered Bob Benson, a sympathetic faculty member at Florida State, an extra $100,000 to be chair of the Economics Department in order to get the agreement signed. In addition, Charles Koch is on the board of directors at various universities, including George Mason University's Mercatus Center. A student commented, "It is as if our university's name and prestige is being used to push forth ideology and research that benefits the corporations that are funding it, which I believe is a significant conflict of interest."[99] Indeed, these conflicts of interest render academia a whore for hire.

---

93   Domhoff, 2010.
94   Goldenberg, 2015.
95   Ibid.
96   Ferguson, 2011.
97   Myers, 2015.
98   Ibid.
99   Ibid.: 7.

Structural conditions force educational institutions to accept ideologically conditional charity. When elites and corporations reduce their tax burden through for-sale legislators, lobbyists, and tax lawyers, they effectively reduce government revenue. The resulting budget deficits are used to justify cuts to education. As taxes on the elite drop, state support of public colleges drops accordingly. As a result, 47.1 percent of public higher education expenses in the United States were covered by tuition in 2014 compared to 24.5 percent in 2000.[100] The City University of New York, where I teach, was founded as a tuition-free workers' college. Now it is mostly supported by constantly rising student tuition that prices higher education out of reach for poor people.

Simulacrum education for the masses guts critical thinking in favor of job training and renders the population receptive to propaganda. Students are socialized to respect authority figures and accept the legitimacy of the social order:

> In the Brave New World, no citizens belonging to the lower castes ever gave any trouble. Why? Because, from the moment he could speak and understand what was said to him, every lower-caste child was exposed to endlessly repeated suggestions, night after night, during the hours of drowsiness and sleep. These suggestions were 'like drops of liquid sealing wax, drops that adhere, incrust, incorporate themselves with what they fall on, till finally the rock is all one scarlet blob. Till at last the child's mind *is* these suggestions and the sum of these suggestions *is* the child's mind. And not the child's mind only. The adult's mind too—all his life long. The mind that judges and desires and decides—made up of these suggestions.'[101]

Aristotle and the ancient Athenians considered pedagogy to be the foundation of substantive democracy, in which all children were trained to govern as adults. Education was supposed to cultivate democratic citizenship as an ingrown habit, a peoples' "constitution." Modern schools, in contrast, seek to squash any possibility of a self-governing demos. H. L. Mencken observed:

> [The] erroneous assumption is to the effect that the aim of public education is to fill the young of the species with knowledge and awaken their intelligence, and so make them fit to discharge the duties of citizenship

---

100   Ibid.: 9.
101   Huxley, 2004 [1958]: 312.

in an enlightened and independent manner. Nothing could be further from the truth. The aim of public education is not to spread enlightenment at all; it is simply to reduce as many individuals as possible to the same safe level, to breed and train a standardised citizenry, to put down dissent and originality. That is its aim in the United States, whatever the pretensions of politicians, pedagogues and other such mountebanks, and that is its aim everywhere else.[102]

Another latent function of institutions of higher education is to reduce poor people to debt bondage via student loans that require a lifetime to repay and cannot be discharged through bankruptcy—unlike corporate debt. As reported in early 2018, two-thirds of graduating US college students had over $1.5 trillion in combined educational loans.[103] That amount does not include money from retirement savings, parents, and credit card accounts that students use to finance their education. Student debt has surpassed credit card debt, making it the second highest form of consumer debt behind mortgages. The economic insecurity that debt entails guarantees a docile workforce whose education is largely limited to vocational training.

Public institutions have become increasingly privatized in all but name. For example, public universities in New York have had their property seized, in a perverse enclosure of the educational commons to benefit for-profit corporations. Corporations are invited under the SUNY Tax-Free Areas to Revitalize and Transform Upstate New York, established by New York governor Andrew Cuomo, to relocate to SUNY campuses for a ten-year tax exemption.[104] Public K–12 schools are being privatized by the charter school and voucher movements spearheaded by elites and their foundations. This is crowned with the appointment of billionaire Betsy DeVos as the secretary of education in the Trump administration. She and her children never set foot in public schools. To the contrary, DeVos has devoted her life to campaigning against public schools in favor of privatization schemes like voucher programs. One highly active nonprofit creating public educational policy is the Bill and Melinda Gates Foundation. These billionaire-backed education schemes are imposed upon the public by corporate politicians including "Wall Street" Cuomo and New Jersey district superintendent Cami Anderson in Newark, both of whom have embraced charter schools.[105] In contrast to foundations' and politicians' claims,

---

102   Quoted in Leithner, 2010.
103   Borodovsky, 2018.
104   Myers, 2015.
105   McCauley, 2015; NJTV News, 2017.

charter schools usually perform worse than their public counterparts.[106] Their true intent is to subvert collective bargaining, since most charters are exempt from unionization laws governing public institutions. They also undermine public control over curricula. For example, Bill Gates spent $2.3 billion to promote the Common Core program despite the fact that educators overwhelmingly opposed it on pedagogical grounds.[107]

Curricula are also privatized for profit, transferring power from faculty to corporations. Pearson's motto, "always learning," is commonly détourned to "always earning." As an example, the British-based corporation made a £4.9 billion profit in 2013.[108] In addition to overpricing textbooks, Pearson owns imprints such as Penguin, Prentice Hall, FT (Financial Times) Press, and Adobe Press. It profits from selling tests such as the Miller Analogies and assessments such as the Partnership for Assessment of Readiness for College and Careers, including tutoring guides, test preparation aids, teacher evaluation materials, and curricula.

Corporate control of curricula threatens academic freedom. This includes refusal to hire critical professors, as the Koch financing cases demonstrate. Critical professors are routinely harassed by outside groups (and often administrators) and fired. However, the greatest threat to dissent in academia is the casualization of the professoriate leading to precarity. Now adjunct, temporary, and non-tenure-track college teaching positions far outnumber tenure-track and tenured positions that were once the norm. Tenured positions provide greater job security and the freedom to critique. Increasing time on the tenure track, sometimes as long as ten years, undermines academic freedom too. This gives administrators and conservative faculty time to weed out critical voices and condition those who remain into obedient silence. Lengthening the tenure process represents the slow death of tenure.

3.2   Economic Institutions

As if straight out of Orwell, corporations are now people! Corporations have evolved into symbolic (simulated) legal persons based on a bastardized interpretation of the Fourteenth Amendment. In the 1886 case *Santa Clara v. Southern Pacific*, the chief justice of the Supreme Court stated that the Fourteenth Amendment applied to natural persons and corporations.[109] Two years later in the 1888 case *Pembina Consolidated Silver Mining Co. v. Pennsylvania*, the

---

106   Kirp, 2013.
107   Green, 2014.
108   On Campus, 2015: 12.
109   Calvert, 2016.

court affirmed: "Under the designation of 'person' there is no doubt that a private corporation is included. Such corporations are merely associations of individuals united for a special purpose and permitted to do business under a particular name and have a succession of members without dissolution."[110] The Supreme Court's ruling in *Citizens United v. Federal Election Commission* in 2010 went further. It allowed corporations to make political contributions citing First Amendment rights, originally understood to apply to natural persons.

Financial markets like the New York Stock Exchange are capital incarnate. One of their functions is to promulgate the illusion that capital (stock) ownership is widely dispersed among the demos, implying economic democracy. This masks extreme stock concentration. In 2013 the top 1 percent and top 10 percent of households owned 49.8 percent and 91 percent respectively of all stocks and mutual funds, while the bottom 90 percent accounted for only 9.1 percent (see Table 2.1). As for the broad-based ownership widely reported, it is mostly through measly amounts in 401(k) retirement accounts.

Economic regulation is performed by the invisible hand (as described by Adam Smith), a symbolic entity assigned as regulator (a third-order simulation). Markets ostensibly symbolize fairness based on competition. In reality, markets have always been regulated to benefit elites. For example, the Securities and Exchange Commission (SEC) functions as symbolic regulator to convince people that markets are not rigged. Yet one of the world's greatest Ponzi schemes was orchestrated by Bernie Madoff, former chairman of the NASDAQ stock market, right under the SEC's nose despite warnings from whistleblowers.[111] The staff members of these agencies are not necessarily to blame.

TABLE 2.1   Wealth distribution in 2013 for the bottom 90%, top 10% and 1% of households.

Percent	Bottom 90%	Top 10%	Top 1%
Total net worth	22.9	77.1	36.7
Stocks and mutual funds	9.1	91	49.8
Business equity	6.2	93.8	62.8
Financial securities	5.7	94.3	54.7
Non-home real-estate	22.2	77.8	33.7
Debt	73.5	26.5	5.4

Source: WOLFF, 2014.

110   Justia, B.
111   Ferguson, 2011.

Elites eliminate regulation by gutting the budgets necessary for agencies to perform their tasks. It is telling that at the time of the 2008 financial collapse, the staff at the SEC had been reduced to one person, rendering regulatory oversight illusory.[112]

The Federal Reserve regulates the economy through monetary policy. It is a "quasi-independent" institution to prevent manipulation for political purposes, consisting of private banks and a politically appointed president and charged with protecting the entire economy. In reality it only represents elite interests. Most Fed presidents and officials are corporate executives from the financial world. Clearly regulation in favor of the majority is symbolic when the decision-makers overwhelmingly represent capital. For example, in response to the economic collapse of 2008 caused by financial institutions, the Federal Reserve implemented a six-year bond-buying program (printing money under its "quantitative easing" program—QE) to prop up the economy. The cost was $4 trillion, not counting the value of free money at zero interest for major financial institutions and banks. These policies almost exclusively benefited stock owners, who are mostly elites.

However, in a depression the problem is insufficient aggregate demand. Trickle-down economic policies retard GDP growth, as the International Monetary Fund has admitted.[113] Instead of the $4 trillion QE, the Federal Reserve could have issued every American a check for $12,837.[114] This would not have created inflationary pressures, given that the problem was deflation due to collapsed aggregate demand. Keep in mind, the Federal Reserve's mandate is to promote sustainable growth *and* high levels of employment. Clearly, the Federal Reserve's policies assisted capital, not labor, given an environment of stagnant wages amid inflation due to QE. The destruction of house values when the housing bubble burst, losses in 401(k) retirement accounts, and monetary policy favoring upper castes resulted in historic concentration of wealth. This represents the greatest financial enclosure of the twenty-first century.

In addition, the twenty-first-century spectacle has destroyed traditional employment models. Many industries employ just a fraction of the labor force employed a few decades ago or have replaced their workforce through digitization and automation. High unemployment is hidden through statistical manipulation (e.g., by not counting *discouraged workers*).[115] Consequently,

---

112   Ibid.
113   Dabla-Norris et al., 2015.
114   This figure represents $4 trillion divided by a population of 311,591,917 as reported by the 2011 US Census.
115   A discouraged worker is a person who has given up looking for employment, typically after long periods of time.

the labor force participation rate reached historic lows at 62.6 percent of the population.[116] This prompted books with titles such as *The Jobless Future* and *The End of Work*, books questioning the very model of employment-based societies.[117] Employment rates also hide that many are underemployed, work for poverty wages at dead-end jobs, or are college graduates taking positions that do not require degrees, often not even in their fields of study. Therefore, postmodern labor markets are simulacrums of Fordist production.

Even core workers, the most necessary, could be replaced by automation or have their compensation reduced to poverty levels. The reason this does not happen is that core workers function as symbols—they show many that the system provides opportunities for better lifestyles. The hope of winning the employment lottery renders the unemployed and exploited obedient—quieting, for example, an adjunct professor hoping for a tenure-track position. This is what sociologists term "anticipatory socialization." Those who are employed become docile because the last thing they want is to lose that lottery ticket, their job. Labor markets transform the demos from collaborators into competitors. After all, *we can't all hit the (employment) lottery.*

3.3   Political Institutions

"Nobody has ever seen Big Brother," George Orwell wrote in *Nineteen Eighty-Four*. "He is a face on the hoardings, a voice on the telescreen. We may be reasonably sure that he will never die, and there is already considerable uncertainty as to when he was born. Big Brother is the guise in which the Party chooses to exhibit itself to the world. His function is to act as a focusing point for love, fear, and reverence, emotions which are more easily felt towards an individual than towards an organization."[118] Likewise postindustrial democracy is symbolic. It vaunts governance by the demos to hide caste-based rule. The concept of representative democracy sustains the fiction that a smaller group embodies the will of all—another way of legitimizing governance by the few.[119] At a minimum, industrial democracy implies the rotation of political power through elections. However, if politicians are always drawn from the elite or those beholden to them, then power is not truly rotated. When all options are variations of the same ideology, choice is illusory, for example, the Democratic and Republican Parties. Rather, it is the face of Big Brother that is rotated. As Debord and Castoriadis observe, this is also true of revolutionary parties that

---

116   Data for 2015. US Department of Labor, n.d.
117   Aronowitz and Difazio, 1994; Rifkin, 1996.
118   Orwell, 1992 [1949]: 216–217.
119   Asimakopoulos, 2016.

enter formal political participation because that is by definition acceptance of the structure. The experience of Greece's SYRIZA party, a hodge-podge of communist groups, is indicative. It came to office in 2014 as a grassroots social movement opposing austerity and EU bailout packages. Predictably, SYRIZA too was forced into the same structural bondage as the capitalist and socialist governments that it had criticized.

Social movements and protests have been sanitized and regulated to occur within circumscribed parameters to thwart substantive challenges to elite interests. Organizers of protests and marches are required to obtain permits that spell out in detail what is and is not allowed. Mass protests, which used to be, by definition, autonomous expressions of the demos, are thus transformed into a regulated third-order simulation carried out by an audience. In turn, the audience is pacified with the satisfaction that it had its say by practicing its constitutional right of free expression. Similarly, spectacular socialism or communism (e.g., that of the former Soviet Union and contemporary China) permit only state-sponsored mass gatherings. Should unsanctioned protests get out of hand, a so-called peoples' party sends out tanks *against* the people, as with the Tiananmen Square massacre of 1989.

Therefore, all parties and politicians are reformist at best. It is the elites who determine the options. This is true of all hierarchies. For example, under Chinese rule, 0.29 percent of the people in Hong Kong select the political candidates permitted to run for high office.[120] In the United States, 0.2 percent of the richest funders determine the "viable candidates."[121] Laura Cha, who was in China's parliament and at the same time a member of the board of HSBC Holdings, a British multinational banking and financial services company headquartered in London, stated, "American slaves were liberated in 1861 but did not get voting rights until 107 years later, so why can't Hong Kong wait for a while?" Cha's comments came after Hong Kong leader Leung Chun-ying stated that free elections were unacceptable, in part because they risked giving Hong Kong's poor and working-class people a dominant voice.[122] In China and Cuba it is the politburo that selects who can be a candidate for political office. In Russia it is Big Brother, currently Vladimir Putin, representing the remnants of the Communist Party turned fascist, that determines viable candidates.

Plato observed that in oligarchic societies wealth determines access to political participation.[123] Postmodern democracy is nominal, given extreme

---

120   Moyers & Company, 2014.
121   Ibid.
122   Downes, 2014.
123   Plato, 1970.

economic inequality: the richest 1 percent own 42.1 percent of all wealth, while the bottom 60 percent of Americans hold 3 percent of the wealth.[124] Elites, epitomized by kings, have always controlled political systems. Now they do so through symbolic democracy, which they purchase. There is no pretense that democracy is not purchased. The infamous *Citizens United* ruling led to a deluge of money entering the electoral process, often by anonymous billionaires through super-PACs. Thus, the contradictory situation where in a democracy there is a principle of one person, one vote, but in this democracy with as much free speech to deliberate in the political process as one has money. Ironically, this is congruent with market ideology according to which you can have any and as many goods and services that you are willing and able to pay for. This constitutes the political exclusion of the third estate.

During the 2012 presidential election, elites contributed millions to Republicans and Democrats.[125] Casino magnate Sheldon Adelson spent over $150 million, promising to double that in the future.[126] Elites also get the ear of candidates at costly fund-raising events that are beyond the reach of the majority. In 2010 President Obama attended a fund-raiser dinner at $30,400 a plate at a time when the minimum wage was $7.25 an hour.[127] In 2016 Democrat presidential candidate Hillary Clinton was beholden to Wall Street for her campaign financing, as her husband Bill Clinton and Obama had been.[128] The payoff for legalized bribery is substantial. From 2007 to 2012, the top two hundred corporations spent $5.8 billion on campaign contributions and lobbying.[129] The return on their investment exceeded $4.4 trillion in government contracts and assistance. In comparison, during that time the federal government paid $4.3 trillion in Social Security for fifty million recipients.

Purchasing political office has been common practice. In 2010 Republican Meg Whitman ran for governor of California, spending $119 million of her own money, breaking a record by billionaire Michael R. Bloomberg who spent $102 million for his successful reelection campaign for mayor of New York in 2005.[130] Historically, running for high political office represents upper-caste status competition. In the past, noble families wanted to produce generals, cardinals, popes, governors, and kings. Now Ivy League schools and elite families brag about how many generals, Supreme Court justices, senators, and presidents

---

124   *Global Wealth Databook 2016*, 2016.
125   Blumenthal, 2012.
126   Wing, 2012.
127   H. Friedman, 2010.
128   Open Secrets, n.d.
129   Allison and Harkins, 2014.
130   Barbaro, 2009; Nagourney, 2010.

they have produced. But how many generals, Supreme Court justices, senators, and presidents did the welfare mothers of the South Bronx, New York or Paterson, New Jersey, produce?

In 2008, two-thirds of US senators were millionaires.[131] In 2014 federal lawmakers as a group were worth about $4.4 billion, the median net worth among senators was $2.9 million, the median wealth for members of Congress was $1.1 million (in 2013 more than half were millionaires), and all nine Supreme Court justices were multimillionaires. In comparison, less than 1 percent of Americans have $1 million or more in financial assets.[132] Political and corporate elites are one and the same. Hank Paulson, treasury secretary under George W. Bush, was a CEO at Goldman Sachs. His successor as the first treasury secretary under Obama, Tim Geithner, was another Goldman Sachs executive. With the presidential election of Trump, Steven Mnuchin became the treasury secretary. Mnuchin too once worked at Goldman Sachs—for seventeen years, including as chief information officer.

Hillary Clinton's 2016 presidential campaign epitomized the merger of politics and spectacle with free concerts (actually political rallies) featuring music superstars Beyoncé and rapper husband Jay Z, Stevie Wonder, Bon Jovi, R&B singer Ne-Yo, singers Cher and Jennifer Lopez, pop star Katy Perry, and basketball superstar LeBron James, to name just a few.[133] Donald Trump, on the other hand, was a reality TV superstar who carried that persona (a real-world media avatar) into his presidential campaign. Trump revolutionized US political campaigning by running his as a movie promoter, relying heavily on Twitter and sensationalism.

Elections are symbolic rituals, simulations disconnected from any original meaning. According to Aristotle, elections are not democratic but an element of aristocracy, thus caste. For him, substantive democracy meant "participation in giving judgment [judicial authority] and in holding office [having equal chance to participate in governing bodies]."[134] According to Castoriadis:

> Scholars merely repeat today that Aristotle's preferred constitution, what he calls politeia, is a mixture of democracy and aristocracy, and forget to add that for Aristotle the "aristocratic" element in this politeia is the election of the magistrates—for Aristotle clearly and repeatedly defines election as an aristocratic principle. This is also clear for Montesquieu and

---

131 Rampell, 2009.
132 Center for Responsive Politics, n.d.
133 Lerer and Colvin, 2016.
134 Aristotle, 1981: 169.

Rousseau. It is Rousseau, not Marx or Lenin, who writes that Englishmen believe that they are free because they elect their Parliament, but in reality are only free one day every five years. . . . representation is a principle alien to democracy.[135]

Simulated democracy, however, alienates citizens, leading to low voter participation rates and further enabling elites to rule.[136] For example, the voter participation rate of the 2014 midterm elections was 37 percent, the lowest since 1942.[137] Low participation rates reflect a withdrawal of the body politic from politics—and for good reason. Research demonstrates that representative democracies respond to and represent only elite interests.[138] One study based on 1,779 variables for policy issues from 1982 to 2002 found the US system to act more as an oligarchy than a democracy: "Multivariate analysis indicates that economic elites and organized groups representing business interests have substantial independent impacts on U.S. government policy, while average citizens and mass-based interest groups have little or no independent influence. The results provide substantial support for theories of Economic-Elite Domination and for theories of Biased Pluralism, but not for theories of Majoritarian Electoral Democracy or Majoritarian Pluralism."[139] These findings are supported by a survey based on data from 2001 through 2010. The survey compared the views of ninety thousand voters with their senators' voting records. The study found that both Republican and Democrat senators voted in the interests of their richest constituents while ignoring those of the poor.[140] Therefore, Orwell's line from *Animal Farm*, "some animals are more equal than others," is a sentiment shared by modern elites.[141] According to venture capitalist Tom Perkins, "Only taxpayers should have the right to vote . . . wealthy Americans who pay more in taxes should get more votes."[142] Let us not forget that the Founders required that voters be property holders. Elites are now abandoning the pretense of democracy altogether, arguing that less democracy would be beneficial for the demos. The title of an article is indicative: "Professor at Koch-Funded University Department Calls for 'Less Democracy.'"[143]

---

135   Castoriadis, 1991: 107–108.
136   United States Elections Project, 2017.
137   Associated Press, 2014.
138   Bartel, 2005.
139   Gilens and Page, 2014: 564.
140   Hayes, 2012.
141   Orwell, 1993 [1945].
142   Riley, 2014.
143   Zaid, 2015.

Elites see democracy as a problem to their "plutonomy." According to an infamous Citigroup confidential memo to premium clients:

> Our thesis is that the rich are the dominant drivers of demand in many economies around the world (the U.S., U.K., Canada, and Australia). These economies have seen the rich take an increasing share of income and wealth over the last 20 years, to the extent that the rich now dominate income, wealth and spending in these countries.... Asset booms, a rising profit share, and favorable treatment by market-friendly governments have allowed the rich to prosper and become a greater share of the economy in plutonomy countries.... Tech whizzes ... lawyers and bankers who intermediate globalization and productivity, the CEOs who lead the charge in converting globalization and technology to increase the profit share of the economy at the expense of labor, all contribute to plutonomy.[144]

A structural safeguard against radical politicians taking office in the United States is the Electoral College that selects the president. The Electoral College is feudal in nature, conceived by the oligarchic Founders, who did not trust the rabble to make the right choice. The Electoral College has overturned the popular vote five times (1824, 1876, 1888, 2000, and 2016), as if that mattered. The US Senate is also a feudal element tied to land. For example, sparsely populated conservative Wyoming has two senators, just as the most populated states, like liberal California.

Ultimately, even if undesirables win office they can sometimes simply be replaced by appointed representatives of elites. This is worse than in feudal times when peasants had political representation as an estate. Detroit is indicative how the democratic process is voided for lower castes by decree:

> For more than a decade now, Michigan governors have been appointing so-called "emergency managers" (EMs) to run school districts and cities for which a "state of financial emergency" has been declared. These unelected administrators rule by fiat—they can override local elected officials, break union contracts, and sell off public assets and privatize public functions at will. It's not incidental that the vast majority of the people who have lived under emergency management are black. Flint, whose population was 55.6 percent black as of the 2010 census (in a state

---

144 Kapur, Macleod, and Singh, 2006.

whose population is 14.2 percent black overall), was under emergency management from December 2011 to April 2015. . . . It was during that period that the decision was made to stop purchasing water from Detroit and start drawing water directly from the Flint River.[145]

3.4 Legal Institutions

Guy Debord writes, "We can see the profound truth of the Sicilian Mafia's maxim . . . : 'When you've got money and friends, you can laugh at the law.' In the integrated spectacle, *the laws are asleep*. . . . In many fields, laws are even made precisely *so that they may be evaded*, by those who have the means to do so."[146] Legal rights and protections are symbolic. As in any caste system, there are two sets of laws: one for the nobles and another for everyone else. This was formal during feudalism as it was during US slavery, whereas today it is informal. This includes disparities in sentencing according to caste—for example, prison terms for crack, used primarily by poor people of color, versus misdemeanors for cocaine, used mostly by affluent whites. The modern justice system is rigged, based on money for lawyers and political power to pressure judges or prosecutors. Unemployed people, those on assistance, and people earning poverty wages are barred from exercising their rights. A low-wage laborer or professional (most of whom have little to no savings) who was illegally fired or sexually harassed would not be able to afford a lawyer's exorbitant retainer fee to fight a case with minimal odds of success in the pro-business judicial system. Poor people and minorities are more likely to be arrested as suspects (due to racial profiling, for example) and to be shot for suspicion of minor crimes. White suspects are arrested without harm and well treated, even when suspected of violent crimes. White-collar criminals are rarely investigated, let alone prosecuted, because they are likely to hire competent lawyers and avoid convictions. Such cases would require an inordinate amount of the prosecutor's time and resources. A prosecutor's career often depends on obtaining high conviction rates, and focusing on crimes by the powerful would result in fewer convictions. The lower castes are targeted because they are less likely to afford competent legal representation and are therefore likely to accept fast plea bargains, even if innocent, to avoid potential lengthy sentences—resulting in high conviction rates.

The financial collapse of 2008 is indicative. Wall Street institutions were engaging in industrial-scale fraudulent mortgage practices. These practices included creating worthless financial instruments that eventually caused the

---

145 Third Coast Conspiracy, 2016.
146 Debord, 1990: 70.

collapse of the global financial system. No one was charged, prosecuted, or sent to prison in the aftermath. Why? Because upper castes who were involved in structural fraud would not prosecute themselves. Elites profited at the expense of the lower castes' taxes, savings, house values, and pensions that were heavily invested in the vast Ponzi scheme. Systemic corruption included that at major banks, financial institutions, credit rating houses, the Federal Reserve, and government regulatory agencies, and by politicians, police, and major business and news media.[147] For example, it was revealed that JPMorgan Chase corrupted and colluded with lawyers, regulators, judges, politicians, and even the attorney general to hide its fraud, leading to the epic collapse.[148] Attorney General Eric Holder testified before the Senate Judiciary Committee that financial institutions were "too big to jail" in the aftermath of the 2008 financial collapse.[149] After public uproar, Holder backtracked, saying he meant *not* too big to jail. He then returned to the Wall Street firm that he had worked for before becoming attorney general.

As for judges and prosecutors, most of them are from privileged castes, not the oppressed from the ghettos. Like Clarence Thomas of the Supreme Court, most judges were corporate lawyers representing the interests of companies whose cases they later rule on. In addition, politicians, who also represent the interests of the corporations that they worked for, appoint many judges.

3.5 *Protective Institutions*

The function of protective institutions is to manage the marginalized through violence. No hierarchical system can rule without a military or security forces. Without the use or threat of violence, it would be impossible to maintain extreme inequality. Members of protective institutions are recruited from the ruling, noble, and oppressed castes.[150] The foot soldiers and low-level bureaucrats are from the oppressed; officers and mid-level and technical staff are from the privileged caste; and executives and policy makers are from the ruling and noble castes.

In the United States, as of 2016, there were 3,351,620 people in civilian protective service occupations such as police, correctional officers, bailiffs, private detectives and investigators, and security guards.[151] In 2017, in addition, there were 2,175,332 military personnel not counted by the Bureau of Labor Statistics

---

147 Ferguson, 2011.
148 Taibbi, 2014a.
149 Democracy Now, 2015.
150 See Chapter 5 for the breakdown of postmodern caste groups.
151 U.S Department of Labor, 2016.

(comprising over 1.3 million people in the active services across all military branches, 826,000 in the National Guard and reserve forces, and 49,332 in the US Coast Guard).[152] This brings the total employed in protective services and military personnel to 5,526,952. In addition, there are 3 million civilians employed by the defense industry directly, making things like weapons, and indirectly, such as working in local businesses supported by a defense contractor's location in a town.[153] This brings the grand total to 8,526,952. That is 2.7 percent of the population whose means of survival depend on the status quo, and more than that when the families of these workers are factored in.[154] This is a far larger percentage of the population than such workers comprised during feudalism. An additional function of these institutions is to co-opt members of other castes through employment.

Law enforcement symbolizes peacekeeping, but its real function has been to act as a domestic occupation force, safeguarding elite interests against direct action. Now police forces are militarized with surplus arms and equipment from the twenty-first-century neocolonial wars. The military symbolizes national defense, but it really is an imperial army securing elite interests abroad and domestically when needed. As in Orwell's *Nineteen Eighty-Four*, constant war justifies a militarized society and increased control over the demos.[155] As Aldous Huxley explains: "Liberty, as we all know, cannot flourish in a country that is permanently on a war footing, or even a near-war footing. Permanent crisis justifies permanent control of everybody and everything by the agencies of the central government." Later in *Brave New World Revisited* Huxley writes about Ivan Pavlov's experiments with conditioning, experiments in which dogs were the subjects: "It has been found that the deliberate induction of fear, rage or anxiety markedly heightens the dog's suggestibility. If these emotions are kept at a high pitch of intensity for a long enough time, the brain goes 'on strike.' When this happens, new behavior patterns may be installed with the greatest of ease. Among the physical stresses that increase a dog's suggestibility are fatigue, wounds and every form of sickness."[156] A sinister function of war includes the deflection of citizen anger. We are told to believe that the lack of investment in infrastructure, education, health care, housing, and more are not due to the greed of ruling elites. Instead, the culprit, deserving of one's hate, is the enemy of the hour—to justify a massive military budget.

---

152 US Department of Defense, 2017.
153 Rizzo, 2011.
154 Based on the 2015 population of 321,773,630.
155 Orwell, 1992 [1949].
156 Huxley, 2004 [1958]: 246–247, 290.

Violence has become normalized and glorified through entertainment that desensitizes us. Examples include wrestlers who are a third-order simulacrum reminiscent of Roman gladiators that can be recycled rather than consumed (killed) in the arena, as Baudrillard would point out; Hollywood movies in which the hero kills the most people and causes the greatest destruction; "reality" police shows; and simulated violence in video games. For example, the Atlantic Council hired the creators of the popular video game Call of Duty to consult them on ideas regarding the future of war, given that the game was a hit among both US soldiers and jihadists.[157] Ultimately, as Brad Evans and Henry Giroux write in *Disposable Futures*:

> The spectacle of violence represents more than the public enactment and witnessing of human violation. It points to a highly mediated regime of suffering and misery, which brings together the discursive and the aesthetic such that the performative nature of the imagery functions in a politically contrived way.... The spectacle works by turning human suffering into a spectacle, framing the terrifying moment of violence, and in doing so renders some lives meaningful while others are viewed as disposable.... It works precisely at the level of subjectivity by manipulating our desires such that we learn to consume violence, becoming fascinated by its horrors, and reducing brutality to the level of entertainment divorced from ethical considerations and political contextualization. The spectacle forces us to experience a brutalizing simulacrum, positively invested in its occurrence.[158]

Moreover, Debord argues that the sham of democracy is based on terrorism: "Such a perfect democracy constructs its own inconceivable foe, terrorism. Its wish is *to be judged by its enemies rather than by its results*. The story of terrorism is written by the state and it is therefore highly instructive. The spectators must certainly never know everything about terrorism, but they must always know enough to convince them that, compared with terrorism, everything else must be acceptable, or in any case more rational and democratic."[159] Postmodern states themselves engage in terrorism, including ecological terrorism. Giroux writes, "In New Orleans, state violence took the form of a refusal by the Bush administration to invest financially in infrastructure designed to protect against floods, a decision that was as much about saving money as it was about

---

157   BBC, 2014.
158   Evans and Giroux, 2015: 32.
159   Debord, 1990: 24.

allegiance to a brutalizing racist logic, cloaked in the discourse of austerity, and willfully indifferent to the needs of the powerless and underserved in black communities."[160]

A function of terrorism is to legitimize (and normalize) constant surveillance made possible by technological advances. Reporter Glenn Greenwald, former CIA employee Edward Snowden, and US soldier Chelsea (formerly Bradley) Manning revealed that the US National Security Agency was collecting data around the world, including emails, internet searches, and phone calls—and covertly activating mobile phone, computer, and TV microphones and cameras, tracking geographic movement, and more on a daily basis.[161] We are surveilled in public even without suspicion of illegal activity. In the panoptic state, ubiquitous police cameras overlook city blocks while mobile watchtowers are deployed in various areas of New York City.

Not to be outdone, spectacular socialism/communism has surpassed the surveillance states of the West. China has 170 million closed-circuit TV cameras (by comparison, the United States has 50 million), with 450 million more to be added by 2020.[162] Of these, 20 million use an artificial intelligence system called Sky Net, which is capable of facial recognition and identification of age, gender, ethnicity, clothes, and movement via GPS. Life imitates art in this case, since Skynet is the name of the artificial intelligence system that destroyed the world in the *Terminator* movie franchise starring Arnold Schwarzenegger. In a demonstration of the system, it took seven minutes for Chinese authorities to track down a BBC reporter who tried to remain undetected.[163] Big Brother would be proud.

Government-corporate collusion to monitor and control the demos is rampant. For example, banks collaborated with law enforcement to arrest and disrupt Occupy Wall Street (OWS) activists. As journalist Naomi Wolf reveals:

> DHS [Department of Homeland Security], FBI, police, regional fusion center, and private-sector activity so completely merged into one another that the monstrous whole is, in fact, one entity: in some cases, bearing a single name, the Domestic Security Alliance Council. And it reveals this merged entity to have one centrally planned, locally executed mission. The documents, in short, show the cops and DHS working for and with banks to target, arrest, and politically disable peaceful American citizens.

---

160   Giroux, 2017: 10–11.
161   Greenwald, 2014.
162   BBC, December 10, 2017; Chin and Lin, 2017.
163   Ibid.

> ... [The documents] show a nationwide meta-plot unfolding in city after city in an Orwellian world: six American universities are sites where campus police funneled information about students involved with OWS to the FBI, with the administrations' knowledge; banks sat down with FBI officials to pool information about OWS protesters harvested by private security; plans to crush Occupy events, planned for a month down the road, were made by the FBI—and offered to the representatives of the same organizations that the protests would target; and even threats of the assassination of OWS leaders by sniper fire—by whom? Where?—now remain redacted and undisclosed to those American citizens in danger, contrary to standard FBI practice to inform the person concerned when there is a threat against a political leader.[164]

Law enforcement agencies even engage in preemptive arrests, as in the movie *Minority Report* starring Tom Cruise. Police in the UK identified and preemptively arrested protesters before a protest of a royal wedding.[165] More than eighteen people were preemptively arrested in New York City during the 2004 Republican convention.[166]

Monitoring eliminates free speech and silences dissent through the chilling effect of self-censorship. A surreal example is provided by a secret memo that was leaked in Britain. According to the memo, President George Bush wanted to bomb the offices of Al Jazeera because it contradicted US propaganda to justify invading Iraq.[167] British prime minister Tony Blair had to dissuade Bush, explaining he could not do that because Al Jazeera was a legitimate news organization like the BBC.[168] The British government denied the existence of the memo, although the British attorney general, Lord Goldsmith, threatened newspapers with prosecution under the Official Secrets Act if they revealed any further details of the document that supposedly did not exist. Al Jazeera reporters were killed and their facilities were bombed by the United States on various occasions—though this was said to have been accidental or "collateral damage."

---

164 Wolf, 2012.
165 Laville, 2012.
166 Draznin, 2014.
167 Maguire and Lines, 2005.
168 Leigh and Norton-Taylor, 2006.

CHAPTER 3

It's All Spectacular

1   **Spectacular History**

History ended when societies divided between oppressors and oppressed. It is the legitimizing ideology, technology, resources, and level of propaganda that change the outward appearance of hierarchy. Social relations, however, remain unchanged: based on unequal distribution of power, authority, and material resources. Our perception of the historical past is a simulacrum framed by our contemporary knowledge base and system of discourse.[1] It is patched together by documents and fragments that either misrepresent or are totally detached from the actual history they purport to represent. This means that our concept of caste is just as mystified as that of capitalism and class.

Theorists such as Castoriadis and Banaji—and even history itself—demonstrate that Marx got history wrong.[2] There is no inevitable proletarian revolution or successive modes of production determined by technology (the forces of production bursting at the seams). In fact, Marx himself tells us not to take him seriously when it comes to any "scientific" notions in his theories. Debord informs us:

> [Marx] clearly never fell prey himself to such illusions. In a well-known letter of 7 December 1867, accompanying an article criticizing *Capital* which he himself had written, and which Engels was supposed to publish as if it were that of an opponent, Marx clearly indicated the limits of his scientific stance: "The author's *subjective* tendency (imposed on him, perhaps, by his political, position and his past)—that is to say, the way in which he himself pictures, and portrays for others, the ultimate outcome of the present movement, the present social process has nothing whatsoever to do with his real analysis."[3]

For spectacular Marxism, the form of exploitation is dependent upon the mode of production, but historical accounts show that particular forms of

---

1 Foucault, 1977.
2 Banaji, 2011.
3 Debord, 2012: 58–59.

exploitation do not depend on the mode of production.[4] Wage, bonded, and slave labor coexisted throughout every historical era within the same communities.[5] Bonded labor and slavery were practiced in the United States and the Caribbean under a supposedly capitalist mode of production. Further, the idea that the emergence of capitalism required free or wage labor—or that it contributed to the liberation of slaves and emancipation of serfs—is contradicted by historical facts. As David Graeber writes:

> It is the secret scandal of capitalism that at no point has it been organized primarily around free labor. The conquest of the Americas began with mass enslavement, then gradually settled into various forms of debt peonage, African slavery, and "indentured service." . . . The peasants of Russia and Poland, who had been free landholders in the Middle Ages, were only made serfs at the dawn of capitalism. . . . Colonial regimes in Africa and Southeast Asia regularly demanded forced labor from their conquered subjects, or, alternatively, created tax systems designed to force the population into the labor market through debt.[6]

The reverse holds true as well. Particular modes of production do not depend on the forms of exploitation.[7] Free/wage labor existed in antiquity without constituting a capitalist mode of production. Slave labor existed in the Middle Ages without constituting a slave mode of production. Debt bondage, found in all epochs, is fundamentally a capitalist mode of production with precapitalist forms of exploitation—debt representing wages and interest/profit representing surplus labor.[8] Today there are slaves and peasants alongside industrial workers and computer programmers within the same nation, each corresponding to a different epoch or mode of production—ancient slave, feudal, capitalist (industrial), and postindustrial/postmodern. The reason various forms of exploitation existed in all epochs or modes of production is because they are part of the same system. The only difference has been their outward manifestation. The only persistent characteristics are structures that reproduce hierarchical relations.

Hierarchical societies are either an established caste system or one in the making, as Weber and Castoriadis argued.[9] What passes as historical change

---

4 Banaji, 2011.
5 Graeber, 2011; Moulier-Boutang, 1997.
6 Graeber, 2011: 350–351.
7 Banaji, 2011.
8 Banaji, 2011; Graeber, 2011.
9 Castoriadis, 1993: 223; Gerth and Mills, 1946.

is intra- or inter-elite conflict that may lead to exchanges of personnel in positions of power and authority. The dominant ideology, however, remains unchanged during intra-elite conflicts but with alternate figureheads, (e.g., a monarchy under a new dynasty). Inter-elite conflict leads to new ideologies to legitimize the rule of a different caste—for example, a bureaucratic caste replacing aristocrats in Russia. This represents an alternate hegemony rather than a new epoch because relations remain hierarchical regardless of changes of personnel in positions of domination or technological changes. Such inter-elite exchanges are mistaken as mobility. But, once all positions of power and authority are staffed by new elites and their supporters, then a process of hardening starts—the structural embedding of privileges—forming a caste system, as Weber demonstrated.[10]

Dahrendorf, like Debord, considers the bourgeois ascendance to be an example of epochal change because of a total exchange of personnel in positions of authority.[11] He argues that the old customs, norms, and legitimizing ideology (e.g., of tradition) buttressing feudal society were replaced by new bourgeois norms and ideology. In reality, however, it was neither a revolution nor was there a total exchange of personnel in positions of domination. For example, only a few aristocrats were executed after the French Revolution. It was an intra-elite conflict for suffrage, struggle between a ruling urban sub-caste (merchants or haute bourgeoisie found throughout history) and their rural counterpart. The latter monopolized political positions of authority legitimized by royal titles tied to land ownership. This conflict did not even result in a new hegemony by new personnel in positions of authority. It was a merger of ruling sub-castes, often merging literally through marriage and business partnerships. Historical documents list the number of non-nobles who married nobles as in Sweden.[12] The postmodern caste of Swedish elite is indicative. Tyler Cowen writes in 2014: "The upper class in Sweden today consists of the nobility and of wealthy bourgeoisie families that socially merged with them. Wealthy bourgeois families live in the same neighborhoods and have adopted similar behavior and identity as the nobility. Despite long Social Democratic dominance they remain a coherent social group, with a distinct and recognizable accent, way of dressing, values etc."[13] The Swedish example also demonstrates the continuation of the merger between the feudal past (the descendants of aristocrats) and the postmodern bourgeoisie. In addition, from

---

10   Gerth and Mills, 1946: 188, 194
11   Dahrendorf, 1959,
12   Bengtsson, et al., 2017.
13   Cowen, 2014.

antiquity (e.g., ancient Rome) to the present, aristocrats who fell on hard times would often marry those who were affluent (typically merchants) who in turn married for the status of the aristocratic title.

Landed elites also found it more profitable to devote their fields to the production of raw materials instead of subsistence crops—for example, grazing sheep for wool to feed insatiable factory demand. This incentivized them to collaborate rather than compete with their bourgeois counterparts. Factory owners also happened to be landed wealth-holders, thus blurring caste divisions between landed nobles and haute bourgeoisie. In the end, the social order remained hierarchical, based on ascription reproducing structural privileges and disabilities between rulling and other castes. Feudal monarchies (under various dynasties) that go back hundreds or even thousands of years exist to this day in England and Japan. A third of all land in Britain is still owned by aristocrats (numbering less than half a percent of the population), dating back hundreds of years.[14]

Another example of intra-elite conflict is the US Civil War. It was not over slavery—the North abolished it in the South but technically not in Northern states. The war was over Northern versus Southern hegemony, representing intra-elite rivalry. It is indicative that both sides continued to participate in federal political institutions after the conclusion of the war. The North could have barred Southern elites from Congress. Instead Southern elites were quickly permitted to participate, indicating that this was a reconciliation of equals, namely ruling elites. The result was identical to that of the bourgeois revolution analyzed by Dahrendorf insomuch as it was a merger of elites but not an exchange. The Civil War actually pitted elite family members against each other. Therefore, a major deficit of Marxism is its confusion of a merger or exchange of elites within a hierarchical system as the birth of a new epochal mode of production.

Textbook capitalism is an economic system in which the means of production are largely or entirely privately owned and the goal of life is the accumulation of profit. But how is this different from feudalism or other past systems? Feudal lords did not have the technology to intensify exploitation—serfs had animal-driven plows, not tractors. However, if one insists that feudal economies were stagnant, one would have to admit that so sometimes is capitalism. The Japanese economy, which is the second or third largest in the world, has been stagnant since 1991. The first twenty years of that period, since 1991, are referred to as the Lost Score or the Lost Twenty Years. The US economy, which is the largest for a single nation, has been experiencing low to no real growth

---

14   Cohen, 2010.

for decades as well, leading pundits since 2008 to think that low growth is intensifying into a "new normal." Low annual growth of 1 to 3 percent represents little to no growth, since, for one thing, the rate of population growth is about 1 percent. Second, the Gross Domestic Product (GDP), typically reported as a measure of growth, is not adjusted for inflation, which always runs above 2 percent. Contraction and low growth has also been the norm throughout the "socialist" European Union, which when combined represents the first or second largest economy in the world. Stagnation also characterizes bureaucratic capitalism—for example, that of the Soviet Union. The Era of Stagnation, also called the Brezhnevian Stagnation, was a period of contraction starting in 1964 and continuing until the system's collapse in 1992.

Under capitalism, goods and services are exchanged within markets. Yet markets have existed in just about every historical period after the hunter-gatherer era. During feudalism, villages were able to have a marketplace by permission of the king, who chartered it. In addition, there have always been markets for labor—for example, the labor of the blacksmith, carpenter, et cetera. In feudal times, workers such as masons and general laborers were not slaves but paid employees, no different than now.

Michael Perelman documents the birth of spectacular capitalism as a theoretical construct of seventeenth- and eighteenth-century political economists rather than a natural progression of history. Their stated purpose was to increase the extraction of labor (i.e., the rate of exploitation) from the peasantry through increased work hours and intensification of work. Sir William Temple (1628–99), who employed Jonathan Swift as his secretary, was clear: "For by these means, we hope that the rising generation will be so habituated to constant employment that it would at length prove agreeable and entertaining to them." Not to be outdone, John Locke, often seen as a philosopher of liberty, called for the "commencement of work at the ripe age of three."[15]

Eighteenth-century political economists believed freemen and subsistence peasants were lazy and difficult to force into longer hours of work. Arthur Young (1741–1820) thought that "everyone but an idiot knows that the lower classes must be kept poor, or they will never be industrious."[16] Economists' solution was to increase surplus labor through enclosure laws to evict peasants from their ancestral lands. This forced them to seek wages in manufacturing under new conditions of production, including more and longer workdays. The masses went from being agricultural to industrial serfs. According to Perelman:

---

15   Perelman, 2000: 19.
16   Ibid.: 98.

To make sure that people accepted wage labor, the classical political economists actively advocated measures to deprive people of their traditional means of support. The brutal acts associated with the process of stripping the majority of the people of the means of producing for themselves might seem far removed from the laissez-faire reputation of classical political economy. In reality, the dispossession of the majority of small-scale producers and the construction of laissez-faire are closely connected, so much so that Marx, or at least his translators, labeled this expropriation of the masses as "primitive accumulation."[17]

Policies included deliberate starvation to intensify exploitation and increase control. Perelman writes: "In this vein, Sir William Temple . . . suggested that the community would be well served if food were taxed when harvests were plentiful lest the working class sink into sloth and debauchery. David Hume, for his part, asserted that such policies would even be in the interests of the poor: 'Tis always observed, in years of scarcity, if it be not extreme, that the poor labour more, and really live better.'"[18] Reverend Joseph Townsend (1739–1816) concluded that direct control of labor through legal means "is attended with too much trouble, violence, and noise, . . . whereas hunger is not only a peaceable, silent, unremitted pressure, but as the most natural motive to industry, it calls forth the most powerful exertions. . . . Hunger will tame the fiercest animals, it will teach decency and civility, obedience and subjugation to the most brutish, the most obstinate, and the most perverse."[19]

German socialist and government minister Johann Karl Rodbertus (1805–1875) explained:

> Originally this compulsion was exercised by the institution of slavery, which came into existence at the same time as tillage of the soil and private ownership of land. . . . When all the land in a country is privately owned, and when the same title to all land has passed into private ownership of land and capital exerts the same compulsion on liberated or free workers. . . . the command of the slave owner has been replaced by the contract between worker and employer, a contract which is free only in form but not really in substance. Hunger makes almost a perfect substitute for the whip, and what was formerly called fodder is now called wages.[20]

---

17 Ibid.: 2.
18 Ibid.: 92.
19 Ibid.: 102.
20 Ibid.: 103.

As Blau stipulated, those who can offer valued things in social exchanges to those who need or want them but do not have them obtain a privileged position resulting in the formation of hierarchical relations.[21] The architects of capitalism engineered a way to make everyone dependent upon the ruling caste for their means of subsistence. It was clear that their new system would not include structural (vertical) mobility of the peasantry turned factory workers.[22] Quite the contrary, the structure was designed to maintain and harden existing caste rankings while intensifying exploitation, thus inequality of power, authority, and resources. The only mobility discussed was locational, from farms to factories. Material mobility was added much later as a characteristic of spectacular capitalism, to legitimize the system.

2   Postmodern Spectacles

"Struggles between forces [that] been established for the purpose of running the same socioeconomic system," Debord writes, are:

> officially passed off as real antagonisms. In actuality these struggles partake of a real unity, and this on the world stage as well as within each nation. This is not to say that the spectacle's sham battles between competing versions of alienated power are not also real; they do express the system's uneven and conflict-ridden development, as well as the relatively contradictory interests of those classes or fractions of classes that recognize the system and strive in this way to carve out a role for themselves in it. Just as the development of the most advanced economies involves clashes between different agendas, so totalitarian economic management by a state bureaucracy and the condition of those countries living under colonialism or semi-colonialism are likewise highly differentiated with respect to modes of production and power. By pointing up these great differences, while appealing to criteria of quite a different order, the spectacle is able to portray them as markers of radically distinct social systems. But from the standpoint of their actual reality as mere *sectors*, it is clear that the specificity of each is subsumed under a universal system as functions of a single tendency that has taken the planet for its field of operations. That tendency is capitalism.[23]

---

21 Blau, 1992.
22 Perelman 2000.
23 Debord, 2012: 36–37.

Socialism and capitalism share the same imaginary. They define progress in terms of industrial development and technological progress. Proponents of both, including Marxism, believe in the scientific management of production and society as the way to promote social welfare. They also share what Castoriadis called technique (methods of production—for example, Taylorist factory production), considering it neutral in regard to social relations. Debord and Castoriadis argue that market and state or bureaucratic systems have morphed into an integrated spectacle. China is an example where political and business castes have merged, draped in spectacular communism as the ideological basis of legitimization, whereas the US caste system is draped in spectacular capitalism and liberal democracy for legitimization. Both claim to fulfill vague values of equality, justice, and fairness that are third-order simulacrums detached from their original meanings. The antagonism between capitalism and socialism is a simulation of an antagonism between simulacrum values and ideals. Spectacular socialist bureaucracies participated in international capitalist markets. Famously, the Soviet Union would import US grains. In China, a so-called peoples' party embraced free markets and global participation with capitalist trade structures and institutions. Baudrillard writes:

> The nonintervention of China obtained and secured after many years, China's apprenticeship to a global modus vivendi, the shift from a global strategy of revolution to one of shared forces and empires, the transition from a radical alternative to a political alteration in a system now essentially regulated (the normalization of Peking-Washington relations): this was what was at stake in the war in Vietnam.... That theirs is a Communist order is not serious in the end: it had proved itself, it could be trusted. It is even more effective than capitalism in the liquidation of "savage" and archaic precapitalist structures.[24]

In both systems the state is the center of formal power to maintain the illusion of representing the good of society. Gilman-Opalsky put it well: "Democratic leaders in capitalist societies must play the part of officials governing in a representative system, much the same as the Stalinists pretended to do with the proletariat. But they are both actors in this regard. Despite real differences over the question of state administration of capitalist production and the market economy, they both hold a 'form of power founded on the position of a national state,' which they protect and reproduce through nationalist

---

24 Baudrillard, 1994: 36–37.

bureaucracies.'"[25] Both systems hold illusory elections for the benefit of the masses to legitimize their rule. How can an election be democratic when the only parties and candidates permitted to participate are those sanctioned by the state, as in the Soviet Union, China, and Cuba? Or when mass media exclude opposing voices—for example, socialists or communists who are never invited to political debates in the United States (state media in China and Russia do the same with their real opposition)?

In order to control disobedience, the West developed the prison industrial complex, while the socialists had Siberian Gulags and Chinese labor camps. Both West and East used security forces to suppress popular revolts and protests. The socialist peoples' governments crushed peoples' uprisings as with Soviet tanks during the Hungarian Revolution of 1956. The Tiananmen Square protests of 1989 were crushed with Chinese People's Liberation Army tanks. The United States used the National Guard and federal troops to suppress popular uprisings during the ghetto revolts of the 1960s and 1970s.[26] The United States uses the FBI and CIA and the Soviet Union used the NKVD and KGB (now FSB in Russia), to spy on (even assassinate) their own people as much as on other nations. The US Army is an international enforcer of US interests just as the Red Army was for the Soviet Union and just as China's imperial forces currently in the making.

2.1 Doubleplusgood: Spectacular Capitalism

Textbook capitalism (also known as classical economics) has been long dead, if it ever existed. In its place emerged neoliberal economics—pure ideology no different than religion. It is propaganda to conceal a solidifying caste order bearing no resemblance to a class system. The difference is that this caste system does not wish to be identified as a caste order, fearing popular revolt or resistance to its propaganda.

According to classical economics, capitalism is based on private property, commonly interpreted to mean private ownership of the means of production, associated with Marxist analysis. But the interpretation of private property as ownership of the means of production is false because private property includes personal private property such as one's car or house. In fact, private property originally meant protection from arbitrary seizure of the aristocrats' property by a sovereign. Here we see a contradiction of spectacular capitalism. How can the system be based on private property if it eliminates it for the majority of society through its natural workings and policies such as enclosures?

---

25   Gilman-Opalsky, 2011: 79.
26   Asimakopoulos, 2011.

Thomas Piketty's seminal data-driven study confirms that the rate of capital (wealth) concentration increases over time.[27] Most Americans own no private property. The bottom 20 percent have -0.3 percent wealth (in other words, has debt exceeding assets), and the second-lowest quintile owns 0.5 percent (see Table 5.1). Early advocates of capitalism were clear that private property was reserved for the ruling caste:

> Poverty is that state and condition in society where the individual has no surplus labour in store, or, in other words, no property or means of subsistence but what is derived from the constant exercise of industry in the various occupations of life. Poverty is therefore a most necessary and indispensable ingredient in society, without which nations and communities could not exist in a state of civilization. It is the lot of man. *It is the source of wealth,* since without poverty, there could be no labour; there could be *no riches, no refinement, no comfort,* and no benefit to those who may be possessed of wealth.[28]

Here we see the historical transformation of the discourse on private property. Furthermore, natural resources such as forests and bodies of water were considered part of the commons. Capitalist ideology did the exact opposite of protecting peoples' property. It robbed them of their property using fictions to justify expropriation of the commons through enclosures.

Another tenet of spectacular capitalism is that people are rational actors who wish to maximize their utility (satisfaction) from the consumption of goods and services. Yet studies in the new field of behavioral economics developed at the Chicago School of Economics, ironically the birthplace of rational economics, demonstrated that people ask for different amounts of money when selling (or buying) based on their level of emotional attachment to the item being sold. Therefore, people act on emotive rationality, not calculative, scientific rationality as assumed by economists. It is also assumed that people have *perfect information* that allows them to make the best value-maximizing choices. Yet it is widely acknowledged that pricing in the United States is not transparent. This is demonstrated by minute-to-minute price changes on Amazon and complex promotions by retailers involving fake manufacturers' suggested retail prices and coupon discount games.[29]

---

27 Piketty, 2014.
28 Patrick Colquhoun (1745–1820), London police magistrate, quoted in Perelman, 2000: 23.
29 Tuttle, 2016.

Related is the concept of marginal analysis, also developed by the Chicago School. Accordingly, a firm should hire additional workers until the wage of the last worker equals the (marginal) value of what she adds to output. Castoriadis demonstrates that the whole theoretical framework is flawed in a world where the division of labor leads to the interdependence of all work: "If, in a coal-fired locomotive, the train's engineer is eliminated, one does not 'reduce a little' of the product (transportation), one eliminates it completely; and the same thing is true if one eliminates the fireman. The 'product' of this indivisible team of engineer and fireman obeys a law of all or nothing, and there is no 'marginal product' of the one that can be separated from that of the other. The same thing goes on the shop floor and ultimately for the modern factory as a whole, where jobs are closely interdependent."[30]

Self-interest leading to society's welfare is another capitalist tenet founded on a fallacy. An economy based on fossil fuels is in the best interest of oil and coal companies. But burning fossil fuels has created climate change, threatening all life on the planet. It is in the Koch brothers' best interest for their paper factories to dump chemicals in rivers rather than dispose of them in an environmentally safe if costly manner.[31] These pollutants have caused cancer clusters downstream, affecting poor communities. The private owners profited at the expense of communities. This violates another tenet of capitalism, by which the full cost or benefit of a transaction should be borne only by the transacting parties. This means that there should be no "externalities." Clearly, environmental pollution is an example of an externality, in this case a "spillover" cost borne by people who were not involved in the transaction.

Limited government intervention in markets (laissez-faire or contemporary deregulation and liberalism) is also a key tenet of spectacular capitalism. Markets are supposedly self-regulating, according to Adam Smith's invisible (simulacrum) hand. Capitalist theory assumes that there is a firewall between government and the economy. It ignores that in the real world one deals with a political economy rather than just politics or economics alone. In reality, all economies throughout history have been constructed by and heavily regulated to the advantage of elites. In industrial and postmodern times, those who amass wealth turn to protecting and enlarging it by capturing the political process—for example, through lobbying and election financing.[32] This is the exact opposite of laissez-faire.

---

30   Castoriadis, 1993: 213.
31   Greenwald, 2012.
32   Whitehouse, 2017.

In addition, financial crises in the form of recessions and depressions are assumed to be unique to capitalism (though it is also said that these should never occur in self-regulating markets). However, there were many panics, depressions, and stagnations before capitalism's rein. Historian Tacitus (AD 56–117) provides detailed accounts of the AD 33 financial panic caused by the mass issuance of unsecured loans by Roman banking houses.[33] In 1345 there was a crash caused by the Peruzzi and the Compagnia dei Bardi banks. In 1637 there was the crash of the market during the "tulip mania." Then there was the international post-Napoleonic depression, circa 1815. From 1873 to 1896 there was the global Long Depression. In the midst of the 1929 Great Depression, John Maynard Keynes observed this contradiction with the ideology of self-regulating markets in which panics and depressions should never occur but regularly do—as had Marx and others earlier. This led to the birth of Keynesian economics (also capitalist economics), according to which government must intervene in times of depression or inflation with monetary or fiscal policy (or both). This is in addition to the financial regulations and intervention in the economy by central banks. Yet, when capitalist ideology was being constructed, there was no mention of any type of Federal Reserve or central banking system. Therefore, in practice, capitalism depends on government intervention to avoid collapse, while in theory the government should not interfere with the economy. Interestingly, neoliberalism has done away with Keynesianism, relying exclusively on monetary policy that is but pure illusion.

The idea of self-regulating markets is partly based on the assumption of competition between producers. This is another pillar of capitalist theory and has commonly been acknowledged to be a lie. In reality, small producers are structurally at a disadvantage relative to large corporations for a number of reasons. Large companies can lobby and purchase politicians to pass legislation favorable to them, such as government subsidies to agribusiness and fossil fuel companies.[34] These corporations take advantage of economies of scale and employ armies of tax lawyers and accountants to obtain a competitive advantage. General Electric received a tax refund despite billions in profits—in addition to savings from offshore tax havens. Corporations also have access to capital markets. Walmart demonstrates the consequences of unfair competition.[35] Whenever it moves into a small town, most shops on Main Street go bust within a year.

---

33 Taylor, 2013.
34 Whitehouse, 2017.
35 Frontline, 2004; Greenwald, 2005.

Ironically, unregulated free markets and unfettered competition result in monopolies and oligopolies that represent a breakdown of capitalism because they limit competition, offering even more proof of the invisible hand's inadequate regulation. In reality, individuals, dominant groups, and states have riddled capitalism with efforts to establish and maintain monopolies, and such efforts extend far back before capitalism. Throughout antiquity to modern times, kings and states chartered monopolies for their cronies. The British East India Company exemplifies a state-chartered monopoly backed by government military operated by private interests in a capitalist system. In the aftermath of the global financial collapse, it was acknowledged that the financial industry was dominated by a few companies (an oligopoly) that were "too big to fail." This led them to engage in risky investments, betting that the government would bail them out if disaster hit in order to avoid global economic meltdown. This represents what is termed a *moral hazard* in economics. When the global economy did collapse, these companies were bailed out with tax money. Yet, years after the bailouts, these financial institutions became even bigger rather than being broken up as per capitalist theory and antitrust laws.[36]

Competition is also fictitious on a global scale. Free trade is regulated trade through international agreements as with the World Trade Organization (WTO), North American Free Trade Agreement (NAFTA), and many more. To say that trade is free also ignores differential power relations among states that wish to exploit other states, exemplified by colonialism and neocolonialism. Now this is manifest in institutions such as the World Bank and IMF dominated by the United States (that constructed them) and its EU satellite.[37] The World Bank and IMF function as global enforcers and disseminators of neoliberal ideology.

Stratification of wages and labor is another tenet of capitalism, and it is justified on the basis of skill and scarcity. Davis and Moore famously argued that there are important positions in society that few have the talents and abilities to train for and perform.[38] Rewards (e.g. wages) are stratified, based on the relative scarcity of people for positions. Important positions offer greater rewards as incentives for those who are capable to undergo cumbersome training. The argument, however, ignores that many people who are highly capable choose a calling regardless of compensation—professors, for example. Castoriadis puts it well: "For the rare individuals who are exceptionally gifted, what really matters is not monetary 'reward' but creating what they are irresistibly driven to

---

36 Cho, 2009.
37 Black, 2003.
38 Schaefer, 2017.

create. If Einstein had been interested in money, he would not have become Einstein—and it is likely that he would have made a rather mediocre boss or financier."[39]

Regardless, in examining stratification of labor based on demand for skills and human capital investment, it is important to keep in mind that not everyone has access to educational opportunities that would put them in a position to compete for higher-waged positions. Castoriadis is clear:

> Even if academic or Marxist theory offered an *explanation* of wage differentiations, they would in any case be unable to furnish a *justification* for them. For, in both cases, the existence of different skills is accepted ... as a *given* beyond debate, whereas in fact it is only the result of the overall economic and social system and of its continued reproduction. If skilled labor is "worth" more, it would be ... in the Marxist view, because the family of this laborer has spent more for his training (and, theoretically, has to "recoup the costs"—which in practice signifies that the skilled worker will be able in his turn to finance the training of his children, etc.). Why, however, has this family been able to spend more—something that other families were not able to do? Because it was already privileged from the standpoint of income.... Let us add that if it is no longer the worker himself or his family but society that assumes these training costs ... there is no reason for the person who has already benefited, at society's cost, from professional training guaranteeing him a more interesting and less arduous job to profit a second time around in the form of a higher income.[40]

Castoriadis goes further, demonstrating that in capitalist societies, ideologies justifying income hierarchy based on differential levels of knowledge, qualifications, talents, responsibilities, or skill shortages are not only fictitious but contradictory.[41] He notes that scientists have great knowledge but little power or income; air traffic controllers are directly responsible for thousands of lives every day but are paid far less than CEOs of airline companies. Regarding scarcity, there is a shortage of some semiskilled workers relative to a glut of lawyers, yet the lawyers always earn more. Similarly, the argument that it is a weighted balance of many variables that determine income levels is based on arbitrary considerations, mystification to justify unequal distribution of social

---

39   Castoriadis, 1993: 224.
40   Ibid.: 213.
41   Ibid.

surplus. Therefore, market or wage-based distribution is rigged to privilege the ruling caste.

Capitalism supposedly differs from other systems in that it provides the possibility of mobility based on achievement. Yet every introductory sociology textbook states that ascription continues to be a significant factor of stratification under capitalism, which is an element of caste. The ideology of mobility became a tenet of capitalism after the mid-nineteenth century. Examples include nineteenth-century Horatio Alger dime novels. However, there are different types of mobility based on various criteria—for example, material mobility and status mobility. In this context, mobility is commonly understood as a change in one's material situation (not social status), for better or worse. Another type of mobility is horizontal, leaving a person in the same material situation, more or less. But a hierarchical system without vertical material mobility is by definition a caste system.

According to Gregory Clark, medieval England and pre-industrial Sweden had more mobility than the United States today.[42] Clark finds that one's economic status in the United States will determine that of one's descendants for four or more generations and concludes that the American Dream was always an illusion. OECD studies confirm that industrialized nations experience limited mobility—the United States being among the least mobile.[43] The Financial Security and Mobility Project of Pew Charitable Trusts supports these crossnational comparisons as well, with the United States consistently ranking at the bottom.[44] In addition, Howard Friedman reviewed multiple quantitative studies, all of which come to the same conclusions.[45] These studies looked at whether a son's income can be predicted by the father's. They found that 42 percent of American sons born to fathers in the bottom quintile remained there. The percentage of sons born to fathers in the bottom quintile that rose to the top quintile was 7.9 percent. Worse, the data show mobility to be decreasing.

Because substantive material mobility does not exist, it is replaced with symbolic status mobility to mitigate the cognitive dissonance between ideology and reality. For example, the educational system offers symbolic status opportunities. A low-status working-class autoworker with a high school degree may eventually obtain a PhD, becoming a high-status professor working as a full-time adjunct at various universities while living on food stamps. Such a person experienced vertical status mobility but materially earned more as an

---

42 Clark, 2014.
43 OECD, 2010.
44 Financial Security and Mobility Project.
45 Friedman, 2012.

autoworker. At best she will have the same levels of power, authority, and material resources with or without that degree. The proliferation of workplace positions and titles also serves as an illusion of mobility despite offering no substantive difference in life chances. The legitimacy of the postmodern spectacle depends in part on simulated opportunity for simulacrum mobility.

2.2 Plusgood: Spectacular Socialism/Communism

Castoriadis, Debord, Baudrillard, and many others demonstrated throughout their work that socialist or communist societies such as the Soviet Union were a variant of capitalism, what Castoriadis referred to as bureaucratic capitalism. Both share the same imaginary. Debord defined such so-called socialist societies as representing a "concentrated spectacle," seeing this also in fascism—which is authoritarian market capitalism. As Gilman-Opalsky explains: "Much of what has passed for socialism, communism, and Marxism in the 20th century (and now in the 21st century) has in fact been one or another variation of capitalism itself.... These administrative differences, which often amount to bureaucratic modulations in policy position and rhetoric, with varying degrees of efficacy, *have never undermined the logic of capitalism....* In short, spectacular socialism has been nothing other than the presentation of state-administered capitalism as the vile apex of anticapitalist politics."[46] Accordingly, the spectacular socialism of the Soviet Union also assumed that people are rational actors. However, people were not to act in their self-interest—that was considered sick and immoral. Rather, people were assumed to instinctively organize on a communal basis as the way to promote not society's self-interest but the interest of the party (and therefore, it was said, everyone). This, of course, does not jibe with the existence of greedy bastards called capitalists and party officials.

A major tenet of spectacular socialism is the abolition of private property. Neither individuals nor the masses own the means of production. These were concentrated into communal property controlled by the party. In twenty-first-century Russia and communist China, much of the ideological pretense has been dropped. Amazingly, the means of production have been partly privatized, transferred to inner party members (in Russia and China), while other firms remained state-owned. Production has been and is hierarchically organized as under capitalism, while its social surplus (surplus labor/profits) has been usurped by either party or market elites. "Communist" China has embraced market production and distribution, calling it good for the people (in classic Orwellian fashion). Amazingly, China's wealth Gini (a measure of

---

46   Gilman-Opalsky, 2011: 16.

inequality) was 0.82 in 2016, about that of the United States at 0.86.[47] Inequality in communist China mirrors the capitalist United States.

In theory, competition did not exist. The official party line was that people were collaborators, not competitors. In reality, there has been competition for bureaucratic positions. For the masses, it has been competition for scarce goods and sheer survival. Factory (market) competition did not exist either, which is true of capitalist markets, as shown. For one thing, private property was expropriated under the control of the party acting as a monopoly, and production was based on quotas. Competition has been mostly framed in terms of status—honor accorded to those producing more than other factories or coworkers.

Regulation has been performed by the state, as under capitalism, but, in contrast, done formally, demonstrating that the party knows best. One difference has been that in theory the United States opposes monopolies, whereas the ruling socialist party embraces them as the expression of collective property that they manage. As with capitalism, though, aggregate supply never equaled aggregate demand, although theoretically it should have. In a capitalist system, free markets should always *clear*, meaning that supply will equal demand. History shows that this is not the case, as demonstrated by recessions, depressions, and periods of long stagnation. In the Soviet system, the bureaucracy determined supply quotas based on projections (estimations) of demand. However, the technocrats' calculations and projections were always inaccurate, often producing oversupplies or undersupplies of goods and services. In addition, factories often did not produce as much as expected—productivity was notoriously low following the first few years of the revolution—given job security and workers' ideological disillusionment.

The formal position of spectacular socialist or communist societies was that there were no classes. In reality, there were a number of castes: politburo (inner party), party functionaries (outer party), and industrial and peasant proletarians. Class, or the lack of it, is a spectacular illusion sold by both systems to the masses. The purpose is to hide the ultimate truth that these are caste systems hidden behind capitalist, socialist, or communist ideology. Mobility was therefore a non-issue, since officially there were no classes. However, one could improve one's condition by rising through the ranks of the state bureaucracy, although this was an impossibility for the masses. Such mobility was typically conditioned on having a relationship with an existing member of the bureaucracy—a relative. In fact, material inequality, in addition to inequality of power and authority, has grown exponentially under the twenty-first-century

---

47   *Global Wealth Databook 2016*, 2016.

spectacle. For example, in one of China's scandals, the news broke that children of party elites who earn £6000 a year were driving £500,000 Lamborghinis.[48]

Hierarchy of labor and wages is found in socialist and communist systems as under capitalism, but this has been detached from class, which did not officially exist. Not surprisingly, state bureaucrats (i.e., capitalists) are better compensated, with pleasant jobs relative to those of the masses, just as with privileged labor castes in the West. In the former Soviet Union, stratification of labor included nonmonetary benefits. Party elites enjoyed summers at their dachas. They also did not have to share their primary residence with strangers assigned by the party as did the masses, because their work was more important, requiring a level of privacy—like the pigs in Orwell's *Animal Farm*.[49] Their homes were also quite different in size and quality, often former palaces and bourgeois mansions. The masses had to live in communal apartments (*kommunalka*) after the Russian Revolution. Between two and seven families had to share a single apartment. Each family had its own room. Hallways, kitchens, and bathrooms were common areas. In the 1950s these apartment blocks were called "khrushchyoby," a combination of Khrushchev's name and the term for slums.[50] The difference between the two spectacles was that the US variant allowed proletarians to select their own roommates as a means to offset rents for tenement apartments owned by capitalists or the government while the socialist variant selected the roommates and government-owned tenement apartment on behalf of the citizenry. All the while, the socialist/communist inner party enjoyed all domestic and Western luxuries while people faced chronic shortages of basic goods such as sugar and expensive black markets.

3 Spectacular Class

The term "class" was not coined by Marx. It has been used since ancient Rome for tax purposes. Ralf Dahrendorf writes: "The Roman censors introduced the word *classis* to divide the population into tax groups. Yet even their classification implied at least the possibility of evaluative distinctions: on the one end of their classification were the *assidui*, who might well be proud of their 100,000 *as*; on the other end were the *proletarii*, whose only 'property' consisted in their numerous offspring—*proles*—and who were outdone only by

---

48 Simpson, 2012.
49 Orwell, 1993 [1945].
50 Attwood, 2010.

the *lumpenproletariat* of the *capite censi*, those counted by their heads."[51] Class took on new meanings over time, varying from philosophers to political economists to sociologists, as Dahrendorf adds:

> When more recently sociologists remembered the word, they naturally gave it a slightly different connotation. Initially the word "class" was used—for example, by Ferguson and Millar in the eighteenth century—simply to distinguish social strata, as we should say today, by their rank or wealth. In this sense the word "class" can be found in all European languages in the late eighteenth century. In the nineteenth century the concept of class gradually took on a more definite coloring. Adam Smith had already spoken of the "poor" or "labouring class." In the works of Ricardo and Ure, Saint-Simon and Fourier, and of course in those of Engels and Marx the "class of capitalists" makes its appearance beside the "labouring class," the "rich" beside the "poor class," the "bourgeoisie" beside the "proletariat" (which has accompanied the concept of class from its Roman origins). Since this particular concept of social class was first applied in the middle of the nineteenth century, its history has been as eventful as that of the society for which it was designed.[52]

Weber argued that economies throughout history had all the elements associated with capitalist stratification: "The creditor-debtor relation becomes the basis of 'class situations' only in those cities where a 'credit market,' however primitive, with rates of interest increasing according to the extent of dearth and a factual monopolization of credits, is developed by a plutocracy. Therewith 'class struggles' begin."[53] Graeber confirms that all financial elements associated with capitalism (e.g., central banks, credit, and bond markets) existed before wage labor.[54] Class and class struggle have herefore existed throughout history even by Marxist criteria and have taken multiple meanings depending on one's assumptions and criteria.

What then is class? Marx did not offer a clear definition because he "postponed the systematic presentation of his theory of class until death took the pen from his hand. The irony has often been noted that the last (52nd) chapter of the last (third) volume of *Capital*, which bears the title 'The Classes,' has

---

51 Dahrendorf, 1959: 3.
52 Ibid.: 4.
53 Quoted in Gerth and Mills, 1946: 183.
54 Graeber, 2011: 345.

remained unfinished."[55] He also conceptualized it differently throughout his work, often contradicting himself in the same work. In *Capital* he writes that under a capitalist mode of production there are only two classes, the bourgeoisie, comprising those who own the means of production, and the proletariat that owns only its labor that it must sell to survive.[56] In the introduction, however, Marx mentions three classes—capitalists, proletarians, and (feudal) landowners. In volume three of *Capital*, in an addendum by Engels, Marx defines class based on revenues, identifying rural elites as a class. He notes, "The owners of mere labour-power, the owners of capital and the landowners, whose respective sources of income are wages, profit and ground-rent—in other words wage-labourers, capitalists and landowners—form the three great classes of modern society based on the capitalist mode of production."[57] He also mentions landowners as a third class in other works—for example, *A Contribution to the Critique of Political Economy*.[58] However, the early Marx considered them part of the bourgeoisie—for example, in *The Eighteenth Brumaire of Louis Bonaparte*.[59] Marx believed feudal elites were alive and well and ruling either without capitalists or side-by-side with capitalists.

Additionally, in *Capital* Marx wrote of the petite bourgeoisie and peasants, whom he referred to as a "class of barbarians," bringing the various "social groups" to five (capitalist, landlord, petite bourgeoisie, proletarian, and peasant). To confuse matters further, he sometimes considered peasants to be outside the proletariat, and at other times he viewed them as a sub-segment of it, as in the *Communist Manifesto*.[60] Then there are "the 'dangerous classes,' the social scum (Lumpenproletariat), that passively rotting mass thrown off by the lowest layers of old society."[61] It is not clear who he includes here, but perhaps he viewed the lumpenproletariat as the mixed caste of rural and urban untouchables, bringing the number of classes to six. Furthermore, Marx considered professionals, such as doctors, lawyers, journalists, professors, writers, and priests, to be the ideological class or defenders of capitalism, bringing the number of "classes" to seven (landlord, capitalist, petite bourgeoisie, ideological, proletarian, peasant, and lumpen). Note that the "ideological" class is not based on material resources or power but rather ideas, thus contradicting

---

55 Dahrendorf, 1959: 8.
56 Marx, 1977 [1867].
57 Marx, 1981 [1895]: 1025.
58 Marx, 1970 [1859].
59 Marx, 1994 [1852].
60 Marx, 1973 [1848].
61 Ibid.: 20

Marx's assumption that classes are based on economic relations. Bertell Ollman writes,

> Marx also speaks of a 'lower middle class' which includes 'the small manufacturers, the shopkeeper, the artisan, the peasant.' This class, it appears, picks up some members from all the economic classes mentioned earlier. What is the criterion by which Marx determines who belongs to the lower middle class? Judging by its membership, it could be income, power, or even distance from the extremes of involvement in the class struggle.... [Marx uses the term 'class'] loosely, often putting it forward as a synonym for 'group,' 'faction,' or 'layer.' This was only in keeping with the imprecise use of class which Ralf Dahrendorf informs us was typical of this period. Where Marx speaks of 'ruling classes,' 'groups' or 'factions' could be substituted for 'classes' without any alteration of the meaning. Marx himself uses 'ruling class' and 'ruling faction' interchangeably in one instance to refer to the same peoples. 'Groups' could also be substituted for 'classes' without any change of meaning in the expression 'ideological classes'; and either 'group' or 'layer' would serve for 'class' where Marx talks of the 'dangerous class.' With all due allowance made for loose word usage, however, Marx cannot escape the more serious accusation of having a litter of standards for class membership and of changing them without prior warning.[62]

Marx may have been observing established feudal castes and rebranding them for his era. We have seen him referring to the following as "classes." One is that of landowners—that usage seems to reflect the ruling caste. Second is the bourgeoisie/capitalist class, which he treats as a mix between ruling (landlord) and noble castes. Third, he considers the petite bourgeoisie, which could represent freemen. Proletarians seem to form a fourth class, including industrial workers and sometimes peasants, which seems to equate to villeins (see Chapter 5 for a discussion of freemen, villeins, bordars and cottars). The lumpenproletariat easily matches the description of bordars and cottars, forming a fifth class. Finally, Marx was well aware of institutional slavery. Few may know that he cooperated with Abraham Lincoln to eliminate it.[63] However, slavery was practiced in all eras, including that of feudalism, and slaves could be Marx's eighth class.

---

62 Ollman.
63 Heartfield, 2012.

Then there is the curious case of tsarist Russia, a feudal state with remarkably little industry, let alone an urban proletariat. Spectacular Marxism required an industrial base, with a national population of proletarians moving through the stages of historical evolution toward socialism and eventually communism. But Bolshevik Russia went from tsarist feudalism to an industrial socialist state, evidently skipping a stage of development. This also puts into question historical materialism since forces of industrial production were just incipient then at best. This apparent skipping of a stage of development sparked intense debates among Left scholars as to whether that was possible. Gramsci observed that the Russian Revolution happened out of order, arriving before any great capitalist antagonisms. Rather, "In Russia, Marx's *Capital* was more the book of the bourgeoisie than of the proletariat. It stood as the critical demonstration of how events should follow a predetermined course: how in Russia a bourgeoisie had to develop, and a capitalist era had to open, with the setting-up of a Western-type civilization, before the proletariat could even think in terms of its own revolt, its own class demands, its own revolution."[64] If Russia went from an agrarian economy to industrial socialism, what happened to the peasants? They remained where and as they were—just like the majority of China's population today, who remain subsistence farmers.

Relatedly, according to the commonly accepted myth, capitalist production began in the 1760s with industrialization. However, it was not until the late twentieth century that most people in the West became engaged in nonagrarian based activities.[65] Specifically, US employment in industrial production did not exceed that in agriculture until after 1910. Agricultural employment as a percentage of all employment in the country did not drop to single digits until after 1962. Interestingly, from 1850 to 1900, employment in services (considered a dominant sector in postindustrial societies) mirrored that in industry. Another curiosity is that from 1910 and after, employment in the service industry has always exceeded that of the industrial sector. Industrial production did not become the dominant employer until the mid-twentieth century, and, even then, during 1952–57 almost twice as many people were employed in services as in industrial production.

Weber pointed out that stratification is not only based on relations in production (class) but also on the social order—for example, the status situation. Marx, however, contradicted himself again because he thought relations in production defined the entire social structure, though he also appears to have accepted that other social relations outside of production matter. However,

---

64 Gramsci, 2000: 32–36.
65 Urquhart, 1984.

these hierarchical relations persist throughout history. It is irrelevant whether the forces of production incorporate power tool use or use hand tools—because social relations remain the same, namely those of oppressors and oppressed.

Another example of Marx's contradictions is that postmodern working classes do not exist, according to his own criteria. One fundamental requirement for class formation is that the oppressed obtain consciousness of their common interests and express them in organized political struggle: becoming a *class for itself* rather than a *class of itself*. According to Marx: "Individuals form a class only in so far as they are engaged in a common struggle with another class. . . . Thus this mass is already a class in opposition to capital but not yet a class for itself."[66] Yet the demos met Marx's criteria for class in many epochs during many modes of production. Before the bourgeois revolutions, serfs had more substantive political participation and representation than citizens do today. Serfs under the estate systems were organized into a self-conscious group (an estate) that acted politically, sometime revolting. In ancient Athens, the demos practiced direct democracy while constantly battling the antidemocratic aristocrats. In 1215, the king of England was forced to cede absolute rule by signing the Magna Carta, as a result of the baronial revolt. England's two-estate system evolved into Parliament, established in the eleventh century. By the fourteenth century Parliament had evolved into bicameral legislature consisting of the House of Lords (nobles and high clergy) and House of Commons (everyone else).

France is a representative example of a three-estate (three-caste) system. The First Estate comprised the clergy, traditionally divided into higher and lower clergy. The Second Estate comprised the nobility, who were divided into nobles of the sword (military) and nobles of the robe (government bureaucrats). The third estate represented everyone else, including urban bourgeoisie and wage laborers, rural freemen, villeins, bordars, and cottars. There were also slaves, the only group without political representation. The king was outside the estate system as a sovereign, while nobles effectively ruled. However, the third estate yielded more political power than postmodern audiences (citizens) through direct participation in assemblies of the estates known as Estates General (citizens' assemblies). In 1302 King Philip IV convened the first Estates General. In the period leading up to the Estates General of 1789, France was experiencing a severe economic downturn. This led the third estate to demand reforms, opposed by King Louis XVI and the Second Estate. In response, Louis XVI attempted to disband the Estates General. The third estate refused

---

66   Marx, *The German Ideology*, quoted in Dahrendorf, 1959: 14.

to abdicate their right to representation and vetoed the king! When the upper and lower clergy and some nobles ultimately joined the third estate, the king was forced to yield. Eventually the Estates General became the National Assembly (June 17, 1789), then the National Constituent Assembly (July 9, 1789), and eventually the foundation for a legislative system. Most of these assemblies based on estates evolved into what are parliaments today. Events in England and France predate capitalism by hundreds of years. Thus, representative democracy and political action by a conscious proletariat predate industrial capitalist societies. To the contrary, capitalism retarded the expansion of political franchise.

Marx also contradicted himself by assuming the universality of classes, which for him were based on property. According to Dahrendorf:

> The dogmatic conjunction of classes and effective private property documents in itself a betrayal of sociology. Perhaps a Marx without the Marxian philosophy of history would have realized that power and authority are not tied to the legal title of property. Marx himself could not realize this, and certainly could not admit it, for had he done so, his philosophical conception of the classless society would have become impossible both empirically and intellectually.... There is, moreover, a strange irony in the fact that the same Marx who so often attacked the uncritical assertion that private property is universal, introduces the same assertion in a concealed way but equally uncritically by speaking of the universality of classes, which for him are tied to the presence of private property.[67]

Another problem is that according to economics textbooks a class system provides the potential for material mobility based on achieved status. Yet data indicate that there is almost no mobility in the United States.[68] If such mobility is structurally absent it is defined as a "closed system" (e.g., caste), as opposed to an "open system" (e.g., capitalism, supposedly). Flipping the question, was there no mobility at all in traditional caste systems?

Spectacular accounts of caste envision strict boundaries without mobility, but in reality there was always a degree of fluidity, mixing at the caste boundaries. In antiquity it was common for people to fall into and out of slavery—for example, becoming enslaved through conquest or obtaining liberty by purchasing it. Sons of farmers could become wealthy merchants as in ancient

---

67 Dahrendorf, 1959: 31.
68 See, for example, Clark, 2014; Financial Security and Mobility Project; Friedman 2012; OECD, 2010; and Reeves, 2017.

Athens. There was mobility in feudal times too. Every now and then a peasant made it to the feudal middle castes as an officer, priest, merchant, et cetera. It was common in England for some villeins to become wealthy, while freemen often fell on hard times, becoming unfree peasants, typically villeins. In England, any free man could become a knight, the lowest title of nobility, by serving first as a page and then as a squire. Kings would regularly remove and award ranks and titles (along with land) as people fell from or rose to favor. In 1066 England, William the Conqueror replaced the defeated nobles with those who supported him during the Norman Conquest, rewarding fourteen hundred men with land.[69]

In France the aristocrats had been reconstituted a number of times by different kings. A French duke could be an Ancien Regime duke, a Restoration duke, a Napoleonic duke, or a Papal duke. Men who were wealthy or who distinguished themselves in combat could become knights. During the Ancien Regime, a non-noble could become one through Acquisition by Letter Patent (by decree of the king) or Acquisition by Office, obtaining a title by serving in certain positions—for example, courts. Most of these positions and attached titles could be purchased for status, especially by the non-noble wealthy, and made hereditary for additional fees.

Throughout feudalism, aristocrats would also experience downward mobility as a result of financial mismanagement or hard times such as crop failures causing land rents to either fall or not be paid. Stories of pauperized aristocrats seeking to marry affluent non-aristocrats (industrialists/urban elites) were commonplace.[70] In France, aristocrats were notorious for their profligate conspicuous consumption that was requisite as a marker of their noble status. This routinely bankrupted nobles, making the practice of marrying wealthy non-aristocrats common.

Centuries later there were free blacks in the US South, where some were even prosperous enough to have owned slaves, while some had families with white partners. Thomas Jefferson is a famous example of this latter situation. Even if the marriages were not sanctioned, they indicated a blurring of the slave/free and black/white caste boundaries in a feudal caste system. Consequently there was mobility under caste systems, although ascription remained the primary determinant for the life chances of the majority. This is exactly the same as under capitalism. The difference is that traditional caste systems openly enforced and acknowledged formal boundaries, whereas postmodern spectacular societies hide it. The blurring of caste boundaries has been relabeled

---

69 National Archives (UK).
70 Ward, 2013.

by political economists as class mobility. That blurring does not constitute a new system based on class, since it predates the capitalist system. Marginal mobility is a historical constant rather than exclusive to capitalism.

If capitalism can evolve and be reborn out of its own collapse, why wouldn't caste systems be able to do the same? We envision caste in its idealized medieval form rather than what it could look like in the society of the spectacle. Of course it would not resemble its feudal ancestor. For example, in the United States after Reconstruction, also referred to as the "Great Compromise of 1877," the North removed troops from the South, effectively allowing it to pass a series of state constitutional amendments and electoral laws disenfranchising blacks and many poor whites. This post-1877 caste system was as formal as its pre-1864 version. Jim Crow did not end formally until the 1954 Supreme Court ruling on *Brown v. Board of Education of Topeka* and the Civil Rights Act of 1964. However, slavery continued into the 1960s. Historian and genealogist Antoinette Harrell discovered black tenant farmers who were unaware that they were free to leave. These farmers were forced to work, tortured, and raped. Harrell recounts:

> I met about 20 people, all who had worked on the Waterford Plantation in St. Charles Parish, Louisiana. They told me they had worked the fields for most of their lives. One way or another, they had become indebted to the plantation's owner and were not allowed to leave the property. This situation had them living their lives as 20th-century slaves. At the end of the harvest, when they tried to settle up with the owner, they were always told they didn't make it into the black and to try again next year. Every passing year, the workers fell deeper and deeper in debt. Some of those folks were tied to that land into the 1960s.[71]

Michelle Alexander further demonstrates how a caste system for blacks evolved from slavery, into Jim Crow, and now into the postmodern prison Jim Crow:

> What is remarkable is that hardly anyone seems to imagine that similar political dynamics may have produced another caste system in the years following the collapse of Jim Crow—one that exists today.... The fact that some African Americans have experienced great success in recent years does not mean that something akin to a racial caste system no longer exists. No caste system in the United States has ever governed all black people; there have always been "free blacks" and black success stories,

---

71   Harrell, 2018.

even during slavery and Jim Crow. The superlative nature of individual black achievement today in formerly white domains is a good indicator that the old Jim Crow is dead, but does not necessarily mean the end of racial caste. If history is any guide, it may have simply taken a different form.[72]

4 The Quantum Mechanics of Value and Capital

4.1 *The Relativity of Value*

Value resides in the domain of quantum mechanics. Like particles, value can exist in multiple places simultaneously. Value obtains a fixed position only when seen by an observer. Therefore, value is in the eye of the beholder. As with freedom, liberty, and justice, value is not something tangible found in nature. Value is a mental construct varying in meaning and contingent upon people, place, and discourses of the time, as Foucault would point out. The founders of classical economics—Adam Smith, David Ricardo, Thomas Malthus, and James Mill—created modern fictions of value that Marx and socialists perpetuated. They considered nature a limitless factor of production, representing value, although land is finite. The fictitious transformation of land, sea, and air into commodities was accompanied by fictions of labor value.

It was not Marx who first conceived of a labor theory of value but David Ricardo. If labor itself had value, it should retain it regardless of what it produces. But, if labor is expended to dig a ditch in the desert, it would have no value, regardless of the labor expended. This is why the political economists had to legitimize the theory with qualifications, such as labor for what people demand. Thus, labor value is relative, since people may demand (or not demand) goods and services based on arbitrary preferences and needs, regardless of the labor time required to produce them.

Industrial capitalism derived profits from selling commodities, denoted by Marx as *M-C-M'*—money (M) tranformed into commodities (C) and then back into money (M') of altered value. Marx considered financial capital as indicative of an advanced form of capitalism. Financial capital derives profits detached from the production of real things by selling simulacrums of value for larger simulacrums of value: *M-M'* (money making more money). The spectacle of postmodern capitalism derives profits by decree, M' where something (not necessarily tangible) is turned into a money equivalent or value. Baudrillard argues that the spectacle is no longer based on real commodities but on images

---

72   Alexander, 2012: 21.

as simulacra of value that may or may not have any connection to anything real including any objective value: "Only to value is capital capable of offering a fantastic spectacle of its decomposition—only the phantom of value still floats over the desert of the classical structures of capital, just as the phantom of religion floats over a world now long desacralized, just as the phantom of knowledge floats over the university.... Surrounded by the *simulacrum* of value and by the *phantom* of capital and of power, we are much more disarmed and impotent than when surrounded by the law of value and of the commodity."[73] Baudrillard argues that capitalism is no longer a capitalist system. Rather, it is a representation of it, a third-order simulacrum. Value is whatever the spectacle decides it to be in its next reincarnation, whether as capitalism, socialism, neoliberalism, or some known by another name. For Baudrillard, value in postmodern society is derived from sign-values, which are normative status rankings similar to those in Veblen's and Weber's analyses. Additionally, even possession has been replaced by the "appearance" of possession.

Currency is a major component of all spectacles representing simulacrum value. According to Aristotle, all money, including commodity money like gold, is symbolic of value and has no value itself.[74] The Bank of England acknowledged in a report that money is imaginary and does not work at all as presented in textbooks.[75] Rather, value has been determined by those in power, based on legitimizing value fictions ultimately backed by violence. The first fiction of value transformation was barter, equating unrelated things through social exchanges. The second fiction of value transformation was the equivalency of things indirectly through commodity money, typically precious metals as a universal medium of exchanged. Fiat money (from the Latin *fiat* "let it become") is a third fiction of value transformation. It is currency declared legal tender by government decree. It is not backed by a physical commodity. It is paper with value because the government said "let there be value." US currency was transformed into purely symbolic value when the United States went off the gold standard, promising to maintain the currency's purchasing power (value)—although this never happens, exemplified by inflation and deflation.

The fourth fiction of value transformation eliminated physical currency altogether. Only a small fraction of money in circulation is physical. Most of it is virtual, on electronic spread sheets of financial institutions representing whatever value is assigned to them by symbolic institutions. The US Federal Reserve creates trillions of dollars by typing on a computer screen the number 1

---

73 Baudrillard, 1994: 153.
74 Graeber, 2011: 298.
75 Graeber, 2014.

followed by a number of 0s. Digital currency such as Bitcoins, created in 2008, comprise a decentralized bookkeeping system for peer-to-peer payments. They are crypto-currency that uses cryptography to secure transactions and to control the creation of new currency. This currency is not made of paper or metal, and it is not a computer entry as that of the Federal Reserve. Bitcoins are not issued by any government or institution. They are constructed out of algorithms produced by anyone's computer by performing complex calculations referred to as *mining*. Thus, crypto-currency represents an anarchist simulacrum currency, existing solely on the internet as digital value (which has fluctuated widely). On December 8, 2017, the market price for one Bitcoin surpassed $17,000, equal to that of an ounce of gold.[76]

Monetary systems in general (e.g. a fractional reserve and central banks), enable the mystification of currency as value. According to Graeber, money represents debt. It is created by elites who have a monopoly on the printing press through central banking systems. In early US history, there was no central banking system, and many banks issued their own currency. With the advent of central banks, currency was monopolized into legal tender, meaning that financial transactions required it. This monetary debt backed by faith (note the "in God we trust" on all US currency) would be worthless without the elites' monopolization of state violence—the currency's true banking. As Graeber writes, "There's a reason why the wizard has such a strange capacity to create money out of nothing. Behind him, there's a man with a gun."[77] Monetary systems are thus forced upon populations as looting mechanisms to extract people's labor time (surplus).

Major contributors to the financial collapse of 2008, including that of Lehman Brothers, were securitized mortgages and credit default swaps. Mathematical gurus took many traditional mortgages (financial instruments representing house values) with good and bad ratings and blend them together into mortgage sausage.[78] The logic was that "risk was spread" sufficiently among A-rated mortgages, constituting a new financial instrument of greater value than its parts. Value was created by arbitrary value assignments from the financial industry. Mortgages, which represent debt, were monetized. However, the algorithmic formulas had been deliberately written to be virtually undecipherable to all, including those with PhDs in math. This was done to hide that A-rated mortgages were actually *junk-rated*, of which the involved institutions were aware. This value fiction was backed by all major financial ratings houses,

---

76   Coindesk, 2017; Gold Price, 2017.
77   Graeber, 2011: 364.
78   Ferguson, 2011.

paid by companies on which they reported. Private and government regulatory agencies were symbolic. When many mortgages started to fail, the illusory bubble popped.

Credit default swaps (CDSs) created by J.P. Morgan in 1994 also contributed to the disaster. Sellers of CDSs agree to pay off third-party debt if the third party were to default on the loan. Buyers of CDSs often bet that the third party will default. However, multiple parties could insure the same asset upon which a CDS was based. These financial wizards created value worth many multiples more than the actual value upon which it were based. In 2001, the value of outstanding CDS was $918 billion. By the end of 2007 it reached $62.2 trillion—the 2007 GDP by comparison was $14.99 trillion.[79]

In the wake of the 2008 collapse, the Federal Reserve's policy included a six-year bond-buying program, for which it printed money under its QE policy in order to prop up the economy. The cost was $4 trillion, an amount created by decree out of thin air on its electronic spreadsheets to buy government bonds (representing debt) with arbitrary value. In a surreal twist, all that newly created money had nowhere to go for a decent return other than the stock market. This led to an artificial inflation of stock values beyond what would be justified by company revenues or productivity.

4.2 There Is No Spoon: Capital(ism)

> SPOON BOY: Do not try to bend the spoon. That is impossible. Instead, only try to realize the truth.
> NEO: What truth?
> SPOON BOY: That there is no spoon.[80]

What is capital(ism)? This simple question does not have a definitive answer to this day. As Graeber explains, there is no consensus on what constitutes capital.[81] However the word itself goes back to the Latin *capitale*, meaning "funds, stock of merchandise, sum of money, or money carrying interest."[82] The term appears in English during the mid-sixteenth century, meaning a grant of land from the king or "head/capita." The English is borrowed from the Italian bookkeeping term for net wealth or net balance. But, if capital is accumulated wealth expressed through currency, financial instruments, or landownership

---

79 ISDA Market Survey, 2010.
80 Wachowski and Wachowski, 1998: 70.
81 Graeber, 2011.
82 Ibid.: 445.

(simulacrums of value), then capital itself is a simulacrum of wealth. This is why Castoriadis considered the Marxist concept of capital to be fictitious, a fetish.

Therefore, one of capitalism's greatest achievements was to convince people that there is such a thing as capital, making it all a mystification of exploitation based on fairy tales by eighteenth-century classical economists. In fact, Adam Smith—often considered the intellectual father of capitalism—never used the term "capital" and was not aware of anything called capitalism. In his oft-cited *Wealth of Nations* published in 1776, Smith referred to an emerging new system of political economy as "mercantilism."[83] This had nothing to do with what is considered capitalism today. Forms of mercantile capital, however, were found in pre-capitalist modes of production such as in the late medieval Islamic world, Sung (Song) dynasty China, and trading states such as Venice and Genoa. Ironically, mercantilism was declared antithetical to capitalism after the 1944 Bretton Woods Accord.

The word "capitalist" was first used in English with its modern meaning in 1792 by Arthur Young in *Travels in France*. The word "capitalism" was first employed with its modern meaning in French, by Louis Blanc in *Organisation du Travail*, published in 1851. According to the *Oxford English Dictionary* the word "capitalism" appears in English in 1854 in William Makepeace Thackeray's novel *The Newcomes*. Marx used the term in German in *Capital*, published in 1867. That is around a hundred years after the supposed birth of capitalism. The ambiguous meaning of "capitalism" lead Dahrendorf to distinguish between Marx's conceptualization of capitalist societies and the more analytically accurate term "industrial societies."[84]

Furthermore, the definition of capital/wealth is a historically contingent mental construct derived by the discursive systems of different societies at different times. In some tribal societies, including that of the Pacific island of Yap, seashells and monumental stone discs that were never physically moved functioned as capital/wealth, a store of value. Capital in antiquity and the early United States included land, buildings, machinery, and slaves. Piketty includes slaves as part of US capital stocks, calculating that they accounted for roughly 30 percent of all capital's value in 1770, equal to that of land. Piketty also calculated that slaves represented a significant portion of all US capital value well

---

83   Mercantilism is a system in which the goal of a country is to accumulate wealth (typically gold and precious metals) through trade with other countries, by exporting more than it imports. This leads to trade imbalances, which have been identified as one cause of World War I, when nations engaged in "beggar-thy-neighbor" trade policies. Modern capitalism considers trade imbalances to be antithetical to the functioning of the system.

84   Dahrendorf, 1959.

into 1880, although the Civil War concluded in 1865.[85] Therefore, anything can be capital, including people.

In Marx's writings, "capital" refers to all resources involved in economic production, such as land, labor, buildings, machines, and currency. Marx and contemporary thinkers added power to the definition of capital.[86] As such, the term "capitalism" would apply to all Marxist epochs.

What about capitalism's uniqueness as a system of perpetual accumulation? It is intellectually disingenuous to assume this or to argue that this is so. If capital is to be understood as accumulation of resources (i.e., land, labor, raw materials, power, etc.), then capital(ism) has been in existence since the demise of widespread hunting and gathering communities. For example, the Roman Empire was largely dependent on expansion through conquest to acquire more land for food production, in order to feed a growing urban population, slaves, and conscripts, and to acquire more resources in general. All hierarchical systems maximize accumulation, whether the system in which feudal lords sought more land, rent, and surplus labor or the system of merchants using the abstraction called money—no different than under capitalism. It is equally disingenuous to assume that all capitalists follow the ideology of perpetual accumulation. Many, including their heirs, are content and enjoying the lives wealth has afforded them, leaving the management of their economic affairs to functionaries.

What about capitalism's supposed uniqueness regarding the use of money as capital and a means of circulation, especially virtual money, and a financial system that suggests credit? According to Graeber, financial systems identical to those of modernity—including systems with credit and money as capital and as a means of circulation (both as commodity and virtual money)—have existed on and off for at least the last five thousand years: "It would seem that almost all elements of financial apparatus that we've come to associate with capitalism—central banks, bond markets, short-selling, brokerage houses, speculative bubbles, securitization, annuities—came into being not only before the science of economics ... but also before the rise of factories, and wage labor itself.... [but, if all this is the "real base,"] how can it be that the superstructure came first?"[87]

At least the concept of "fractional ownership" through stocks based on the legal fiction of a corporation must be unique to capitalism, right? No—corporate charters are feudal in origin. The king offered them in exchange for

---

85 Piketty, 2014: 160.
86 See for example the introduction in Asimakopoulos and Gilman-Opalsky (2018).
87 Graeber, 2011: 345.

service to him. These charters had shareholders. The only difference is that today corporations are immortal, whereas in the past they expired after a specified amount of time. Graeber reminds us: "Joint-stock corporations were created in the beginning of the colonial period, with the famous East India Company and related colonial enterprises, but they largely vanished during the period of the industrial revolution and were mainly revived at the end of the nineteenth century, and then, practically at first, in America and Germany . . . [which] spent the first half of the twentieth century battling over who would replace Great Britain as hegemon, that included modern bureaucratic corporate capitalism."[88]

Is capitalism not distinct because it is derived from industrialization? No—industrialization is not identical to capitalism. This is true because, for example, a socialist, communist, or anarchist society could also be industrialized. Plainly, industrialization is production based on the use of machinery. Machinery, however, has been used throughout history, the only difference being its outward manifestation, based on technological development, and need at the time (e.g., cranes and engines powered by slaves, animals, watermills, or steam). However, according to history textbooks, industrialization was sparked by the "spinning jenny" invented in 1764 by James Hargreaves in England.[89] Note that the spinning jenny was wooden, powered by watermills, and operated by workers. Clearly, industrial machinery need not be made of metal parts or powered by fusion. People think of industrialization as the birth of mass production. Yet many things have been mass-produced since antiquity relative to the production techniques and output of typical smaller producers at the time. Therefore, industrialization is a historically contingent evolution of technology in general that reduces necessary labor time. This more accurate definition would apply to most societies since antiquity, rather than capitalist societies alone.

In terms of capital being a distinct social relation, Marx posited:

> Wakefield discovered that, in the colonies, property in money, means of subsistence, machines, and other means of production does not as yet stamp a man as a capitalist if the essential complement to these things is missing: the wage-labourer, the other man, who is compelled to sell himself of his own free will. He discovered that capital is not a thing, but a social relation between persons which is mediated through things.

---

88 Ibid.: 449.
89 The spinning jenny was a multi-spindle spinning wheel for cotton that allowed for workers to spin eight threads at once with a single wheel.

A Mr Peel, he complains, took with him from England to the Swan River district of Western Australia means of subsistence and of production to the amount of £50,000. This Mr Peel even had the foresight to bring besides, 3,000 persons of the working class, men, women and children. Once he arrived at his destination, "Mr. Peel was left without a servant to make his bed or fetch him water from the river." Unhappy Mr Peel, who provided for everything except the export of English relations of production to Swan River![90]

Capital is indeed built on social relations but between oppressed and oppressors rather than between classes. What Marx observed were various manifestations of hierarchical relations expressed through technology at that time while assuming these relations had economic foundations. He then assigned various types of social relations corresponding to each of his technological periods. In the end, however, social relations are between those that command their own and others' time and those who have little, if any, control over theirs. Therefore, it is a fallacy to look at someone dressed in tattered, clothes toiling on the land, and assume that he or she is in a different situation from a factory worker or a Walmart employee in tattered clothes. This is why limiting analysis of power and authority relations, including their material expressions, to the sphere of production/economics is a doomed endeavor. Exploitation is a social relation permeating all spheres of hierarchical orders.

Postmodern social relations are between the issuer or debtholder and the individual attached to it, the debtor. The debtholder owns fictitious (simulacrum) capital functioning as postmodern means of production. The masses possess no resources, have no jobs, and, unlike the ruling caste, cannot create value/capital by decree. Their primary means of survival is access to credit, servicing it for a lifetime as profit for the debtholder. This forced bondage is driven by neoliberal globalization. As globalization increases unemployment and destroys income in developed and developing regions, those regions' populations are forced into various credit or debt arrangements. This can range from credit card debt, student loan debt, and medical debt to farm and human trafficking debt.

These social relations are a contemporary incarnation of structural debt bondage.[91] Since the 1980s, most, including the middle class, have amassed

---

90   Marx, 1977 [1867]: 932–933.
91   For example, Graeber (2011) argues that wage, slave, and bonded labor are created through debt and monetary systems by elites to force the population into submission and to finance wars. Further, this has been the state of affairs for the last five thousand years.

more debt than assets. Overall household debt as a percentage of after-tax income was 30 percent in 1950.[92] The deb-to-income ratio for households rose to 68.4 percent by 1983, peaking at 127 percent in 2010 before falling to 107.3 percent by 2013.[93] The middle class has treated debt as income to try to sustain a level of consumption that is unsustainable because real incomes have stagnated since the 1970s.[94] Overall, the bottom 90 percent of society carries 73.5 percent of all debt, while the top 10 percent carries 26.5 percent of all debt; the wealthiest 1 percent of the population carries 5.4 percent of all debt (see Table 2.1). The transformation has taken us from being wage slaves in Marxist terms to being postmodern debt slaves.

All this is made possible by technological advances and the increasing rationalization of society based on measurement and calculability, which increase the levels of control.[95] People are transformed through their debt into financial products whose value is best represented by their credit score. Modern debt bondage in the United States can be measured by wage garnishing, which has been on the rise. According to a study by the ADP Research Institute on payroll data, more than one in ten US employees ages thirty-five to forty-four had their wages garnished for credit card, medical, and student loan debts in 2013.[96] It is also important to note too that student loan debt has been increasing dramatically in recent years and cannot be forgiven even under bankruptcy. More wages are garnished for consumer debt than for child support for people earning $25,000 to $40,000 annually. In 2013, four million employees, or 3 percent of all US workers, had their wages garnished for consumer debt. In the Midwest that figure reached over 6 percent, or one in sixteen workers.[97] Worse, many workers have up to 25 percent of their pay (the federal maximum limit) garnished for debt.

According to Graeber, "All this raises the question of what 'capitalism' is to begin with, a question on which there is no consensus at all."[98] If there is no such thing as class, value, capital, or history determined by productive forces, then what are we left with? Whatever it is, it's not capitalism.

---

92   Leicht and Fitzgerald, 2007: 59.
93   Wolff, 2014.
94   See, for example, Mishel et al. (2012).
95   This process has been discussed by Weber, famously expressed through his concept of the "iron cage" in *The Protestant Ethic and the Spirit of Capitalism* 2001 [1930]. The concept has been further developed by contemporary thinkers such as George Ritzer through his concept of the "McDonaldization of society" in his book of the same title (2008).
96   Kiel and Arnold, 2014.
97   Ibid.
98   Graeber, 2011: 345.

CHAPTER 4

The Monetization of Everything

Guy Debord writes:

> The spectacle corresponds to the historical moment at which the commodity completes its colonization of social life. . . . the spectacle is another facet of money, which is the abstract general equivalent of all commodities. But whereas money in its familiar form has dominated society as the representation of universal equivalence, that is, of the exchangeability of diverse goods whose uses are not otherwise compatible, the spectacle in its full development is money's modern aspect; in the spectacle the totality of the commodity world is visible in one piece, as the general equivalent of whatever society as a whole can be and do. The spectacle is money *for contemplation only,* for here the totality of use has already been bartered for the totality of abstract representation. The spectacle is not just the servant of pseudo-use, it is already, in itself, the *pseudo-use* of life.[1]

Commodification is making formerly non-sellable or non-market things sellable in markets. It includes charging fees for what used to be free. Historically, commodification has been intensifying, encroaching into more spheres of society. The postmodern spectacle has moved from Baudrillard's hypercommodification to universal monetization, transforming everything directly into legal tender/value. An example of the degree and extent of monetization is represented by actuarial science, assigning values to anything. Bodies, society, the environment, and space-time are monetized through Wall Street, pawnshops, eBay, and Craigslist. Amazon claims to be an online store where anyone can sell or purchase anything and have it delivered virtually anywhere. The US government monetized debt itself after the 2008 collapse, sparking complaints from China.[2] According to Graeber, no central bank had ever before monetized or created new money, value, and/or capital out of debt.[3]

---

1 Debord, 2012: 29, 32–33.
2 Graeber, 2011; O'Grady 2009.
3 Graeber, 2011.

1   Life, Flesh, and Death

In *Diamond v. Chakrabarty* (1980), the Supreme Court decided that life can be patented.[4] General Electric engineered a bacterium capable of breaking down crude oil for use in oil spills. The application was rejected by a patent examiner because under patent law at the time, living things were considered unpatentable under Section 101 of Title 35 U.S.C.[5] The Board of Patent Appeals and Interferences agreed with the original decision, but the United States Court of Customs and Patent Appeals overturned the case. The Commissioner of Patents and Trademarks appealed to the Supreme Court, which decided in favor of General Electric.

Monetization of life has been extended to human genes and sequences of DNA with patents to those who identified them, typically corporations, good for twenty years. Gene patents have often resulted in companies having sole ownership of genetic testing for patented genes. Over forty-three hundred genes have been patented. However, in 2013, in the case of *Association for Molecular Pathology v. Myriad Genetics, Inc.*, the Supreme Court ruled that genes cannot be patented because DNA is a "product of nature."[6] Yet the ruling permitted patents for DNA manipulated in a lab because altered sequences are not found in nature, such as a type of DNA known as complementary DNA (cDNA). Yet this type of DNA is produced from molecules that carry instructions for producing proteins (messenger RNA) that are products of nature.

With cloning, the spectacle transformed plants, animals, and humans into Baudrillard's second-order simulacrums. These are living things that are indistinguishable genetic copies of originals, patented and owned by their manufacturers. In theory, workers need not be replaced in the Marxist tradition by raising their children. They could be cloned to order as fully developed adults when the previous copy of that worker dies. Researchers in Japan produced twenty-six generations of mice (598 total) cloned from a single mouse. In 2008 researchers created the first mature human embryos using somatic cell nuclear transfer where the nucleus of a somatic cell was taken from a donor and transplanted into a vacant host egg cell.[7] Now the consumer is a commodity and the commodity a consumer.

Life is also monetized by the health-care industry. In the United States, health care is formally considered a commodity for profit. Prescription drug pricing

---

4   Justia, A.
5   Justia, B.
6   National Institutes of Health, 2016.
7   Dvorsky, 2014.

offers an example in which life depends on the ability to pay. In 2016 a scandal broke when it was reported that life-saving EpiPens had gone from $100 to $608 for a two-pack over the preceding decade.[8] Heather Bresch, CEO of Mylan, which produces the epinephrine auto-injector, saw her pay increase by 671 percent over the period when the device's price rose by 400 percent.[9] The price of Daraprim, a sixty-two-year-old drug widely used for treating life-threatening parasitic infections, went from $13.50 a tablet to $750 overnight.[10] Martin Shkreli, the CEO of the drug company, became infamous for arguing that the price was set at what the market could bear, while mocking investigators at a congressional hearing. Bill Ackman, CEO of Valeant Pharmaceutical, testified before Congress that his company would buy niche drugs and then raise the price up to 3,000 percent. The pharmaceutical industry as a whole raises the average price of drugs by 10 percent per year, far above inflation or production costs. None of this should be surprising given that the industry spends $235 million a year on lobbying—more than any other special interest group.[11] In addition, drug companies focus their research on "treatments" that make you dependent on them for life instead of on vaccines or cures.

In the United States, those with or without health insurance can be legally denied medical care by hospitals or private practices if they do not pay upfront their co-pay—or full fee if uninsured. The only exception: hospital emergency rooms, which are prohibited from turning away patients. However, emergency rooms are only obligated to "stabilize" the patient, so that they do not die there. For medical procedures required beyond this, patients are advised as to what type of care to seek upon discharge from the emergency room. Worse, many hospitals serving poor communities are shuttering their emergency rooms to avoid serving those who cannot pay. Life matters only if it can be monetized.

The human body has always been a source of profit, but the postmodern spectacle has monetized the entire body. Slavery is the most common example of bodies as commodities. Postmodern slavery is instituted through the criminal justice system commodifying the bodies of inmates in addition to expropriating their labor. The institutionalization of profits in criminal justice has led to historically high incarceration rates that are far above and beyond those of feudal times. Rates were fairly stable in modern times, ranging from 79 per 100,000 males in 1925 to a high of 139 in 1980. During 1981 and 1982, however,

---

8   Popken, 2016.
9   Ibid.
10 Perrone, 2016.
11 Ibid.

the rate spiked to 171, and by 2010 the male incarceration rate reached 497.[12] In 2013, the rate of incarceration for black males was an astonishing 2,805 per 100,000, and it was 1,134 per 100,000 for Latinos.[13]

While incarceration rates and for-profit prisons exploded after the 1980s, trends that appear to have begun in California, crime statistics show downward trends.[14] California had disproportionately benefited from jobs and military contracts related to the Cold War, and the Cold War's end presented an existential threat to the state's military industrial complex.[15] The solution was to wage war on domestic populations, representing a structural shift from externally oriented to internally oriented violence and militarization. It started in the 1980s when President Ronald Reagan, former governor of California, declared his "war on drugs" in combination with increased sentencing guidelines such as the so-called "three strikes" laws.[16] That is when the for-profit prison boom began. Prison profits created a new structural reality, and this was demonstrated by California, which monetized poor people and blacks to replace lost jobs and profit streams at the end of the Cold War.[17] By 2011 the prison industry had over $5 billion in annual revenues, raising fears that it would lead to normalized widespread arrests for minor offenses or made-up allegations.[18] In 2017 it cost California $75,560 per year to keep someone in prison, more than tuition at Harvard.[19]

Monetization of inmates also includes children. Former judge Mark Ciavarella Jr. was convicted for what was dubbed "kids for cash." He illegally sentenced thousands of children to long-term sentences over nothing. He then funneled them to a private for-profit juvenile detention center in exchange for kickbacks.[20] The judge monetized the bodies of these children that were further monetized by for-profit prisons. Indirect benefits for the prisons included full occupancy rates, which increase a corporation's valuation.

Inmates are also alienated and monetized at once via prison transfers to rural areas, far away from their family and friends. Their families either cannot

---

12 Sourcebook of Criminal Justice Statistics.
13 Sentencing Project, 2012.
14 Ibid.
15 Gilmore, 2007.
16 The Violent Crime Control and Law Enforcement Act of 1994, commonly known as "three strikes," imposes mandatory life imprisonment for a person convicted in federal court of a serious violent felony and with two or more previous convictions in federal or state courts, of which at least one is a serious violent felony (the others could be drug-related).
17 Gilmore, 2007.
18 Taibbi, 2014b.
19 Los Angeles Times, 2017.
20 Getlen, 2014.

afford to visit them or must relocate to be near the prison. This provides primarily white rural areas economic benefits for local businesses such as increased demand for goods and services, especially food and housing. Family members moving to live near rural inmates may also provide a source of cheap labor, given that they are likely to lack valued skills. Such transfers, perversely, also monetize inmates of color by deliberately bringing them to white rural areas: the intention is to increase minority demographics so a town can qualify for federal funding intended to assist nonwhite communities in development.[21]

In addition to serving as nearly slave labor, working for pennies without any legal protections, undocumented immigrants are also monetized in the United States through private, for-profit undocumented worker detention centers.[22] For example, the GEO Group is a multinational corporation with facilities in North America, Australia, South Africa and the United Kingdom. These include maximum-, medium-, and minimum-security prisons, immigration detention centers, and mental health and residential treatment facilities. US Immigration and Customs Enforcement (ICE) spends $2 billion per year in taxpayer dollars for immigration detention using private contractors like GEO.[23]

Prisoners today are commodities, just as corn and coffee—and breast milk. Monetization of breast milk is not new. It was practiced since ancient times when families would employ wet-nurses. In more modern times it was especially prestigious for elites to hire wet-nurses who had the best pedigree based on prior customers. In the postmodern spectacle, "physicians increase demand for this commodity—human milk—by identifying it as valuable, and then prescribe it to their patients as a cure for a medical problem," Linda Fentimen writes. "This unacknowledged commodification of mothers' milk . . . garners enormous profits for entrepreneurs in the human milk and infant formula markets. . . . [These include] wet nurses and a corporation that takes donated milk and manufactures it for sale to hospitals for $184 an ounce. Women who donate milk to this for-profit corporation are apparently unaware of the profits made by the corporation when their milk is sold."[24] This is why breast milk is known as "superfood" and "liquid gold" on the commercial market.[25] In the UK, one can enjoy breast milk ice cream, and in the United States one can purchase breast milk lollipops.[26]

---

21 Case, 2009.
22 Fault Lines, 2012.
23 American Civil Liberties Union, n.d. A.
24 Fentiman, 2009.
25 Bindel, 2017; Labrecque and KATU News, 2017.
26 Bindel, 2017.

At a clinic in Phnom Penh, Cambodia, run by Utah-based Ambrosia Labs, poor women sell their breast milk for consumption in the United States. They are paid fifty cents an ounce for milk that the company sells for up to $4 per ounce. Why would the women do this, especially since they are not left with enough milk to adequately feed their babies? Because the alternatives are working at a garment factory or collecting and recycling garbage for $10 to $13 a day, the same as from selling milk. "White" milk, though, costs more. A British model sold her breast milk for $12.50 an ounce to "male milk-fetishists," earning $375 a day.[27]

In 2013 American women could sell their breast milk, usually through online markets, to men for fifty cents to $3 per ounce, with an average of $1.50.[28] Reputable milk banks charged up to $6 per ounce; by comparison the minimum wage at the time was $7.25 per hour. A lactating woman is typically capable of producing twenty-five to forty ounces per day, but women with Hyper Lactation Syndrome, known as "super producers", yield over a gallon and a half per day.[29] Assuming a "professional" can train her body to produce at the high end, 40 ounces per day, $3 an ounce for forty ounces a day equates to potential income of $120 per day, $840 per week, $3,600 per month, or $43,800 per year—more than many teachers earn. A milk bank could theoretically make $87,600 a year in sales (at $6 an ounce) off of one woman, who may not know the profit the milk bank is making.[30] Corporations sell milk to hospitals at $184 an ounce and could theoretically earn a whopping $2,686,400 annually from the milk of one woman (40 ounces per day x $184 an ounce x 365 days), who they may pay a few thousand dollars.

The level of milk monetization reached new peaks (or lows) in Japan. A bar named Bonyu Bar (Mother's Milk Bar) is dedicated to a niche fetish of drinking breast milk.[31] Customers, virtually all men, can either buy shots of milk or get it directly from the nipple. The bar has three lactating bartenders and charges two thousand yen (about eighteen US dollars in 2018) for a cup of freshly squeezed milk and five thousand yen to breastfeed from the nipple. The management encourages patrons to try a sampler shot of each woman's milk before deciding which to order.

The global hair industry is another example of the body's commodification. It too has been a thriving trade for thousands of years. "In Egyptian times,

---

27   Ibid.
28   Spitznagel, 2013.
29   Labrecque and KATU News, 2017.
30   Fentiman, 2009.
31   Shimanaka, 2009.

men and women shaved their heads but wore wigs as protection from the sun. Queen Elizabeth I sported a wig of tight red curls. In India, temple hair has been sold for centuries—mostly to stuff mattresses, or for the chemicals it contains."[32] Currently, human hair is used for weaves and wigs for American and European celebrities, the rich, and poor black women in America.[33] As with breast milk, this industry obtains hair for free. India is a major supplier of hair on the global market, with hair referred to as "temple hair." Here religion is incorporated into the global market, earning pure profit. In India it is customary for women and men to grow long hair that they donate in a religious ceremony. Long hair is considered a form of vanity. Therefore, people often offer their hair as a sacrifice to a deity in exchange for a favor such as recovery of a sick child. This takes part in a ceremony called *mundan*. Thousands of the faithful make the pilgrimage to the Hindu temple of Tirumala Venkateswara daily.[34] Corporations collect the donated hair without the women knowing that it is used to make very expensive wigs, weaves, extensions, et cetera, for Western consumers.[35] The hair is processed by intermediaries in India that employ women in sweatshops. In Britain, extensions made of temple hair cost £3,000, and the average woman's head produces approximately ten ounces of hair, worth about £210.[36] In the United States weaves cost $1,000 to $3,000 without installation and $5,000 installed. People in India who are aware of hair's value are known to steal it sometimes by entering through windows to chop it off sleeping women or from behind a distracted woman in a movie theater.[37]

The hair industry in America for blacks, most of which is owned by non-blacks, is a $9 billion annual business.[38] One of the largest consumer markets for these expensive products is that of poor black women, for whom hair extensions represent a significant proportion of their income. In order to possess "good hair," many of these women enter voluntary debt bondage, as serfs in medieval times, to finance it. The irony of expropriating hair offered by Indians as a personal sacrifice against vanity for the exploitation of poor black women in the name of vanity should be noted. This demonstrates cultural imperialism and its colonizing effect of what is considered beautiful or ugly. Blacks are made to feel that their natural hair and skin tone is inferior to that of Caucasians to the extent that the use of acid to straighten hair is considered a

---

32 Smellie, 2012.
33 Smellie, 2012; Stilson, 2010.
34 Smellie, 2012.
35 Stilson, 2010.
36 Smellie, 2012.
37 Stilson, 2010.
38 Ibid.

necessary evil by men and women, famously including Malcolm X in his youth. The acid is the infamous "relaxer" that burns the scalp, leading to baldness and, fortunately for the industry, to the need for wigs. In addition to beauty, blacks claim to use it so they can "look like," thus "fit in" with, white society that would otherwise feel intimidated by Afros.[39] This feeds into the beauty industry (magazines, television shows, etc.) that profits by destroying women's self-esteem with untenable images of beauty. The global cosmetic industry alone was a $460 billion market in 2014.[40]

Unlike the past, there is now an international industrial-scale organ trade, referred to as the red market. This market has grown to the point of becoming ubiquitous.[41] China is an indicative case. It executes more prisoners than any country by far. Many are executed to harvest their organs for sale without consent, making this a state-operated flesh business. In addition to harvesting organs from prisoners, investigation has found that China is harvesting organs from non-prisoners. Tianjin First Central Hospital, a well-regarded government-backed institution, was reported to have transplanted far more organs in the late 1990s and early 2000s than the supply by executed prisoners, even though China has low rates of organ donation.[42] China also has a booming private-sector organ industry. For example, a teenager sold a kidney to buy an iPhone and an iPad, and others have sold kidneys to pay off debts or to pay for an abortion for a girlfriend.[43]

A police raid on a dairy farm in India found seventeen people in chains.[44] They were bled at least two times per week in what was called "the Blood Factory." The "factory" provided a large percentage of the blood supply to city hospitals. In addition, India is the world's primary source of bones used in medical studies. The bones are obtained by robbing graves. The global trade in kidneys, corneas, and other organs (and human eggs) is also well-documented. An Indian camp for refugees of the 2004 tsunami was known as Kidneyville because many desperate people sold their kidneys. Brokers typically quoted $3,000 for the flesh but paid out much less after surgery. Victims tolerated this because any money was better than no money.[45] The World Health Organization estimates that 10 percent of organ transplants worldwide are black market. Effectively the poor use their bodies as ATMs from which to make withdrawals.

---

39 Ibid.
40 Business Wire, 2015.
41 Carney, 2013.
42 Bilger, 2016.
43 Associated Press, 2012.
44 Carney, 2013.
45 Ibid.

The globalized flesh market includes the fertility tourism industry. In addition to visiting exciting new places, travelers can purchase one-stop baby fabrication, as in Cyprus, which has the most fertility clinics per capita in the world. For $8,000 to $14,000, full service includes fertilized egg implantation at prices 30 percent cheaper than in Western countries.[46] The flesh donors, however, are eastern European women in dire straits who are paid a few hundred dollars. The customers are typically from western Europe. India legalized surrogacy in 2002 to attract medical tourism. At an Indian infertility clinic featured on *Oprah*, surrogates are paid $5,000 to $6,000 and are kept prisoner in residences during their entire pregnancy, like cows.[47] The clinic charges $15,000 to $20,000 per human "unit," a bargain compared to the United States, where the average cost of surrogacy ranges from $98,000 to $140,000.[48] The surrogate mother is paid between $39,450 and $52,450 for what is called "gestational surrogate cost", not including the cost of donated eggs—or sperm, when needed. Donated eggs run between $5,000 and $10,000 on average.[49] Sperm can run from $300 to $700, although donors typically earn about $50 per ejaculation.[50] The high cost of these services has also led to companies offering surrogacy *financing*.

US consumers often demand eggs and sperm from donors who are tall, thin, and athletic and have characteristics such as white skin, high IQs, and high SAT scores. Customers can request that donors have a certain color hair and eyes, and donors submit details not only about their job history and hobbies but also those of their immediate family members.[51] All this, of course, comes at a premium. In fact, now humans can be custom-made, just like in the dystopian film *Gattaca*, starring Uma Thurman. In 2017 scientists manipulated the genetic code in human embryos using a technology called gene editing, which can be combined with cloning. The scientific community declared this a successful example of human genetic engineering.[52] As Baudrillard wrote years before the realization of this technology, cloning (as now with gene editing) is the ultimate simulation of life.[53] It is a second-order simulacrum of original humans. Given that scientists are also successfully combining animal with human DNA, humans are on the fast track to becoming third-order simulacra with no connection to any original.

---

46 Ibid.
47 Ibid.
48 ConceiveAbilities, online.
49 Ibid.
50 Ibid.
51 Hess, 2014.
52 Belluck, 2017.
53 Baudrillard, 1994.

Monetization of ejaculates (semen) and genes is followed by monetization of children. Each child represents a certain level of expenditures, beginning with the likes of diapers, and including toys, clothing, and participation in the educational indoctrination complex. Once birthing took place mostly at home, and no money changed hands. Now birth is medicalized, taking place in hospitals. In 2018 the average cost of giving birth in a hospital was $32,093 for vaginal birth without complications and $51,125 for a standard caesarean section.[54] The education industry alone generates billions of dollars from tuition and books. In the United States it is estimated that the average cost of raising a child born in 2013 till the age of eighteen is approximately $245,340.[55] Such statistics represent the monetized equivalent or cost of reproducing and replacing a worker unit in Marxist terms. Unfortunately, the federal hourly minimum wage in the United States in 2013 was $7.25. During the eighteen years of child-rearing, a full-time minimum-wage worker would earn $271,440 ($7.25 x 40 hours per week x 52 weeks x 18 years) before taxes. Assuming no other living expenditures (an absurdity leaving out the cost of housing, medical care, food, and much more), that worker's income would hardly cover the cost of replacing himself or herself.

Those involved in the global flesh market might consider merging with the customizable sex industry. Pablo Escobar was a Colombian drug lord and one of the wealthiest people in the world. He made it fashionable as a socially acceptable form of conspicuous consumption to "fabricate" women according to idealized Western stereotypes. Ever since, drug lords and other elites commonly purchase women as mistresses if they agree to undergo extensive plastic surgery according to the buyer's specifications regarding tits, ass, calves, face, belly, and the like. This is not a case of women simply undergoing some cosmetic procedures. These are women who are extensively altered, giving rise to the term "narco-aesthetics." Mimi Yagoub writes: "The key change that took place as this aesthetic ideal bloomed was that the millions of dollars flowing into the hands of Colombia's drug barons made this body so easy to obtain by plastic surgery that those who wanted their perfect woman could easily "pimp out"—in vulgar but popularly used terms—any girl they wished, rich or poor."[56] In the United States, trophy wives, strippers, and prostitutes also enhance their bodies—typically tits—to marry a rich man, make more in tips, or charge more for sex. Actors, singers, politicians, news anchors, and celebrities

---

54   Glenza, 2018.
55   US Department of Agriculture, 2014.
56   Yagoub, 2014.

are also big customers of cosmetic surgery because they consider it vital for their careers, making it a financial investment.

Sex has moved from a local to a global trafficking industry, monetized deeper and wider than ever before, with profits exceeding $100 billion per year.[57] Sexually exploited victims yield an average annual profit of $21,800 per head, Belinda Luscombe reports in *Time* magazine. "Shandra Woworuntu, who worked in finance in Indonesia, tells the story of how she was snapped up from the airport and traded from brothel to brothel in a sex trafficking ring in 2001 for several months and finally escaped by jumping from a second story window. What lawless part of the world did this horrific event take place in? Brooklyn, New York."[58] Porn has also exploded—into a $97 billion industry annually with the advent of the internet.[59] The United States accounts for $10 to $12 billion of that. Most internet traffic continues to be porn-related.

In addition to sex for pay, dating and marriage have been commodified and monetized with online sites. In the United States, 15 percent of adults and 22 percent of young adults use online dating sites and apps.[60] The US industry earns $2 billion in revenue each year and expanded at an annual rate of 5 percent between 2010 and 2015. In China revenue was estimated at $1.6 billion for 2016.[61]

The monetization of life does not end at death. Walmart monetized its workers' deaths. The company took out life insurance policies on its employees (about 350,000 workers in the 1990s) and collected when they died. And the company wasn't alone in doing this: in a 1996 memo, an insurance consultant for Winn-Dixie referred to the deceased insured as "Dead Peasants."[62] Walmart even included actuarial estimates of employee deaths in its profit forecasts, thus subsidizing profits by securitizing the lives of its labor force. Now it is commonplace for corporations to take out what is formally called corporate-owned life insurance (COLI). These include corporations such as American Electric Power, AT&T, Ball, Basset Furniture, Dow Chemical, Eaton, Nestlé USA, Olin, Pitney Bowes, PPG Industries, Procter & Gamble, and Walt Disney.[63] Adding hubris, these companies deduct interest payments on COLI loans from their taxes.

---

57   Luscombe, 2014.
58   Ibid., online.
59   Morris, 2015.
60   Cesar, 2016.
61   Ibid.
62   Schultz and Francis, 2002.
63   Ibid.

Traditionally people died at home, where the viewing of the body would also be held, followed by the funeral, without any substantive processing of the body such as embalmment. Capitalism outsourced those family functions to for-profit medical establishments and made dying at home something to be avoided. Inpatient hospice care costs $6,200 per day, and intensive care runs up to $10,000 per day.[64] Total Medicare hospice spending in 2010 was $13 billion, and the average cost per patient was $10,700. Medicare does not limit payments for hospice care but enforces a cap for agencies: $24,500 per person. In addition, the median cost of a funeral in 2014 was $8,508—compared to the much lower cost of a natural burial without "processing" of the commodity-body.[65]

In another category of moneymaking opportunity being seized, death is postponed—by minutes or months—at sometimes astronomical cost and a potentially worse quality of life for patients, who often do not have the right to commit suicide (allowing chattel to self-destruct is not profitable). Of course, the beneficiaries are members of the ruling caste, who own stock in for-profit hospitals and pharmaceutical companies, and the armies of medical and insurance workers, lawyers, judges, regulators, and politicians.

Death is also monetized after celebrities die. A painting of a skull by dead American graffiti artist and painter Jean-Michel Basquiat—the gay Haitian–Puerto Rican high school dropout who was homeless in New York City and survived by selling T-shirts and homemade postcards—sold at Sotheby's in 2017 for $110.5 million.[66] Elvis Presley has been monetized in death even more than he ever was in life. His records still generate massive revenues, while over half a million people visit his Graceland home in Memphis, Tennessee, annually, paying $93.75 for admission, yielding about $46.9 million.[67] However, no one's death has ever been expropriated and monetized more than "Jesus Christ superstar." The relics market, such as countless pieces said to be from the True Cross, which in total would have to add up to a forest worth of wood, is a major example throughout history. The top relic is the Shroud of Turin, a simulacrum of Jesus's image created around 1260 to 1390 AD, which often goes on tour for public viewing as if it were a rock star. From April 19 through June 24, 2015, more than two million people visited it at 6 euros per head, yielding about 15 million euros ($17 million) for the Catholic Church.[68]

---

64 Fay, 2015.
65 National Funeral Directors Association, 2015.
66 Pogrebin and Reyburn, 2017.
67 Price for 2017 (Graceland.com).
68 Shroud.com, 2017.

Still, the most profitable form of monetization of death has always been war. War and dead soldiers are used to justify global military expenditures. In 2012 alone $1.756 trillion was spent on militaries worldwide, representing 2.5 percent of the global GDP.[69] The United States spent as much on its military as the next fourteen nations combined, at $615 billion in 2014—$527 billion for the annual national defense budget and an $88 billion war supplement.[70]

According to Graeber, all financial and monetary systems were created for the extraction of surplus through debt and wage labor to finance wars.[71] This led to an alliance between financiers, politicians, and the military that has continued for the past five thousand years. Examples of profiteering include contracts for weapons rejected by the military and unaccounted billions from military contracts. For example, Pentagon audits found Halliburton had over $1.422 billion in questionable costs.[72] The company was awarded the multibillion-dollar no-bid Iraq contract when its former CEO, Dick Cheney, orchestrated the invasion of Iraq while he was vice president of the United States. Corporations also profit by charging outrageous prices for items found at hardware stores. McDonnell Douglas sold metal nuts worth less than a dollar to the navy for $2,043 each.[73] Another source of war profiteering is outsourcing (monetizing) tasks to corporations that have traditionally been performed by soldiers (including cooking and cleaning), and another is hiring mercenaries as security contractors and soldiers, including employees of the private military company Blackwater, known as Academi since 2011. The top ten weapons contractors have all admitted or been convicted of fraud yet continue to do business with the government. The only company ever suspended was GE, considered the worst offender, although the suspension lasted a mere five days.[74]

2 Food, Water, and the Environment

Food has been a commodity since ancient times. However, it was produced and traded as food, not as a financial instrument. In modern times, the global food regime evolved from colonial trading systems to state-directed development

---

69 Stockholm International Peace Research Institute.
70 US Department of Defense, 2013.
71 Graeber, 2011.
72 Pleming, 2005.
73 Zepezauer, 2004.
74 Ibid.

to corporate control.[75] Now most of the food sold in US grocery stores is produced by just ten corporations: Nestlé, Associated British Foods, Coca-Cola, Danone, General Mills, Kellogg, Mars, Mondelēz International (formerly Kraft Foods), PepsiCo, Unilever, and Wrigley.[76]

Food is sold through commodity futures markets, whose purpose initially was to stabilize price fluctuations and benefit farmers as well as investors. But, as of the 2008 global economic collapse, food has been globally "financialized" (monetized) with risky derivatives, self-referential trading systems, hedging, arbitrage, and index speculators severing markets from actual food demand.[77] Food has been transformed into a speculative investment separated from its qualities as food, with the explicit purpose to make profits. All this leads to increased price volatility. Here the market logic of growth, meaning increasing prices, is applied, putting food out of reach for many of the world's poor, leading to supply shortages, price spikes, and food riots.

Food financialization includes food chains created by manufacturers and supermarkets. This has moved food production from local small-scale, autonomous, and ecologically sustainable production to a global industrial agribusiness based on patents for genetically modified crops and financed through corporate debt. Corporations such as Monsanto have developed genetically modified crop seeds that can resist high levels of weed killer, typically Monsanto's Roundup. The offspring of these plants can be made to produce sterile seeds that force farmers to keep buying them from the companies. Whether or not the seeds are sterile, these companies prevent farmers from harvesting the seeds under a patent agreement that forces them to buy new seeds every year. Monsanto introduced this system in 1995 and by 2012 had received over $23.5 million from patent infringement lawsuits against farmers. This is big business, representing the global colonization of food crops in such a way that Monsanto, DuPont, and Syngenta control 53 percent of the global commercial seed market.[78] Since the introduction of these seeds, the average cost to plant one acre of soybeans increased 325 percent, while corn costs increased 259 percent.

Monetization of food also leads to land being diverted from production of human food and animal feed for the production of fuel additives such as corn for ethanol and jatropha for diesel and jet fuel, all in further pursuit of higher

---

75   Russi, 2013.
76   León, 2014.
77   Russi, 2013.
78   Paul and Cummins, 2013.

profits.[79] This has been associated with land grabs in developing countries. In the United States, where the government encourages such practices through legal mandates and subsidies, 40 percent of corn is dedicated to the production of ethanol.[80] And, over a couple of decades, Archer Daniels Midland, Bunge, Cargill, Caterpillar, John Deere, Monsanto, and Syngenta received over $596 million in subsidies from state and local governments. This pales in comparison to over $18.5 billion since 2000 in federal support.[81] In this regard, the US government is paying corporations to privatize and control food production.

Worldwide, 15 percent of corn production is for fuel. This accounts for 20–40 percent of price increases in 2007–8, when many food crops doubled in price. Increasing land use for biofuels in the United States leads to greater food insecurity in developing countries that depend on food imports. This expansion has increased the price of corn in Mexico, costing the country $1.5 billion over six to seven years (and costing $6.6 billion for all developing countries and $11.6 billion for all net corn-importing countries), with tortilla prices rising 69 percent.[82]

Eighteenth-century political economists who declared that nature is a factor of production, with made-up economic value, transformed the environment into a commodity. But in postmodern society the environment as a whole is monetized. A History Channel documentary titled "What's the Earth Worth" indicates the mind-set that comprehends the planet as a commodity and evaluates it in terms of monetary sums.[83]

Water has been monetized since ancient times, especially in parts of the world where it is scarce. In postmodern societies, it is monetized as part of the production process. An example is fracking, a subterranean mining process that uses water to let loose natural gas trapped in rocks. Fracking is big business in that it accounts for much of America's recent energy independence. Water is also expropriated outright. Towns and cities continue to fight with fracking and bottling corporations over contracted water rights at times when reserves run low. Nestlé, for example, in the middle of a historic drought and with water restrictions in place, was bottling water in California from groundwater because it was on Indian land that exempted the giant multinational from oversight.[84] Nestlé was working from a relatively old script: locating

---

79 Wise and Brill, 2012.
80 Ibid.
81 Holly, 2015.
82 Wise and Brill, 2012.
83 History Channel, 2012.
84 Abrams, 2014.

production in an impoverished community that had been historically targeted with genocide.

An infamous example of water appropriation and financialization was Bolivia's privatization of its water supply.[85] Law 2029 was passed by the Bolivian government in 1999 as demanded by the World Bank and neoliberal institutions to raise funds. The law offered rural areas no guarantees of water distribution. Worse, all water systems built and operated by local communities were declared illegal and confiscated without reimbursement. People with house wells were not permitted to use them, and they were also not allowed to use rainwater collection tanks. The company that purchased the water rights was Aguas del Tunari, a phantom holding company masking its true owners: Bechtel and crony politicians, including those from the Movement of the Revolutionary Left (MIR) party. In Cochabamba, the third-largest city in Bolivia, with over one million residents, the average person earned around $41 per month, while teachers and pensioners earned about $80. The new privatized water rates increased by $30 per month and were pegged to the value of the US dollar against the local currency. In response, the residents of Cochabamba revolted.

According to the organization Food and Water Watch, water and sewer privatization in the United States leads to loss of public control, accountability, and transparency as corporations cherry-pick service areas to avoid low-income low-profit communities while limiting access through price gouging. For example, private companies charge an average of 59 percent more than public utilities. For sewer service they charge an average of 63 percent more, ranging from 7 percent more in West Virginia to 154 percent more in Texas. A survey of eighteen municipalities that took control back from private companies showed that they operated water and sewer services for an average of 21 percent less. In addition, privatization can increase the cost of financing water projects from 50 percent to 150 percent.[86] Local governments use municipal bonds to finance these projects at an average interest rate of 4 percent. Private companies use equity and corporate debt, costing from 7.5 percent to 14 percent more. The financing costs can add $0.8 to $2.5 million over thirty years per $1 million in investment.[87]

Today's financial markets provide investments based on instruments such as derivatives, hedges, and weather-linked bonds that transform thin air into

---

85 Olivera, 2004.
86 Food and Water Watch, 2015.
87 Ibid.

a monetary value.[88] Emissions trading, also known as "cap and trade", is an example of the monetization of air. It is a market-based approach to regulate pollution with incentives for reductions in emissions. Greenhouse gas emissions are capped and then markets are used to allocate emissions permits or allowances. Carbon trading is an example. Emissions trading is a perverse monetization not of the environment but of the pollution that will destroy it. One carbon credit—that is, the right to emit one ton of carbon dioxide or another greenhouse gas equivalent to one ton of carbon dioxide—is worth €3 to €6 in the European Union's Emissions Trading System (ETS).[89] However, who determines the price and based on what criteria? As Peter Teffer observes: "According to experts, a price of around €30 is needed for the scheme to have an effect on companies. Now, polluting is simply too cheap to work as an incentive. The ETS price has been low for years, due to a glut of credits, or EU allowances (EUA's), in the market. The economic downturn, combined with a fixed number of new credits being created every year, led the price down. However, 6€ is still above the record low in 2013, when EUA's were around €3."[90]

If the cost/value of these credits was determined by what is needed to reduce emissions, the price would change only when the level of pollution changes. Clearly, this is not the case. In the above quote, the drop in the price of carbon credits was partly due to overproduction of such credits, not improvement in the environment. These are the legitimate credits created by international agreements. Unfortunately, there is also a bootleg market selling a simulacrum of simulacrums: bogus carbon credits/value simulating legitimate simulacrum credits/value. Russia, the Ukraine, China, and other countries have been creating bogus carbon credits under a UN agreement called Joint Implementation. The credits were sold in the EU carbon market, where corporations purchased them instead of creating their own emissions cuts to save money. Thus, countries have literally monetized thin air into fictitious value. Perversely, these credit schemes led to increased emissions.[91] Their true function is the legitimization of pollution through simulated regulation and the generation of profits.

3 Cities, Nations, and Culture

Entire cities and even nations have been liquidated for profit since ancient times. This once was typically in the form of forced taxation or looting from

---

88   Muller and Marcel, 2000.
89   Teffer, 2016.
90   Ibid., online.
91   Kollmuss et al. 2015.

conquering armies that sometimes razed them to the ground when done. Now there are no conquering armies or cities burned to the ground. Instead, corporate armies of lawyers, lobbyists, and puppet politicians are used to monetize them more efficiently. The Flint experience is exemplary. As Michael Moore writes:

> When Governor Snyder took office in 2011, one of the first things he did was to get a multi-billion-dollar tax break passed by the Republican legislature for the wealthy and for corporations. But with less tax revenues, that meant he had to start cutting costs. So, many things—schools, pensions, welfare, safe drinking water—were slashed. Then he invoked an executive privilege to take over cities (all of them majority black) by firing the mayors and city councils ... the local people had elected, and installing his cronies to act as "dictators" over these cities. Their mission? Cut services to save money so he could give the rich even more breaks. That's where the idea of switching Flint to river water came from. To save $15 million! It was easy. Suspend democracy. Cut taxes for the rich. Make the poor drink toxic river water. And everybody's happy. Except those who were poisoned in the process. All 102,000 of them. In the richest country in the world.[92]

Correcting the damage from Flint's contaminated water supply will cost over a billion dollars, most of which will be given to private contractors. The homes of the affected residents are now worth nothing. This has cleared the way for corporate land grabs of poor communities, for cents on the dollar, which will likely result in gentrification. The deliberate neglect of infrastructure in poor communities represents the monetization of cities through a process of "accumulation by dispossession"—part of neoliberal policies of disposability.[93] In New Orleans, the biggest damage from Hurricane Katrina was in the predominantly black ninth ward as a result of neglected levees. What came after was not a rebuilding of the community. Henry Giroux writes: "In both New Orleans and Flint, the ruin unearthed by the politics of disposability created the conditions for markets and profits. Austerity politics was the basis for refusing to invest in protecting New Orleans and the destruction following it was used to justify multiple forms of privatization that were politically untenable before the storm including vouchers, charters, and no-bid contracts. Similarly, the human made disaster of Flint and the politics of austerity was the basis for the

---

92   Moore, 2016.
93   Harvey, 2005.

emergency management of the cities and schools that created the conditions for the water poisoning."⁹⁴

Conquest, whether traditional colonialism or more modern neocolonialism, is an older form of liquidating nations and continents. Greece demonstrates the newest version of liquidation through the monetization of an entire nation, including cultural symbols, world heritage sites, and national territory. German suggestions during the 2010 bailout negotiations on how Greece should cope with its international debt, much of which was held by German banks and the German government, are representative:

> Alongside austerity measures such as cuts to public sector pay and a freeze on state pensions, why not sell a few uninhabited islands or ancient artefacts, asked Josef Schlarmann, a senior member of Angela Merkel's Christian Democrats, and Frank Schaeffler, a finance policy expert in the Free Democrats. The Acropolis and the Parthenon could also fall under the hammer, along with temptingly idyllic Aegean islands still under state ownership, in a rush to keep bankruptcy at bay. "Those in insolvency have to sell everything they have to pay their creditors," Schlarmann told Bild newspaper. "Greece owns buildings, companies and uninhabited islands, which could all be used for debt redemption." . . . "The chancellor cannot promise Greece any help," Schaeffler told Bild in a story under the headline: "Sell your islands, you bankrupt Greeks! And sell the Acropolis too!"⁹⁵

As a condition of continued bailout loans from the EU and IMF in 2016, the Greek government placed public assets it was forced to sell in a private holding company or "privatization fund." The country had to do this because Germany did not believe the Greeks would actually sell anything. Basically, Greece was forced to give its assets to a pawnshop. The assets for the fire sale included various real estate and the country's entire infrastructure:

> 14 regional airports
> Athens International Airport (AIA)
> Piraeus Port Authority (OLP) [one of the largest in the Mediterranean]
> Thessaloniki Port Authority (OLTH)
> Egnatia Motorway
> Athens Water Supply and Sewerage (EYDAP) [largest city]

---

94   Giroux, 2017: 11.
95   Inman and Smith, 2010.

Thessaloniki Water Supply and Sewerage (EYATH) [second-largest city]
Hellenic Gas Transmission System Operation (DESFA)
Hellenic Petroleum (HELPE)
Public Power Corporation (PPC)
Public Gas Corporation (DEPA)
Hellenic Telecommunications Organization SA (OTE)
Hellenic Post SA (ELTA)[96]

In addition, most wages (including the minimum wage), pensions, health care, and public services, were cut, while taxes on the majority skyrocketed. In 2018 Greece exited its financial rescue program but with the agreement to keep severe austerity policies in place beyond 2060 in order to pay off its debt. In an article titled "Greece Was Never Bailed Out—It Remains Locked in an EU Debtor's Prison," the former finance minister of Greece, Yanis Varoufakis wrote: "The world's media have been proclaiming the successful completion of the Greek financial rescue programme mounted in 2010 by the European Union and the International Monetary Fund. . . . A more careful reading of the facts points to a different reality. . . . Greece entered another 42 years of harsh austerity and deeper debt bondage (2018–2060)."[97]

Debord's integrated spectacle leads to global cultural homogenization, expropriates and destroys local cultures, and even co-opts and monetizes its opponents. For example, Hollywood films are increasingly financed, produced, and distributed internationally, often jointly with Chinese companies. Coca-Cola is sold in Vietnam. One can express one's radical politics by wearing a T-shirt emblazoned with Che Guevara's iconic image—purchased at various fine retailers. It is now common to hear anti-establishment music in luxury goods commercials exalting the virtues of being an individual or rebel if only one consumes this or that garbage. As for rap and other anti-establishment music, it is given a space in the culture as another safety valve to release pressure. Of course, this type of cultural expression is marketed to the masses only when profits are to be made.

4   Time and Space

Debord writes: "The development of capitalism meant the unification of irreversible time *on a world scale*. . . . What appears the world over as *the same day*

---

96   Lexology, 2016.
97   Varoufakis, 2018.

is merely the time of economic production—time cut up into equal abstract fragments. Unified irreversible time still belongs to the world market—and, by extension, to the world spectacle."[98] Constructed time is what underlies all movements within the spectacle: time to consume goods or services, entertainment, and political or cultural activity (e.g., going to a protest or play), time for sex, war, work, sleep, and "me time" or "us time." Time is never seen as a state of being but of doing and consumption. How much non-institutionalized or even unstructured free time does a worker have relative to that of a medieval serf? The serf had at least the winter months entirely off. This is why Debord argued that serfs were the last humans to experience natural cyclical time relative to the stream of time generated by the spectacle. This is integral to hierarchical systems, for the fear is, as Proverbs reminds, that idle hands are the devil's workshop. If people have free time to think without stress, they may reflect on the status quo and demand change. Thus keeping the animals constantly occupied is a form of hegemonic defense by pre-empting the oppressed from forming counter-ideologies.

Another example of the unification of time-space and its monetization are international calling centers available anywhere in the world any time. US customer service operators located in India or elsewhere provide service 24/7 at a fraction of the US and EU labor costs. Time (and space) is also disembodied via the internet in the form of email. In the twentieth century employers would only call an employee at home in the case of emergencies. Now everyone is expected to answer text messages immediately. Amazon employees were expected to respond to email after midnight, receiving text messages demanding a swift response.[99] France passed a law in 2016 providing workers with *le droit de la déconnexion*, or the right to disconnect.[100] The law prohibits employers from expecting workers respond to emails or other digital communications when not on the clock. All this represents the obliteration of the distinction between private and public space-time.

As Veblen reminds in his landmark *Conspicuous Consumption*, how one spends one's leisure time, assuming one has any, is an expression of status.[101] This leads to activities expected of status groups, which require monetary expenditures. Postmodern leisure time has been monetized further. We do not play sports at the park or watch local amateur teams and community theater performances. Instead, we "need" to purchase tickets to expensive professional sports games, superstar concerts, and Broadway spectacles where we are transformed

---

98 Debord, 2012: 107.
99 Kantor and Streitfeldaug, 2015.
100 Collins, 2016.
101 Veblen, 2012 [1899].

from active participants into an audience (spectators). Children's playtime is another source of revenue. Now all of a child's life is structured around the clock. Sports are organized as with Little Leagues. Dancing is reserved for ballet classes. Gone is the far more beneficial free, unstructured playtime in which children are socialized through natural interaction with others. Gone is the imagination and with it abstract thinking and thus critical thinking. Imaginative play with others has degenerated into a simulacrum with online video gaming. In those virtual worlds, children and adults can interact virtually in real time with others far, far away who they never met, people they will never know beyond the level of avatar. Leisure is also monetized through norms of vacationing. "The social image of the consumption of time is for its part exclusively dominated by leisure time and vacations," Debord writes.[102] Elites summer at the Hamptons or Fiji, the poor at theme parks or away from home visiting and staying with relatives. Travel time is also monetized, and, on planes, blankets, pillows, meals, drinks, movies, and extra legroom now come at an additional charge.

Even space itself has been monetized, disembodied, and universalized. You do not need to walk to a newsstand to purchase a physical copy of the *Financial Times*. Rather, you can buy and read the publication via the internet from anywhere in the world at any time. This is especially true now that "everything" has been digitized (via the Google Books Library Project, for example). This leads to a continuous state of work, because technology makes it possible to perform it in any space, including the coffee shop and even from one's bed, which demonstrates a colonization of private and public space.

Public space is also liquidated in this manner. Standard IMF policies imposed on periphery nations include privatization through forced fire sales of public assets, including land/space. Public airwaves also demonstrate the monetization of space, which in this case is marked by an appropriation of air. Once treated as a commonly held tool owned by citizens, the airwaves are typically auctioned off to private interests with profit in mind and typically void of any public interest requirements that were once the standard for radio and TV stattions awarded a license.

From antiquity up to the twentieth century, one could go to the agora to shop or, as Socrates, to talk with anyone who cared, because it was a public space. The public, not the merchants, regulated the agora. Now these marketplaces or town centers are enclosed by shopping malls. Courts have ruled that although these spaces are open to the public, they are private property. Therefore, management can restrict public expression or assembly within that space.[103] In other cases, big-box stores like Walmart are the agora.

---

102 Debord, 2012: 112.
103 *Chicago Tribune*, 2017.

In addition, there are the evictions of the public from public space, supposedly in the interests of the public. Occupy Wall Street demonstrated this, as did the wider Occupy movement that followed. Laws relating to health, personal safety, and permits were used to annul constitutional rights such as the freedom to assemble and freedom to speak in public space. In Oakland, New York City, and other cities around the world, peaceful protesters were evicted from public spaces, including parks. Local governments have been increasingly dealing with homelessness by criminalizing it in order to placate shopkeepers (concerned with customer traffic) and residents (with property values in mind). Anti-homeless solutions often include loitering laws, installation of spikes under bridges, the use of narrow benches to deter homeless people from sleeping there, and bans on feeding homeless people or providing services to them.[104] Thus, those who lack personal space are also denied access to many public spaces to which they have the right of access as citizens. One reason is that there is a homelessness industry, which is big business, representing the monetization of dispossession. Examples abound. For instance, in New York City, tax dollars are spent on temporary private housing, such as fleabag motels renting rooms at prices far above what it would cost to rent a quality apartment for a homeless family or individual. Luxury hotel chains also benefit from homelessness. In 2015 New York booked over eight hundred rooms at $600 per night and sixty at $629 to house homeless families in Times Square hotels.[105] That is about twice the rate of the upscale Waldorf Astoria. According to the city's controller it costs $400,000 per night to house homeless families in hotels.[106] In 2015, the city booked over 425,000 hotel rooms at a cost of more than $72.9 per night.[107] That is about $2,187 per month, which could have covered the cost of rental or public housing.

On the comic side, parking meters on public streets monetize both time and space. To park on a public street paid for by taxes, one has to pay for a certain amount of square feet of space for a specific unit of time. Of course, the real payoff is parking tickets, which can result in arrest warrants if not paid.

5   The Global Spectacle

Ancient and colonial empires were international caste systems in which the dominant nation set the rules. Marx understood that hegemonies build intricate

---

104   Luttrell, 2014.
105   Smith, 2016.
106   Ibid.
107   Ibid.

national and world structures based on their organizing principles. This, he argued, assured a system's institutional reproduction and maintenance, rendering alternatives as impractical utopias.[108] In the current system that is the twenty-first-century spectacle, the hegemon is the United States, with the EU functioning as its junior partner. Russia and China represent subordinate nations engaged in hegemonic struggle against the United States. Bureaucratic nations like China are variants within the same hegemonic system. Debord puts it well: "As for the bureaucratic power that rules in a number of industrialized countries, it certainly has its own peculiar spectacle, but this plays an integral part in the overarching spectacle as general pseudo-negation and hence as vital support. So even if in its local manifestations the spectacle may embody totalitarian varieties of social communication and control, when viewed from the standpoint of the system's global functioning these are seen to be merely different aspects of a *worldwide division of spectacular tasks*."[109] The US global regime commonly called neoliberalism functions as a postmodern system of debt bondage or tribute, ranging in scale from the individual to entire nations. It is based on financial deregulation, "free" trade, and globally segmented labor markets.[110]

5.1 Finance

The formation of the postmodern financial structure centers on the IMF, World Bank, and transnational banks originating in the 1980s. Its creation came out of the collapse of the Bretton Woods Accord in the 1970s.[111] At that

---

108 See Marx, 1978: 180, 185, 192–193.
109 Debord, 2012: 37.
110 I originally presented the concept of *globally segmented labor markets* at the conference Growth and Crisis, Social Structure of Accumulation Theory and Analysis, National University of Ireland, Galway, Ireland, November 4, 2006, at a session titled "Property and Its Limits." This was based on the extension of national regionally segmented labor markets developed by Gordon, Edwards, and Reich (1982) and first published in Asimakopoulos, 2009.
111 Under US hegemony, the Bretton Woods system of monetary management established the rules for commercial and financial relations among the world's major industrial nations at the end of World War II. Bretton Woods established the International Monetary Fund (IMF) and the International Bank for Reconstruction and Development, commonly referred to as the World Bank. Chief features of the system were an obligation for each country to adopt a monetary policy that maintained the exchange rate of its currency within plus or minus 1 percent, the dollar backed by gold, and the ability of the IMF to bridge temporary imbalances of payments. On August 15, 1971, the Nixon administration unilaterally terminated convertibility of the dollar to gold, making the promise of the United States the sole backing of currencies. The action is also cited as the end of the Bretton Woods Accord, even though its main institutions continue to function today.

time, transnational banks were forming and ultimately providing offshore tax havens without controls on capital flows for global corporations. The banks accumulated massive reserves from corporate accounts that were then lent to developing nations, laying the foundation for the 1980s debt crises. These developments were a major cause of the demise of the Bretton Woods regime, which had institutionalized the old colonial relations, and financial deregulation, such as of capital flows and currency exchange rates, causing the Mexican currency crisis in 1994 and Asia in 1997. In the wake of the 1980s debt crises, the role of the World Bank and IMF changed qualitatively by adopting policies leading to the formation of the new financial regime. The adoption of the new ideology by these institutions was assured, given that the United States has 16.52 percent of the vote at the IMF and 16.3 percent at the World Bank and had an even larger percentage of the vote at the time, representing a share multiple times that of any other nation.[112] Combined, the United States and European Union have 45.4 percent of the vote at the European-controlled IMF and 43.16 percent at the traditionally US-run World Bank.[113]

Some scholars have argued that the financial regime is not new.[114] Rather, it is a continuation of forces dating to the formation of Bretton Woods, when the financial sector was requesting policies that are associated today with neoliberalism, such as free capital flows. It is no surprise that financial capital or any other capital was opposed to regulation that it did not control. What is important is that Bretton Woods did not include these demands. Therefore, the liberalization of capital flows is more properly dated to the 1980s even though it has its origins in the prior system. Panitch and Gindin acknowledge this qualitative shift: "The impact on American financial institutions of inflation, low real interest rates and stagnant profits in the 1970s accelerated the *qualitative transformations* of these years, which increasingly ran up against the old New Deal banking regulations. . . . This was what prompted the global 'financial services revolution.'"[115]

Specifically, the first major shift occurred when in its *World Development Report* (1980), the World Bank changed the definition of development from "nationally managed economic growth" to "participation in the world market."[116] This was a move away from what in essence were mercantilist (i.e., protectionist) policies used by developing nations and toward neoliberal trade, a reference

---

112   International Monetary Fund (figures for 2017); World Bank (figures for 2017).
113   Ibid.
114   Panitch and Gindin, 2005.
115   Ibid.: 57. Emphasis added.
116   McMichael, 2008.

to capital mobility. Second, the World Bank and IMF went from providing development assistance in the form of project loans to restructuring the economies of poor nations in crisis through policy or structural adjustment loans. Thus, these serve as global disciplining institutions. For example, when poor nations need to seek loans from the World Bank and transnational banks they are required to obtain loans from the IMF first. As a condition for these loans, the IMF requires recipients to implement neoliberal reorganization of their economy.[117] These measures include deregulation, free trade and capital flows, severe reductions in public spending, currency devaluation, tax increases on the masses, wage reductions to attract foreign investment with decreased export prices, and especially privatization (read monetization or liquidation). In effect, the IMF removed monetary and fiscal sovereignty from nationally elected governments through a system of postcolonial debt bondage. On February 21, 2012, Greece marked a historic event when as a condition of the European Union–IMF bailouts, it was required to concede to the humiliating loss of fiscal sovereignty. It accepted permanent unelected monitors with the power to overrule elected governments on budget and spending decisions.

Hegemonic currencies also play a disciplining role. At its foundation the common currency known as the euro was designed to subvert labor in countries where it was strong. The euro's architect was Robert Mundell, a Nobel Prize economist and father of supply side economics for the Reagan administration. Mundell acknowledges that the goal through the euro was for elected governments and labor to be subordinated to markets and businesses. He states: "It puts monetary policy out of the reach of politicians, [and] without fiscal policy, the only way nations can keep jobs is by the competitive reduction of rules on business."[118] Mundell also advocated scrapping labor laws, environmental regulations, and taxes on capital.

Capital mobility and privatization make possible the globalization of production and ownership of national resources in developing regions that are in essence no different from neocolonialism. This is demonstrated by the record level of net foreign direct investment (FDI) inflows to poor nations without facing restrictions on profit repatriation. The threat of capital mobility also enables corporations to extract concessions from host nations and to discipline uncooperative local elites.[119] US global financial interests tie the economies of other nations to it. The globalization of finance is the *Americanization* of finance, and the deepening and extension of financial markets has become,

---

117   Black, 2003.
118   Quoted in Palast, 2012b.
119   Black, 2003.

more than ever, fundamental to the reproduction and universalization of US power.[120]

5.2 Trade

The twenty-first-century trade regime is not "free." It is managed based on free trade agreements (FTAS). The blueprint for FTAS was the North American Free Trade Agreement (NAFTA) in 1994. NAFTA allowed the free flow of goods and capital *but not of people* between an industrialized high-wage region and a developing one with subsistence wages.[121] The establishment of the World Trade Organization (WTO) in 1995 extended these regimes to a global scale, while the number of FTAS increased sharply. FTA rules are typically designed in secret by global elites, represented by their corporations and governments, often with little or no participation of any citizen, environmental, or labor groups. Not surprisingly, the trading rules privilege capital while pitting high-income workers in developed regions against low-income workers in underdeveloped regions. This was the case with NAFTA and the WTO proceedings.[122] The failed 2015 Trans-Pacific Partnership (TPP) negotiated by the Obama administration was one of the worst.[123] According to the consumer advicacy organization Public Citizen: "The TPP text was the result of 500 official U.S. trade advisors representing corporate interests involved in years of closed-door negotiations while the public, press and Congress were locked out. At the heart of the TPP were new rights for thousands of corporations to sue the U.S. government before a panel of three corporate lawyers that could award unlimited sums, including for loss of future expected profits, to be paid by American taxpayers when the corporations claim U.S. policies violate the new entitlements the TPP would provide them."[124]

Under the cover of FTAS, corporations scour the globe for cheap labor and financial incentives such as tax breaks. For example, in 2015 the hourly compensation costs in manufacturing, including wages and benefits, in Mexico and Poland were $5.90 and $8.53 respectively, compared to $23.60 in Japan,

---

120 Panitch and Gindin, 2005: 47.
121 Scott, et al., 2006: 4.
122 O'Hara, 2001.
123 It was also originally supported after Obama by presidential Democrat hopeful Hillary Clinton, who stated that it was one of the best free trade agreements. She flip-flopped when both of her rivals—presidential hopefuls Bernie Sanders and ironically Republican Donald Trump—opposed it as one of the worst ever.
124 Public Citizen, 2017.

$37.71 in the United States, $37.59 in France, $31.44 in the United Kingdom, and $42.42 in Germany.[125] As FTAs increased in number, wages in developed nations have been declining, while incomes of elites rise, leading to growing inequality.

As wages decline in developed regions, those in poor regions have remained flat since the 1990s because other parts of the world offer ever-cheaper labor. In India hourly compensation was $1.59 in 2012, and in China it was $4.12 in 2013.[126] Mexican wages have remained flat despite NAFTA's promises, as employment has increased: "Mexican employment did increase, but much of it in low-wage *maquiladora* industries, which the promoters of NAFTA promised would disappear.... The share of jobs with no security, no benefits, and no future expanded."[127]

In addition to lowering various transaction costs for globalized production, FTAs guarantee that once goods are produced in low-wage regions they can be exported unhindered into developed nations, primarily the EU and the United States. Tariffs, quotas, and other trade barriers would have made this unprofitable. Foreign direct investment flows are indicative. Inflows to low-wage regions reached record levels, leading to higher US trade deficits, as corporations shipped back the output of outsourced production to developed regions for consumption. The US trade deficit with pre-WTO China in 1985 was $6 million, but this reached $29.5 billion by 1994.[128] When China entered the WTO in 2001, the deficit reached $103 billion the next year, and it ballooned to $347 billion in 2016.[129] Theoretically the privileged position of the United States in the global system could allow it to experience perpetual trade deficits that nations like China have no choice but to accept.[130] This is possible given that the international reserve and trade currency is the US dollar backed by warships. Thus, the United States can purchase global goods denominated in its own currency by "printing money" at no cost—it is not even printed but entered on the Federal Reserve's balance sheet.[131] This is a postmodern form of imperial tribute and the grandest illusion and simulacrum of value ever created.

125 Conference Board, 2016.
126 Ibid.
127 Scott, et al., 2006: 2.
128 US Census Bureau C.
129 Ibid.
130 Panitch and Gindin, 2005.
131 Frank, 2006.

5.3   Segmented Labor

The global spectacle elevates national labor market segmentation to a global segmentation of labor.[132] The origins of the new labor accord can be traced back to the 1980s when the United States had to contain inflation to stem capital outflows and balance the international financial system. At the time, taming inflation meant increasing interest rates through the Volcker shock (by reducing the money supply and later increasing Fed rates) and containing wage-led inflation from a moribund US labor and civil rights movement. The latter was achieved by crushing the remnants of the labor movement when Reagan fired the air traffic controllers. This cleared the way for financial capital to expand its global outreach (by securing international confidence in the value of the dollar) and its merger with production capital. Leo Panitch and Sam Gindin write:

> The Volcker shock's contribution to the new priority of "breaking inflationary expectations" in the early '80s depended on something more fundamental still. . . . The real issue was not so much finding the right monetary policy, as restructuring class relations. Breaking inflationary expectations could not be achieved without defeating the working class's aspirations and its collective capacity to act. . . . Volcker would later say that "the most important single action of the administration in helping the anti-inflation fight was defeating the air traffic controllers strike." It was on this basis that the American state regained the confidence of Wall Street and financial markets more generally. This proved pivotal to the reconstitution of the American empire by unleashing the new form of social rule subsequently labeled "neoliberalism"—promoting the expansion of markets and using their discipline to remove the barriers to accumulation that earlier democratic gains had achieved.[133]

Although the new labor accord had been initiated by Reagan in the 1980s, it could not be fully developed into globally segmented labor markets without, first, the financial system to secure capital mobility in the 1980s and, second, the neoliberal trade structure unveiled in 1995 that helped secure mobility of production but not of people. For this reason, the emergence of globally segmented labor markets can be dated to 1994–95 with the establishment of NAFTA and the WTO. This represents a twentieth-century enclosure of national populations, no different than colonial relations.

---

132   Asimakopoulos, 2009; Gordon, et al., 1982.
133   Panitch and Gindin, 2005: 63–64.

The regime creates high-income regions of democratic, market-based consumption, where consumers are given greater sovereignty and consumption choices. However, as workers they experience flat real wages, increasing inequality, and the erosion of social safety nets such as pensions, healthcare benefits, and job security. Low-income regions of authoritarian production such as China are also created, where the majority of people remain subsistence-wage consumers. Worse, global corporations subcontract production to local companies that in turn treat local workers as they would the oppressed in a caste system. In fact, many workers are lower caste members in their countries, where caste is formal, as in India. These employees are often beaten, raped, worked to near-death, kept imprisoned on the worksites, and driven to suicide as part of normalized production relations, which mirror their overall treatment in society.

CHAPTER 5

The Structure of Postmodern Caste

1   Social Order

Social inequality is a condition in which members of a society have different amounts of wealth, prestige, or power. When this is based on categories of people in a hierarchy, it becomes stratification. Stratification is a trait of society. Not based on individual abilities, it carries over from generation to generation, perpetuating inequality. It is universal, although it may vary from one to another society, and it includes beliefs about why the system is legitimate. The foundation of caste systems is social segmentation of society based on ascription rather than achievement.[1]

Many think that the United States and other spectacular postmodern societies are not caste systems because of technological development and representative democracy or politburos. However, India exemplifies what an evolved caste system may look like in the twenty-first century. India is the largest representative democracy in the world, but it incorporates caste distinctions in its constitution, which has an established quota system for jobs and educational admissions. As an example, in 2015, the relatively well-off Patel caste protested a quota system in hiring for government jobs and college entrance based on caste or tribe. As reported in the *New York Times*:

> Taking their cue from the Patels, other prosperous castes have now begun talking about holding similar protests. On editorial pages and TV news programs, debate is raging over the nation's quota system, first codified in India's Constitution 65 years ago. The Indian Express called the Patel protest 'an eruption against growth that has not been inclusive.' ... [In a town near the Patel protest] the fear was palpable in an impoverished, hopelessly overcrowded neighborhood ... named for the principal architect of India's Constitution. Almost everyone in this neighborhood comes from a caste that benefits from the quota system, including Narayan Parmar, 51, who said he felt profoundly threatened by the demands of the

---

1   An ascribed status is a trait that one is born with, such as gender, or a social position that one is born into, such as caste, without regard for that person's unique characteristics or talents. An achieved status is a social position attained by a person through his or her own efforts (e.g., becoming a doctor). Vertical mobility in caste systems is limited.

Patidars [Patel caste]. . . . In this neighborhood the Patel protest is seen as an act of monumental selfishness—just one more way for the haves to have more.[2]

This news article could have easily substituted the word "caste" with "class" or "race." Such quotas exist in many industrial democracies. The US and UK equivalent would be anti-discrimination and affirmative action laws. However, there is no requirement for a caste system to have a formal constitution or bill of rights and obligations for each caste. The US Constitution did not mention slavery as an acceptable institution, while references to 'the people' (and 'men' in the Declaration of Independence) were understood to mean white males, excluding women, blacks, and other groups. To the contrary, postmodern caste systems need the pretense of class and democracy to maintain the illusion of mobility and political equality upon which the system's legitimizing ideology rests. Different privileges and disabilities, such as local school financing, are structural. Regardless, caste differences are culturally understood through the daily practice and reproduction of social relations. Therefore, if caste systems around the world can survive and evolve over millennia as in India, why wouldn't the US and European feudal caste systems survive and evolve? In fact, capitalism's remarkable ability to survive its own demise is in and of itself rather unremarkable. The only change is the outward appearance of the system as presented by propaganda at the time. Under the hood, however, is the same caste engine, suggesting that we are living under twenty-first-century technological feudalism. The technological base changes over time, but social relations remain the same.

1.1 *Privileges and Disabilities Based on Ascription*

Privileges in caste systems are reserved for the upper castes, while disabilities are borne by lower ones. Historically, religion legitimized these relations. Postmodern caste systems use education to legitimize elite privileges as stemming from personal achievement, implying that material inequality is fair. This constitutes symbolic meritocracy. Ivy League students are from privileged castes, not first-generation immigrants or from ghetto heartlands. Their admission into the *right* educational institutions is structurally rigged and in many cases assured as a birthright. Daniel Golden's work describes the blatant corruption in Ivy League admissions policies that privilege higher castes.[3] The fine graduates of Ivy League schools obtain the best positions in society because they

---

2 Barstow and Raj, 2015.
3 Golden, 2006.

possess a passport that signals caste membership rather than ability. The case of President Trump's son-in-law is typical. Jared Kushner was born the son of a billionaire. Young Jared was a mediocre student in high school, yet he was admitted to holy Harvard.[4] What did his teachers have to say? According to one, "There was no way anybody in the administrative office of the school thought he would on the merits get into Harvard. . . . His GPA [grade point average] did not warrant it, his SAT scores did not warrant it. We thought, for sure, there was no way this was going to happen. Then, lo and behold, Jared was accepted. It was a little bit disappointing because there were at the time other kids we thought should really get in on the merits, and they did not."[5] How did this student that would probably be rejected by a state university get in? Daddy Kushner pledged $2.5 million to Harvard after which the doors opened for Jared.[6] Of course, the oligarchs did not see it that way: "Risa Heller, a spokeswoman for Kushner Companies, said [that] 'the allegation' . . . is and always has been false. His parents . . . are enormously generous and have donated over $100m to universities, hospitals and other charitable causes. Jared Kushner was an excellent student in high school and graduated from Harvard with honours. (About 90 percent of Jared's 2003 class at Harvard also graduated with honours.)"[7]

Based on the propaganda that privileges are derived by educational attainment, one would expect economic rewards to be correlated with higher levels of education. Data, however, confirm that there is no correlation between education and income. To the contrary, wages for all workers have been stagnant, while those with the highest education, such as college professors, are increasingly living in poverty. As Paul Krugman notes, economic rewards are correlated with power relations:

> The inflation-adjusted earnings of highly educated Americans have gone nowhere since the late 1990s. So what is really going on? Corporate profits have soared as a share of national income, but there is no sign of a rise in the rate of return on investment. How is that possible? Well, it's what you would expect if rising profits reflect monopoly power rather than returns to capital. . . . As for wages and salaries, never mind college degrees—all the big gains are going to a tiny group of individuals holding strategic positions in corporate suites or astride the crossroads of finance.

---

4 Golden, 2016.
5 Ibid., online.
6 Ibid.
7 Ibid., online.

Rising inequality isn't about who has the knowledge; it's about who has the power.⁸

Even capitalist apologist Thomas Piketty laments that the belief that people earn what they are worth is not evidenced based on data covering three hundred years. Rather, "most meritocratic beliefs are often invoked to justify very large wage inequalities, which are said to be more justified than inequalities due to inheritance."⁹ Cultural identifiers are more important than merit. According to the *Financial Times*, employers in the UK discriminate in favor of upper-caste people when hiring for desirable positions:

> The UK's most elite financial services and legal firms operate a 'poshness test' that systematically locks talented working-class people out of high-flying jobs, an official report has found. Recruiters use criteria skewed towards those from privileged backgrounds such as whether candidates have travelled extensively or display 'polish' and confidence, the government-appointed Social Mobility and Child Poverty Commission reports. ... Alan Milburn, the former Labour cabinet minister who chairs the bipartisan commission, said the research showed that young people with working-class backgrounds were being "systematically locked out of top jobs. Elite firms seem to require applicants to pass a 'poshness test' to gain entry."¹⁰

In addition, valuable internships leading to great jobs (versus free labor, dead-end internships for lower-caste children) are rigged in favor of the elite as well.¹¹

Chelsea Clinton personifies caste nepotism masquerading as meritocracy in the institutions of consequence. The Ivies competed to recruit her as a student when Daddy Clinton was president. Upon graduating with a bachelor's degree, she "signed up with McKinsey, a consulting company known as an elite business training corps. She was the youngest in her class, hired at the same rank as those with MBA degrees. Her interview was more like a conversation, said D. Ronald Daniel, a senior partner."¹² At age thirty-four, she was hired by NBC, a corporate media outlet, as a reporter, even though she neither attended journalism school nor worked in the field.¹³ Her assignment was for

---

8   Krugman, 2015.
9   Piketty, 2014: 416.
10 Neville, 2015.
11 Reeves, 2017.
12 Kantor, 2007.
13 Van Buren, 2014.

fluff pieces, such as when she interviewed the gecko cartoon character of the Geico insurance company. Yet, while typical starting salaries for such positions come in at around $100,000 to $200,000, Chelsea was paid $600,000 a year for what amounted to minimum work. Indeed, in the three years that she was under contract, she aired only fourteen segments, which comes out to roughly $26,724 for each minute, or $445 per second.[14] NBC also hired clueless children of other oligarchs as correspondents, including George W. Bush's daughter Jenna and Senator John McCain's daughter Meghan.

The ascribed privileges of Chelsea Clinton go on. She is vice chair of her parents' renamed Bill, Hillary and Chelsea Clinton Foundation.[15] Chelsea was appointed to the board of directors of IAC/InterActiveCorp, owned by media tycoon Barry Diller, a friend of Daddy Clinton. Her hard-earned compensation included a salary of $300,000, an annual retainer of $50,000, and $250,000 in restricted stock. With a master's degree, she taught graduate courses at Columbia University's School of Public Health at an undisclosed salary. However, it gets more absurd. This super-intellectual was hired as an assistant vice provost for the Global Network University at New York University—also at an undisclosed salary. To be clear, this is analagous to appointing a high school senior as an assistant principal.

Chelsea's success also demonstrates that the institution of the family contributes to the formation and reproduction of a caste system. As Castoriadis noted, studies confirm that it is the natural tendency for parents who possess esteemed skills and knowledge to pass them to their children.[16] Parents with devalued skill sets will wish for their children to learn new more valuable ones. Unfortunately, the opportunity to do so is not equal to that of households that possess those skills—not to mention social and cultural capital, wealth, and power. As a result, disadvantaged children will wind up knowing and doing what their parents did. The son of a factory worker may become a fast-food worker, and the son of a plumber may become an electrician. Children of doctors, lawyers, financiers, and so on become doctors, lawyers, or financiers. The offspring of the elite never experience material limitations for generations, even if they are mentally retarded. This is not mobility but a circulation of bodies within castes. Note that the ranking of labor skills is arbitrary, based on power by the dominant caste to value its own skills.

---

14 Ibid.
15 Ibid.
16 See, for example, Reeves, 2017.

In addition, Piketty demonstrated that the family is a contributor to inequality because of inheritance.[17] He summarizes this in his formula: $r > g$. Accordingly: "The principal destabilizing force [in capitalism] has to do with the fact that the private rate of return on capital, r, can be significantly higher for long periods of time than the rate of growth of income and output, g."[18] Wealth grows at a faster rate than wages rise (which fall at times). As Piketty puts it, "The past devours the future."[19] The long-run trend of this tendency, which occurs on a global scale, is the drastic exacerbation of material inequality, which translates into deepening disparities of political and social power.

Inheritance denotes a characteristic of caste systems in that all strata of society are limited to the material existence and opportunities of the families they were born into. A non-hierarchical system would prohibit the practice of inheritance. Instead, it would recycle inheritance in an egalitarian manner back into society. Perhaps this is why Plato argued that in an ideal society, children would be raised by the state without their biological parents knowing which are theirs.[20] Parents would be prevented from using their wealth, status, power, social networks, et cetera to privilege their own children at the expense of others. This would create equal opportunity at a structural level because all children would obtain the exact same treatment, education, and resources devoted to them as their abilities warrant. Ironically, even the theory of capitalism requires a 100 percent inheritance tax. That is how everyone can compete fairly, based on ability. As parents' efforts and rewards have nothing to do with their children, children throughout a given social order would all be starting from the same place, with the same resources as their cohorts.

1.2   Who Pays the Piper?

One indicator of who rules society is who is required to pay the bills. Rulers outsource such obligations to the oppressed, making the tax code an indicator of power relations. During direct democracy in ancient Athens, rich families were required to finance military ships, major public works, and so on as a form of tax for the public good. In contrast, during feudalism, aristocrats were exempt from the king's taxation and free labor requirements that applied only to serfs. For an aristocrat to be taxed would have been considered insulting. Leona Helmsley continued this tradition. She had a reputation for tyrannical behavior, earning her the nickname Queen of Mean. Because of the brazen

---

17   Piketty, 2014.
18   Ibid.: 571.
19   Ibid.: 571.
20   Plato, 1991.

nature and public awareness of her tax evasion, she was symbolically prosecuted. During her trial, a former housekeeper testified that she had heard Helmsley say: "We don't pay taxes. Only the little people pay taxes."[21]

Traditionally, aristocrats felt obligated to help the poor in times of famine and provide other forms of assistance, summed up by the term 'noblesse oblige.' This was a fully privatized system of voluntary philanthropy. The postmodern spectacle has replaced many of the state's traditional social programs with charity and philanthropy. One reason is that the modern form of noblesse oblige is cheaper than taxation. More importantly, privatization of social welfare programs gives elites control over what programs are created, prioritized, and financed, and how they are managed. The charter school and Common Core curriculum movements in the United States are clear examples of such trends. Public input and control through the democratic process is effectively eliminated, while charities become increasingly privatized and lie shrouded by a lack of transparency.

US tax rates on the rich peaked in the 1940s to 1950s, reaching over 90 percent under Eisenhower's administration, but have been dropping ever since at an accelerating rate from the 1990s.[22] Between 1997 and 2007, the four hundred highest income earners saw their incomes rise by 392 percent while their average tax rate was reduced by 37 percent.[23] In addition, the Bush tax cuts disproportionately accrued to the richest 0.1 percent. Most elites earn their income through investments like stocks and bonds rather than salaries. The maximum capital gains tax is 15 percent, but for wages it can be as high as 35 percent. People earning $16,750 to $68,000 pay 15 percent income tax compared to zero capital gains tax for the same amount. A study found that a New York janitor earning about $33,000 a year had an effective tax rate of 25 percent. In comparison, residents of a building named after Helmsley on Park Avenue earned on average $1.2 million annually at an effective tax rate of 14.7 percent.[24]

The top 1 and 10 percent of households own 49.8 percent and 91 percent respectively of all stocks and mutual funds, whereas the bottom 90 percent account for only 9.1 percent (see Table 2.1). Therefore, the elite also benefit from reduced corporate taxes. For example, corporate taxes in the 1950s were 35 percent, compared to current effective tax rates of 0–10 percent.[25] General Electric paid no taxes for a decade while making billions in profits.[26] Perversely, instead

---

21 Gilson, 2011.
22 Ibid.
23 Ibid.
24 Ibid.
25 Gilson, 2011; Zepezauer, 2004.
26 Gilson, 2011.

of the rich and corporations being taxpayers, they are tax recipients of "wealth-fare" such as government subsidies to agribusiness.

As if minuscule taxation was not enough, elites evade it altogether through illegal means, typically offshore tax havens. In 2016, the European Union fined Apple $15 billion for avoiding taxes thanks to a sweetheart deal with Ireland.[27] The company did not have any employees in Ireland, just a mailbox. Profits from other EU countries were transferred to the phantom Irish division and taxed at less than 1 percent (0.005 percent in 2014) versus Ireland's formal corporate tax rate of 12.5 percent.[28] However, one of the greatest revelations was leaked in what became known as the Panama Papers on April 15, 2016. The Panamanian law firm Mossack Fonseca enabled global elites to establish anonymous shell companies in tax havens.[29] Those implicated included close associates of Russian president (dictator) Vladimir Putin, British prime minister David Cameron's father, Chinese president (dictator) Xi Jinping's relatives and various members of the Chinese Communist Party Politburo Standing Committee, King Salman of Saudi Arabia, Iceland's prime minister Sigmundur David Gunnlaugsson (who resigned after the revelations), Argentina's president Mauricio Macri, and some of the world's wealthiest athletes and celebrities.[30] Overall, 8 percent of the world's wealth, amounting to $7.6 trillion, is hidden in tax havens.[31] This represents $200 billion per year in lost global tax revenues, including $35 billion in the United States and $78 billion in Europe.[32] The Panama Papers were followed a year later by 13.4 million leaked documents from Appleby, a Bermudan law firm, dubbed the Paradise Papers.[33] The documents also exposed epic tax evasion by the global elite and corporations like Apple for decades.

In addition, many corporations depend on tax dollars to subsidize their labor and operating costs because they pay workers below subsistence levels. Over half of all federal and state spending on assistance programs such as Medicaid and food stamps (SNAP) goes to working families, most of which have members who work full-time. This costs California $3.7 billion, New York $3.3 billion, and Texas $2 billion annually.[34] Walmart alone costs taxpayers

---

27   Taylor, 2016.
28   Ibid.
29   New York Times, 2016.
30   Ibid.
31   Zucman, 2015.
32   Ibid.
33   Forsythe, 2017.
34   Jacobs, 2015.

$6.2 billion per year in public assistance.[35] Overall, taxpayers subsidize corporations like McDonald's to the tune of $153 billion a year.[36] These corporations also profit from customers who receive public assistance and can only afford to eat fast food or purchase items from cheap retailers. Walmart alone accounted for 18 percent of food stamp sales. The company acknowledged that in 2013 it accounted for $13.5 billion out of $76 billion in food stamp sales.[37]

1.3 *Extreme Structural Inequality*

Extreme inequality is a characteristic of caste systems demonstrated by statistics. The richest eight people in the world have a net worth equal to that of the poorest half of the world.[38] One thousand ten billionaires on the 2016 Forbes list owned $6.5 trillion, equal to that of the bottom 70 percent of the global population.[39] Eighty-nine percent of these billionaires are males, which is typical of hierarchical societies throughout history. A third of them obtained their wealth from inheritance and 43 percent drew theirs from economic cronyism. On the corporate level, the combined revenue of the ten largest corporations exceeds that of 180 countries combined.

Remarkably, and irrespective of time or place, caste systems consist of the same caste groups that receive almost the same wealth and income shares. For example, there was never a time in the US or elsewhere when the bottom quintile received the same as the top, second, or even third and fourth quintiles. This is true regardless of whether the economic base was ancient slavery in Rome, feudalism in the Byzantium in AD 1000 and England in AD 1086, or postmodernism in 2020. The only change has been a well-documented trend of increasing inequality. That means material shares are based upon power relations between castes more than anything else.[40] There have been minor differences in the distribution of wealth and income across time and countries. However, much of this is explained by historically contingent events and local culture (e.g., population collapse or a militant demos). Yet fluctuations in wealth and income shares for the lower castes are within a much tighter range than that for upper castes. I use the United States, United Kingdom, France, Sweden, Russia, and China as case studies. Because of limited availability, I use a number of different data sets within and across countries that are not fully

---

35 O'Connor, 2014.
36 Jacobs, 2015.
37 O'Connor, 2014.
38 Oxfam, 2017.
39 Ibid.
40 Castoriadis, 1993: 225–226.

compatible. This makes historical and international comparisons imperfect but indicative nevertheless. I start with the architect of the global regime, the United States.

In 1774, the wealth shares for the richest 1, 5, and 10 percent of Americans were 16.5, 41, and 59 percent respectively (see Table 5.1). By 2016, the wealth shares for the richest 1, 5, and 10 percent increased to 42.1, 66.5, and 77.6 percent respectively. Wealth inequality measured by the Gini coefficient almost doubled, from 0.456 in feudal 1774 to 0.862 in postindustrial 2016.[41] Income shares for the bottom 90 percent of the population decreased from 69.2 percent in 1774 to 53 percent in 2016 (see Table 5.2). The income share of the top 1 percent almost tripled, from 7.1 percent in 1774 to 20.2 percent in 2016. The richest 10 percent received 30.8 percent of income in 1774 compared to 47 percent in 2016. The income shares of the next richest 10 percent were nearly halved, from 16.5 percent in 1774 to 4.5 percent in 2016.[42] The income share for the middle 40 percent was 40.3 percent in 1774, dropping to 37.1 percent in 2016 (see Table 5.2). The income share for the bottom 40 percent was 12.3 percent in 1774 and 11.4 percent in 2016. Accordingly, the income Gini coefficient in postmodern 2016 was 0.481—higher than the feudal thirteen colonies at 0.437 in 1774 (Table 5.2).

The United Kingdom reflects the US experience with a twist. The wealth share for the top 1 percent of the population in 1740 was 43.6 percent, but by 2016 it was halved to 23.9 percent (see Table 5.1). The wealth share for the top 5 percent of the UK population was 73.6 percent in 1740 (in 1086 it was about the same, at 80 percent) dropping to 43.7 percent by 2016 (Tables 5.1 and 5.3). Unfortunately, I could not find historical data on wealth distribution for the bottom 90 percent of the population. Nevertheless, the 2016 data are similar to that in 1086. Income shares have fluctuated within a tighter range than that for wealth. In 1759 and 2014, the income share of the top 1 percent in the UK was 17.5 and 13.9 percent respectively, a reduction of 3.6 percentage points (Table 5.2). The income share for the top 10 percent in 1759 and 2014 was 45.1 and 39 percent, a decrease of 6.1 percentage points. The share for the middle 40 percent was 30 percent in 1759, rising 7.8 percentage points to 37.8 percent by 2014. The bottom 40 percent received 12.5 percent of income in 1759 and 19.1 percent in 2014, an increase of 6.6 percentage points. However, it is widely reported

---

41   The Italian statistician Corrado Gini in his 1912 paper "Variability and Mutability" developed the Gini coefficient now commonly used as a measure of income or wealth inequality. A value of 0 indicates total equality, while a value of 1 indicates total inequality.
42   Author's calculations based on data from Table 5.2.

TABLE 5.1 Wealth shares in percentages and Gini for six countries.

	US		UK		France	
Year	1774	2016	1740	2016	1807	2016
Gini	0.456*	0.862		0.732		0.72
Top 0.01%		11.2†				
Top 0.1%		22†				7.2*
Top 1%	16.5*	42.1	43.6*	23.9	45.6*	24.5
Top 5%	41*	66.5	73.6*	43.7	78.7*	44.1
Top 10%	59*	77.6	86*	56.6	79.9*	56.4
9		10.7		16.4		15.5
8		5.6		10.8		10.6
7		3.2		7.3	18.32‡ (Middle 40)	7.7
6		1.9		4.8		5.3
5		0.9		2.8		2.9
4		0.3		1.4		1.2
3		0.2		0.5	2.67‡ (Bottom 50)	0.4
2		0.1		0.2		0.1
1		−0.4		−0.9		−0.1

Sources:
Global Wealth Databook 2016, 2016.
* Roine and Waldenströrm, 2015.
† Saez and Zucman, 2016.
‡ World Wealth and Income Database.
§ Bengtsson et al., 2017.
** Kimball, 2015.
†† Nafziger and Lindert, 2012.
‡‡ Brandt and Sands, 1992.

Notes:
1. Data from Roine and Waldenström (2015) are for private wealth.
2 Data from Wealth and Income Database are for net personal wealth.

THE STRUCTURE OF POSTMODERN CASTE

Sweden		Russia		China	
1750	2016	1870††	2016	1706	2016
0.8§	0.832		0.923		0.819
		1.9**			
29§ (Top 0.4)	7.32*				
	35.9	19.4** (Top 1.4)	74.5	16.4‡‡ (Top 0.8)	43.8
20§ (Top 6.5)	59.5		84.8	37.6‡‡ (Top 6)	63.2
	72.4		89	48.1‡‡ (Top 10.5)	73.2
	13.1		4.2	17.6‡‡ (Next 10.8)	10.6
33§ (Middle 49.9)	6.6	32.3**	2.4	22‡‡ (Next 22.7)	6.1
	3.9		1.7		4
	2.3		1.2		2.7
	1.3	(Bottom 86.1)	0.8	12.4‡‡ (Next 37.6)	1.7
	0.7		0.5		1
	0.2		0.2		0.6
18§ (Bottom 43.4)	−0.1		0.1	0‡‡ (Bottom 18.4)	0.3
	−0.3		0		−0.1

3. US data from Saez and Zucman (2016) are for families in 2012.
4. UK 1740 data are for personal wealth.
5. French data for the top 1 and 10 percent are for 1810; for the top 0.1 percent are for 2010.
6. Russian data for 1870 are for private land distribution (Kimball, 2015). The state, public bodies, and church owned 44.3 percent of all land. Land figures for peasants include peasant allotments (common land) of 31 percent and peasant individuals holding 1.3 percent. Holdings of the imperial family are counted as part of state lands. The holdings of nobles do not include the holdings of the imperial family. Data for the bottom 86.1 percent are for peasants. See Nafziger and Lindert (2012) for population estimates. In 1649 the law turned peasants into serfs owned by estates. Serfs owned nothing until their emancipation in 1861.
7. Chinese data for 1706 are for land ownership by households in Huailu County, Hebei.

TABLE 5.2 Income shares in percentages and Gini for six countries.

	US		UK		France	
Year	1774	2016	1759	2014	1695–1704	2014
Gini	0.437†	0.481‡	0.522†	0.358	0.62**	0.294
Top 1%	7.1†	20.2§ (2014)	17.5†	13.88§		10.8§
Top 5%	22.2†	22.6‡	35.4†			
Top 10%	30.8†	47§ (2014)	45.1†	39.0	66**	32.63§
Highest quintile	47.3†	51.5‡	57.5†	43.1	79**	38.5
Fourth quintile	40.3† (Middle 40)	22.9‡	30† (Middle 40)	21.9	11**	22
Third quintile		14.2‡		15.9	6**	17.3
Second quintile	12.3† (Bottom 40)	8.3‡	12.5† (Bottom 40)	11.9	4** (Bottom 40)	13.5
Lowest quintile		3.1‡		7.2		8.7

Sources:
OECD, 2016.
* IndexMundi, 2018.
† Lindert and Williamson, 2012.
‡ US Census Bureau, A.
§ World Wealth and Income Database.
** Morrisson and Snyder, 2000.
†† Nafziger and Lindert, 2012.
‡‡ Milanovic, et al., 2007.
§§ Novokmet, et al., 2017.
*** Alvaredo, et al., 2017.

THE STRUCTURE OF POSTMODERN CASTE

	Sweden		Russia		China	
1903		2014	1904	2015	1880	2012
		0.281	0.362††	0.412*		0.462* (2015)
8.4§		8.7§ (2013)	13.5††	20–25§§	15.5‡‡ (Top 0.3)	13***
			22.7††		10.3‡‡ (Top 1.7)	
16.8§		30.6§ (2013)	31.9††	29.7*–45§§		31.4*
		36.7	47.7††	45.3*	74.4‡‡ (Bottom 98)	47.9*
		22.8	31†† (Next 40)	21.5*		22.3*
		18		15.2*		14.9*
		13.8	21.3†† (Bottom 40)	11.1*		9.8*
		8.7		6.9*		5.2*

Notes:
1. OECD data are for household disposable income.
2. Data from Lindert and Williamson (2012) are for households. Data for 1774 based on the 13 colonies. UK data for households in England and Wales.
3. Data from US Census Bureau, A are for households.
4. World Wealth and Income Database (2014) data are for personal income.
5. Data from Morrisson and Snyder (2000) are based on capitation assessments. Gini under 1695–1704 is for 1760-90.
6. Data from Novokmet, et al., (2017) are high estimates using tax data versus government surveys.

TABLE 5.3   Feudal caste groups and land/wealth distribution in percentages for five countries.

England 1086		China 1706		Sweden 1750	
Population	Land	Population	Land	Population	Wealth
King's family	17				
Nobility 390 people	80	Nobility 0.8	16.4	Nobility 0.4	29
Freemen 12	3	Next 9.7	31.7	Bourgeoisie 6.5	20
Villeins 40	0 (45)	Peasant farmers 89.5	52	Peasant farmers 49.9	33
Bordars 32	0 (5)			Workers & low middle class 43.4	18
Slaves >10	0				

Sources:

England
Domesday Book.
Note: Data in parenthesis indicate access to land.

China
Brandt and Sands, 1992.
Note: Data for 1706 are based on land ownership by households in Huailu County, Hebei.

Sweden
Bengtsson, 2017.

Russia
Kimball, 2015.
Nafziger and Lindert, 2012.

Notes:
1. Population estimates are from Nafziger and Lindert (2012).
2. In 1649 the law turned peasants into serfs owned by estates. Serfs owned nothing until their emancipation in 1861.
3. Data for private land distribution. The state, public bodies, and church owned 44.3 percent of all land. Land figures for peasants include peasant allotments (common land) of 31 percent and peasant individuals holding 1.3 percent.
4. Holdings of the imperial family are counted as part of state lands. Land holdings for nobles do not include the holdings of the imperial family.

THE STRUCTURE OF POSTMODERN CASTE 153

Russia 1870		US 2019		
Population	Land	Population	Wealth	Income
Imperial family	1.9	Rulers 20-400 people	3	1.2
Nobility 1.4	19.4	Nobility 1%-400 people	39.1	19
Peasant farmers 86.1	32.3	Privileged labor 19	46.2	31.3
		Required labor 20	8.8	22.9
		Precarious labor 60	3	25.6
		Slaves 3	0	0

US
Collins and Hoxie, 2015.
Global Wealth Databook 2016, 2016.
Luhby, 2015.
US Census Bureau, A.
World Wealth and Income Database.

Notes:
1. Collins and Hoxie (2015) estimate 20 individuals own as much as the bottom 50 percent, 400 individuals own as much as the bottom 61 percent.
2. Nobility's wealth share is 39.1 percent. The richest 1 percent hold a 42.1 percent wealth share (*Global Wealth Databook 2016*, 2016) minus a 3 percent wealth share for the top 400 individuals (Collins and Hoxie, 2015) equals 39.1 percent.
3. Privileged labor's wealth share is 46.2 percent. The wealth Share for the top quintile is 88.3 percent (*Global Wealth Databook 2016*, 2016) minus a 42.1 percent wealth share for the richest 1 percent (*Global Wealth Databook 2016*, 2016) equals 46.2 percent.
4. Income data for required and precarious labor are for households from US Census Bureau, A. Income for the richest 400 people from Luhby (2015).
5. The income share in 2015 for Nobility is 19 percent. The income share for the richest 1 percent was 22.2 percent (World Wealth and Income Database) minus a 1.2 percent share for the richest 400 people (Luhby, 2015) equals 19 percent.
6. The income share for privileged labor is 31.3. Income share for the top quintile is 51.5 percent (US Census Bureau, A) minus a 22.2 percent wealth share for the richest 1 percent (World Wealth and Income Database) equals 31.3 percent.

that wealth and income inequality in the UK has been increasing for over the past decade.[43]

Wealth distribution in France has remained virtually unchanged from feudal to postmodern times for the bottom 50 percent of the population (see Table 5.1). They received a 2.67 percent wealth share in 1807 compared to 4.5 percent in 2016. In relative terms, that is 69 percent more, but in absolute terms it is a measly 1.83 percentage point increase. The middle 40 percent of the population fared better, receiving an 18.32 percent wealth share in 1807, doubling to 39.1 percent in 2016. That is a significant increase of 20.8 percentage points, which comes mostly at the expense of the richest 1, 5, and 10 percent, whose shares were halved from 1807 to 2016 (Table 5.1). Nevertheless, the richest 10 percent obtain more than half of the wealth, with the richest 1 percent holding a quarter of it. The income shares of the top 10, and 20 percent were also halved from prerevolutionary 1695–1704 to postmodern 2014 (Table 5.2). The income shares of the lowest four quintiles more than doubled during that period. Unfortunately, as Piketty demonstrated, inequality is rising at an increasing rate. Past gains obtained through direct action are being eroded by neoliberalism. This is demonstrated by the contentious *loi travail* (labor law) signed on August 9, 2016, by President François Hollande, a so-called socialist.[44] The law gives private companies greater powers to fire their employees in the name of "flexibility." This will reduce income for the majority of workers and increase the ranks of the precariat.

Contrary to popular belief, 'socialist' Sweden has been and is as unequal as the United States, if not more so. Swedish income distribution is more egalitarian but wealth distribution is not. In 1750 the nobility constituted 0.4 percent of the population, with a wealth share of 29 percent; the bourgeoisie were 6.5 percent of the population, with a 20 percent share (see Table 5.3). The wealth share for the top 6.9 percent of the population (nobles plus bourgeoisie) was 49 percent in 1750. In 2016 the share of the richest 10 percent was 72.4 percent (Table 5.1). The combined groups of peasants and workers in 1750 constituted 93.3 percent of the population and had 51 percent of all wealth (Table 5.3). In 2016 the bottom 90 percent had 27.7 percent of all wealth, a decrease of 23.3 percentage points—to half what it was. A significant change occurred for the bottom 40 percent of the population. Its wealth share dropped from 18 percent in 1750 to 0.5 percent in 2016 (Table 5.1). Overall, the Gini coefficient was higher in 2016 at 0.832 compared to 0.8 in 1750.

---

43 BBC, June 2017.
44 Boring, 2017.

In 2014 the bottom quintile of Swedes received 8.7 percent of all income (the same share as the richest 1 percent) compared to 30.6 percent for the richest 10 percent and 36.7 percent for the top quintile (Table 5.2). But the income of the top 1 percent was more than halved from 1903 to 2014. That for the top 10 percent was reduced from 46.8 percent in 1903 to 30.6 percent in 2014. Unfortunately, historical income data for the bottom 90 percent of Swedes is not available, thus limiting comparisons. However, according to a study, there is

> new evidence on intergenerational mobility at the top of the income and earnings distributions. Using a large dataset of matched father-son pairs in Sweden, we find that intergenerational transmission is very strong at the top, more so for income than for earnings. At the extreme top (top 0.1 percent) income transmission is remarkable with an intergenerational elasticity of approximately 0.9. We also . . . find that IQ, non-cognitive skills and education of the sons are all unlikely channels in explaining the strong transmission. Within the top percentile, increases in the income of the fathers, if they are related at all, are negatively associated with these variables. Wealth, on the other hand, has a significantly positive association. Our results suggest that Sweden, known for having relatively high intergenerational mobility in general, is a society in which transmission remains strong at the very top of the distribution and wealth is the most likely channel.[45]

Further, inequality is increasing at an accelerating rate. The Swedish newspaper *Dagens Samhälle* analyzed changes in income by municipality from 2011 to 2015.[46] It found that the number of rich households grew in 273 municipalities, while the number of poor households grew in 264. Middle-income households fell in every municipality except for four. A study found that growing inequality is driven by returns to capital due to wealth concentration, not wages that have lagged as per Piketty's formula $r > g$.[47]

One would expect high levels of income and wealth equality under spectacular socialism, exemplified by Russia that has had since the 1917 revolution to create an egalitarian society. To the contrary, Russia remained as unequal after 1917 as under the Tsar. Today Russia is the most unequal among major countries, with a wealth Gini of 0.923 in 2016 (Table 5.1). The richest 1 percent in Russia in 2016 held a whopping 74.5 percent of wealth, compared to 11.1 percent

---

45   Björklund, Roine, and Waldenström, 2012.
46   Roden, 2017.
47   Ibid.

for the bottom 90 percent of the population. One hundred eleven people account for 19 percent of all household wealth in Russia according to a 2014 report. The poorest 60 percent receive a wealth share of only 2.8 percent.[48] Income data mirror wealth inequality. Tsarist Russia in 1904 was feudal, yet the income Gini of 0.362 then was lower than the 0.412 in 2015 (Table 5.2). The income share for the bottom 40 percent was higher in 1904 than in 2015. For the third and fourth quintiles, it was about the same in 1904 and 2015. The highest quintile and top 10 percent also fared about the same. The richest 1 percent, though, receive almost double the income share in Russia today compared to feudal times. Wealth and income inequality continue to rise.

'Communist' China has had since 1949 to create an egalitarian society. Yet in 2016 China's top 1 percent owned 43.8 percent of wealth compared to 16.4 percent in feudal 1706 (Table 5.1). In 2016, the bottom 90 percent had a 26.9 percent share of all wealth (compared to 52 percent in 1706), and the bottom 60 percent had a 6.2 percent share of all wealth (compared to 12.4 percent in 1706) (Table 5.1). As for income, in 2012 the bottom 60 percent received a 29.9 percent share compared to about 13 percent for the richest 1 percent (Table 5.2). In historical terms, the income share in 2012 for the bottom 98 percent was about the same as in 1880 (Table 5.2). Both wealth and income inequality continue to rise.

All these countries have comparable wealth inequality with Gini coefficients over 0.72. Russia is the outlier with exceptional inequality as evidenced by its 2016 Gini of 0.923 (Table 5.1). Interestingly, the United States, Sweden, and China have similar Gini coefficients, above 0.8. The United Kingdom and France experience somewhat less inequality, with Gini coefficients of 0.732 and 0.72 respectively. The wealth share in 2016 for the richest 1 percent in Russia was significantly higher than the other countries, at 74.5 percent. Wealth shares for the top 1 percent in the capitalist United States, socialist Sweden, and 'communist' China are similar, ranging from 35.9 to 43.8 percent, China's being the highest (Table 5.1). The share for the richest 1 percent in France is 24.5 percent, and it is 23.9 in the UK, half the shares of their counterparts in the other three countries. The wealth shares across all six nations for the bottom decile ranged from -0.9 to 0 percent, practically the same. The second-lowest decile had from 0.1 to 0.3 percent of all wealth. The third decile wealth share ranged from 0.2 to 0.6 percent, the fourth from 0.3 to 1.4 percent, the fifth from 0.8 to 2.9 percent, and the sixth from 1.2 to 5.3 percent. The bottom 60 percent in all six countries had less than ten percent of all wealth.

The United States, Russia, and China have an income Gini above 0.4. China's is the second highest of all six countries, at 0.462, after the United States. The

---

48   *Global Wealth Report 2014*, 2014.

bottom 90 percent in the United Kingdom, France, Sweden, and China received similar income shares, ranging from 61 to 69 percent (Table 5.2). The bottom 90 percent in the United States and Russia fare worse, receiving nearly identical shares at 53 and 55 percent respectively. The poorest 20 percent received single-digit income shares across the board, ranging from a low of 3.1 percent in the United States to a high of 8.7 percent in France and Sweden.

2 Caste Groups

Historical examples of nobles acting as the ruling caste, headed by either a sovereign or an oligarchy, abound. There are also numerous times when the clergy have acted as the ruling caste, ranging from the medieval Papal States to contemporary Iran. Historical examples of military dictatorships similarly abound. Bureaucracies have also taken power, as in the Soviet Union and China. Under bureaucratic, clerical, and military rule, an institution governs, not a particular caste. Such institutions tend to be staffed by members of multiple castes. However, there is internal caste-based stratification. Lower castes staff low positions, privileged castes have mid-level positions, and nobles and rulers garner top positions. There has never been an example where the bottom caste became rulers for long. The longest was thousands of years ago, during Athenian direct democracy, which lasted 186 years alongside institutional slavery. Postmodern revolutionary communes, such as those of anarchists during the Spanish Civil War and the 1968 Paris insurrection, lasted for a couple of years—or just months.

Caste systems are composed of three generic groups: ruling, noble, and oppressed. The oppressed group is composed of subcastes: privileged labor, required labor, precarious labor, and slaves. Each caste and subcaste has its own level of wealth, status, and power, resulting in distinctly different life chances and subcultures. In 1086 England these groups were the king and his relatives (the ruling caste), nobility, and the oppressed, the latter consisting of freemen (privileged labor), villeins (required labor), bordars and cottars (precarious labor), and slaves (see Table 5.3).

Stratification is typically measured by dividing the population in ranked quintiles by either income or wealth shares, which is flawed because castes are not numerically equal. Measuring inequality based on equal-size population quintiles incorporates different caste members into the same quintile. This obscures the true level of inequality. Neoliberals argue that, despite any uncertainty, there is mobility between quintiles, unlike with castes. Still, this does not explain why each caste receives relatively fixed shares over generations and across varying economic periods. As shown in other sections above, there is no meaningful mobility beyond downward and beyond that which exists at the caste margins.[49] In reality, the holdings of feudal elites have been transferred to their modern-day descendants. For example, a third of Britain is still owned by the aristocracy:

> More than a third of Britain's land is still in the hands of a tiny group of aristocrats, according to the most extensive ownership survey in nearly 140 years. In a shock to those who believed the landed gentry were a dying breed, blue-blooded owners still control vast swathes of the country within their inherited estates. A group of 36,000 individuals—only 0.6 per cent of the population—own 50 per cent of rural land. Their assets account for 20 million out of Britain's 60 million acres of land, and the researchers estimate that the vast majority is actually owned by a wealthy core of just 1,200 aristocrats and their relatives. The top ten individual biggest owners control a staggering total of more than a million acres between them. These figures have been uncovered by the 'Who Owns Britain?' report by Country Life Magazine, thought to be the most extensive survey of its type undertaken since 1872.[50]

Moreover, as in 1086, the queen of England is not only one of the richest people, but also the largest landowner in the world.

The descendants of the French nobility number around six thousand.[51] For example, Pierre-Louis de La Rochefoucauld, duc d'Estissac, a well-known postmodern noble, is the ninth-generation grandson of François Alexandre Frédéric de La Rochefoucauld. François (who lived in the palace of Versailles) was a noble in charge of King Louis XVI's wardrobe. Pierre-Louis de La Rochefoucauld claims to have proof of his family's lineage dating back more than one thousand years to Foucauld the 1st in 1019. These descendants continue to be among the richest people in France, especially large property owners who acknowledge that their family names provide a business advantage. They intermarry with other wealthy people and perpetuate a closed peasant-free caste. For example, the men-only Jockey Club, consisting of about twelve hundred members, is one of the most elite and hard-to-enter clubs worldwide. The club's liveried servants address members by their aristocratic titles. Members

---

49 See, for example, Clark, 2014; Financial Security and Mobility Project; Friedman 2012; OECD, 2010.
50 Cohen, 2010.
51 Marlowe, 2013.

continue the lifestyles of their conservative ancestors. For example, Pierre-Louis de La Rochefoucauld, who has marched a few times against legalizing same-sex marriage, goes stag hunting every year and laments how he and his friends have to constantly battle draft laws to ban it.[52]

A study based on more than two hundred probate inventories of Swedish nobles for 1750, 1800, 1850, and 1900 found increasing inequality and the bifurcation of the nobility, with most wealth held by a few large landowners.[53] In addition, 80 to 90 percent of wealth is transmitted from generation to generation.[54] The descendants of the nobility, numbering approximately 0.2 percent of the population, continue to hold much of Sweden's wealth.[55] For example, 10 percent of the richest Swedes are nobles, while 20 percent of modern era prime ministers have been nobles.[56] The same is true of income distribution, based on studies that found limited intergenerational mobility.[57]

2.1 *Ruling Caste*

"The integration of state and economy is the most evident trend of the century," Guy Debord writes. "It is at the very least the motor of all recent economic developments. The defensive and offensive pact concluded between these two powers, economy and state, has provided them with the greatest common advantages in every field: each may be said to own the other; at any rate, it is absurd to oppose them, or to distinguish between their reasons and follies. This union, too, has proved to be highly favourable to the development of spectacular domination—indeed, the two have been indistinguishable from the very start."[58] Debord forgets that the economy and state have always been fused. In 1086 England, King William the Conqueror and his family owned 17 percent of the land, although technically all land was the king's.[59] Land was used as a proxy for wealth and income in feudal times. The postmodern ruling caste in the United States is in actuality an oligarchy numbering between twenty and four hundred people.[60] The wealth of the Forbes 400 is equal to

---

52 Ibid.
53 Bengtsson, et al., 2017. European executors of wills had to provide probate courts an inventory of the value of the deceased's property, known as probate inventories. See also, for example, ArkivDigital.
54 Cowen, 2014.
55 Bengtsson, et al., 2017; Cowen, 2014.
56 Ibid.
57 Björklund, Roine, and Waldenström, 2012.
58 Debord, 1990: 12.
59 Domesday Book; National Archives (UK).
60 For a breakdown of the Postmodern US caste structure, see Table 5.3.

that of the bottom 61 percent of the population.[61] In comparison, the median net worth for families was $81,000.[62] In 2013 the average adjusted gross income for the top four hundred US taxpayers was $265 million representing a 1.2 percent income share—almost none of it from salaries.[63] The income threshold for this group was $100 million.[64] In comparison, the average adjusted gross income for all taxpayers was $61,700.[65]

The true kings, though, are the twenty wealthiest people, about the same number that ruled in feudal England of 1086. Eight of the richest people are founders of corporations, two are financiers, one is a casino owner, and nine are heirs from families of dynastic wealth.[66] None of them come from ghettos or uneducated families. Their wealth share is 1.1 percent, as much as the bottom half of the country, approximately 152 million people.[67] Their income is immense and difficult to calculate for many reasons, ranging from tax evasion to data that is not publically available. However, in 2009 the richest seventy-four people had an average income of $518.8 million, more than that of nineteen million workers combined.[68] In 2017 the richest man, Amazon founder Jeff Bezos, earned an average of $107 million per day.[69] Mark Zuckerberg earned $41.1 million per day, Charles and David Koch $32.1 million, Warren Buffett $23 million, Steve Ballmer $23 million, Larry Page $22.2 million, Jim Walton $21.9 million, Larry Ellison $17.3 million, Bill Gates $11 million, and Michael Bloomberg $6.8 million.[70]

They experience spectacular life chances beyond the imagination of the masses—little different in this than Renaissance Italian nobles. Their life expectancy is high because of greater access to health care, healthier and less stressful lifestyles (at least in terms of precariousness), quality food, proper diet, and more. Infant mortality rates for this group are minimal. They eat at state or high society functions and world-class private restaurants. They employ top chefs who cook food grown at their private farms. Their wardrobes are custom-made by international fashion houses unless they wear 'common Joe'

---

61   Collins and Hoxie, 2015.
62   Ibid.
63   Luhby, 2015.
64   Ibid.
65   Ibid.
66   Collins and Hoxie, 2015.
67   Wealth share calculated based on data from *Global Wealth Databook 2016* (2016) and Collins and Hoxie (2015).
68   DeGraw, 2011.
69   Michaels, 2018.
70   Ibid.

costumes in public for their image like the Facebook shit Mark Zuckerberg. They live on huge compounds, in city mansions, or entire penthouse floors. Their children are sent around the world to the most prestigious educational institutions to hang out with the offspring of other elites.

Their status is as high as their wealth. Regardless of whether the oppressed speak of them in negative terms, elites command public respect. Many of the oppressed would be thrilled if visited by the queen of England. Dating from robber barons such as Carnegie and Rockefeller to postmodern rulers, billionaires have been celebrities. Today that includes financiers George Soros and Warren Buffett, financial media emperor Mike Bloomberg, the NBA's Dallas Mavericks owner Mark Cuban, tech icon Bill Gates, and royal families. However, these people are monsters who purchase status through philanthropy and charitable foundations. The despicable Carnegie and Rockefeller had their workers gunned down by private thugs such as the Pinkertons and corrupt local police, yet they were revered before and after they died, Carnegie for building public libraries and Rockefeller, ironically, for funding health-related research.

Their level of political power equals that of ancient emperors and absolute monarchs. They *are* the political system, as per the proclamation of King Louis XIV, "L'État, c'est moi" ("I am the state"). Perversely, this statement would be as accurate in meaning had it been uttered by President Trump. According to one well-publicized study: "Multivariate analysis indicates that economic elites and organized groups representing business interests have substantial independent impacts on U.S. government policy, while average citizens and mass-based interest groups have little or no independent influence. The results provide substantial support for theories of Economic-Elite Domination and for theories of Biased Pluralism, but not for theories of Majoritarian Electoral Democracy or Majoritarian Pluralism."[71]

The new monarchs are a global caste, no different from the network of nobles throughout feudal Europe. They transgress national borders while their populations are either not allowed or unable to afford domestic or international travel. They are the masters of the universe, ruling over various *Animal Farm* nations of various spectacular flavors such as capitalist, 'socialist,' or so-called communist. As with their feudal ancestors, the global elite identify and have more in common with each other than with their national subjects.[72] National and global rulers intermarry, which, combined with inheritance, intensifies the process of accumulation and concentration. Similarly to Mills, Rothkopf calls them the superclass consisting of global corporate, financial, and military

---

71 Gilens and Page, 2014: 564.
72 Freeland, 2013.

elites.[73] However, in contrast to Mills, who included politicians in his power elite model, Rothkopf discounts them as mere power brokers. Domhoff identified elites as the wealthy.[74] In reality, as Debord observed, contemporary elites have morphed into one, regardless of background (political, corporate, military, and cultural). Further, there is well-documented group cohesion and caste consciousness among the elite from the national to the global level. For example, Harvard and Oxford are finishing schools for a global aristocracy, institutions where one may find children of Chinese and Russian oligarchs, European elites, Middle Eastern despots, Latin drug lords, and African warlords. In addition, caste consciousness is cultivated through families, private clubs, social registries, and more, as documented by classics such as Mills's *The Power Elite* and especially William Domhoff's *The Bohemian Grove and Other Retreats* and *Who Rules America*.[75] Business caste cohesion is maintained through interlocking corporate directorates and policy planning networks such as the US Chamber of Commerce, think tanks, and colleges and universities.[76]

2.2 Nobles

In England of 1086, the nobility consisted of 200 bishops and abbots with noble titles (holding 26 percent of the land) and 190 lay tenants-in-chief (holding 54 percent of land, of which the twelve richest barons owned 25 percent).[77] Collectively nobles numbered around 390 people. There were also lower nobles, such as knights. Based on a low-end estimate of the population at 1.25 million, these two groups constituted less than 0.0312 percent of the population and had a combined wealth share of 80 percent.[78]

Today's nobles in the United States are the top 1 percent excluding the four hundred richest people who comprise the ruling caste. Nobles number 1,607,000 families with a wealth threshold of $3,960,000 and an average wealth of $13,840,000 (figures include the richest four hundred people).[79] Their wealth share, excluding that for the richest 400, is 39.1 percent (see Table 5.3). In 2015, the average annual houshold income for the top 1 percent (including the richest 400 people) was $1,363,977 and with an income threshold of $386,000.[80]

---

73 Mills, 2000a [1956]; Rothkopf, 2009.
74 Domhoff, 2010.
75 Domhoff, 1975, 2010; Mills, 2000a [1956].
76 Akard, 1992; Burris, 1992; Domhoff, 2010; US Senate Committee on Governmental Affairs, 1978a; US Senate Committee on Governmental Affairs, 1978b.
77 Domesday Book.
78 Ibid.
79 Data for 2012 from Saez and Zucman (2016).
80 Gold, n.d.

The income share in 2015 for the richest 1 percent was 19 percent, excluding the income share of the richest four hundred people.[81]

However this caste is bifurcated between the high nobles (top 0.01 percent excluding the richest four hundred people) and low nobles (intermediate top 1-0.01 percent). The high nobles (top 0.01 percent) number 16,070 families with a wealth threshold of $111 million and an average wealth of $371 million (figures include the richest four hundred people).[82] Their wealth share, excluding that for the top 400, is 8.2 percent.[83] In 2015 the annual income threshold for the top 0.01 percent was $7.5 million with an average income of less than $31,616,431 because these figures include the richest four hundred people.[84] The income share of the top 0.01 percent, excluding that of the richest 400, is 3.9 percent.[85]

The top 0.01 percent are viceroys who head all institutions of consequence: cultural, economic, military, and political. They are corporate and political elites, large business owners, and coupon-clippers, to use a Marxist term meaning rentiers who live by collecting interest and dividend payments from stocks and bonds that they typically inherit. Their status is consistent with their wealth. They share similar life chances as those they serve. They eat at world-class restaurants and enjoy high-quality home meals cooked by chefs. They shop at top fashion districts. Children are sent to the best prep schools and universities. They have political power, with the rulers' blessings, and often run for political office themselves. Typically they influence the outcome of races for mayoralties, governorships, and seats in state legislatures and Congress. These nobles are system managers, while their masters set the strategic agenda.

Low nobles (intermediate top 1-0.01 percent) consist of 1,590,930 families with a wealth threshold of $3,960,000 million, average wealth between $7,290,00 (the average for the intermediate top 99-99.1 percent) and $39.7 million (the average for the intermediate top 0.1-0.01 percent), and a 30.6 percent wealth share.[86] In 2014 the income threshold for the top 1 percent was $386,000, excluding any capital gains, the threshold for the top 0.1 percent was

---

81 See Table 5.2. Income share for the richest 1 percent was 20.2 percent (World Wealth and Income Database) minus 1.2 percent share for the richest 400 people (Luhby, 2015) equals 19 percent.
82 Saez and Zucman, 2016.
83 The wealth share in 2012 for the richest 0.01 percent was 11.2 percent (Saez and Zucman, 2016) minus 3 percent for the top 400 individuals (Collins and Hoxie, 2015) equals 8.2 percent.
84 Gold, n.d.
85 The income share in 2015 for the richest 0.01 percent was 5.1 percent (Gold, n.d.) minus 1.2 percent share for the richest 400 people (Luhby, 2015) equals 3.9 percent.
86 Data for 2012 from Saez and Zucman (2016).

$1.5 million, and $7 million for the top 0.01 percent.[87] In 2015, the average annual family income for the intermediate top 0.1-0.01 percent was $3,984,218. Therefore, the average income for the top 1-0.01 percent is less given that the average family income for the bottom five deciles of the richest 1 percent was $534,495.[88] In 2015 the income share of the top 1-0.01 percent was 15.1 percent.[89]

2.3 Privileged Labor

The caste of privileged labor in 1086 comprised specialized workers like masons, other builders, millers, and swineherds, but the caste was mostly composed of freemen, also known as freeholders or free tenants.[90] They were the only free peasants, constituting 12 percent of the population and holding approximately 3 percent of the land.[91] They owed little or no service to the lord and had independence and security of tenure. Some were prosperous, especially after the European population collapse caused by the plague in the fourteenth century. As a result of the Black Death, there was ample land available for cultivation by surviving serfs who had become freemen. This reduced the power of feudal lords over serfs who enjoyed social mobility and higher wages due to their short supply.[92] Life for serfs became harder when the population in Europe grew after the plague.[93] Many freemen gave up their freedom, becoming serfs, by bonding themselves to a lord due to hard times. This is from where the capitalist concept of financial bonds is derived.

The postmodern caste of privileged labor, also known as core workers, consists of the top intermediate 80-99 percent, twice as many feudal freemen. Privileged labor's wealth share in 2015 was 46.2 percent with an income share of 31.3 percent (Table 5.3). The average wealth for the top quintile, which includes the richest 1 percent, was $630,754.[94] Therefore, the average wealth of the intermediate 80-99 percent was much lower than $630,754 given that the wealth threshold for the top 1 percent was $3,960,000 with an average wealth of $13,840,000.[95] Privileged labor's income in 2014 was between $112,391

---

87   Gold, n.d.
88   Ibid.
89   The income share for the richest 1 percent was 20.2 percent (World Wealth and Income Database) minus 5.1 percent held by the top 0.01 percent (Gold, n.d.) equals 15.1 percent.
90   Domesday Book.
91   Domesday Book; National Archives (UK).
92   O'Brien and Roseberry, 1991: 25.
93   Hilton, 1975.
94   Data for 2011 from US Census Bureau D. The Census Bureau measures the average American net worth every ten years; the next report will be published after the printing of this book in 2021.
95   Data for the top 1 percent for 2012 from Saez and Zucman (2016).

(the upper limit at the 80th percentile) to under $386,000 (the upper income limit for the top 99th percentile in 2015).[96] The mean household income for the top quintile, which includes the richest 1 percent, was $194,276.[97]

It should be noted that, many in the 99th percentile live in urban areas where property, salaries, and the cost of living are higher. Many homes and condos in urban and suburban areas cost well upward of $1–2 million, as in New York City and San Francisco. In 2017, the median home price in San Francisco was $1.5 million, compared to the average US home price of $245,000.[98] The median price for condominiums was $1.2 million in San Francisco and $1.1 million in Manhattan.[99] Therefore, much of the wealth for the 99th percentile is in their homes—which are not necessarily mansions. Salaries reflect the higher cost of urban living, but the buying power is about the same as those earning less in lower-cost areas of America, such as "flyover country." For example, senior counsel salaries in New York City in 2018 averaged $184,093, the average was $221,000 for assistant general counsel, and $245,000 for associate general counsel.[100] Readers should also note that these are averages in the city; many earn much more.

A large fraction of this caste is privileged structurally by the social order, but this is not necessarily due to skills or labor shortages. For example, Castoriadis observes that there is a glut of lawyers and shortages of some semi-skilled workers, but lawyers always earn more.[101] Other workers are privileged because they have skill sets that are in demand. Privileged workers enjoy greater levels of independence and authority both at work and in society. Therefore, it is not in their interest to change the status quo. They are the high status workforce that can afford to eat at pricy restaurants. Their home food is high-quality and organic, from upscale grocers. They shop at higher-end retailers. Their children may go to private or public schools (since they live in higher-income school districts) and attend prestigious universities.

Privileged labor consists of affluent professionals such as executives, physicians, and lawyers. Chief executives earn an annual mean income of $180,700. They are highly regarded. Physicians and surgeons earn a mean annual income

---

96 Data for income limit at the 80th percentile from US Census Bureau B. Data for upper income limit for the top 99th percentile from Gold (n.d.). I use income data from 2014/2015 to make comparable calculations relative to the gross family income as a modest wage that uses data for 2014.
97 US Census Bureau B.
98 Li, 2017.
99 Ibid.
100 Glassdoor, 2018.
101 Castoriadis, 1993.

of $194,990 and have a status score of 86 (scores range between 0 and 100, with larger numbers indicating higher status).[102] Lawyers earn a mean annual income of $133,470 and have a status score of 79. Technology-related positions are the newest examples of privileged labor, privileged due to demand. The status ranking for computer systems analysts and scientists is 74.[103] Financially, the best company to work for in the beginning of a tech career is Facebook, where the median pay for five years of experience or less is $116,800.[104] The median pay after ten years of experience is $159,600, similar to LinkedIn.

However, in 2014, a family of four needed a gross income of $60,608 to $98,722 depending on the region they lived in, with an average of $70,657 as a modest living wage, which would allow for little if any savings (see Figure 5.1). Therefore, income for privileged labor falls between 1.59 (based on the group's lower income limit of $112,391 at the 80th percentile) and 5.46 times (based on the group's upper income limit of $386,000 at the 99th percentile) the average living wage of $70,657, with an average of less than 2.75 times (based on the mean household income of $194,276 for the top quintile). Yet a study found that nearly 25 percent of households making $100,000 to $150,000 a year claimed not to be able to "come up with" $2,000 cash within a month for an unanticipated expense.[105]

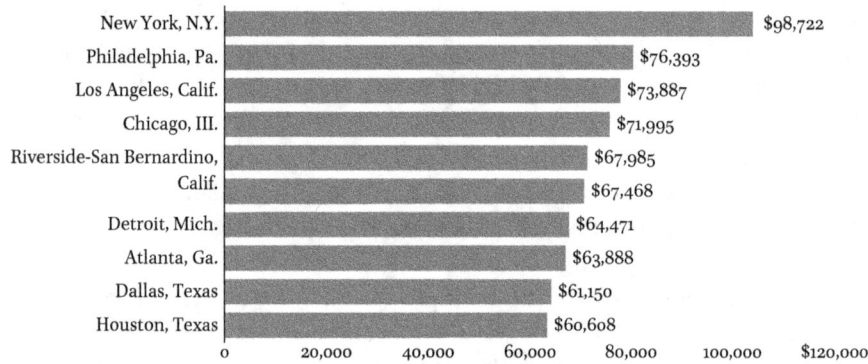

FIGURE 5.1 Annual two-parent, two-child family budgets in 10 largest family budget areas, 2014.
SOURCE: EPI FAMILY BUDGET CALCULATOR (GOULD, ET AL., 2015).

---

102 Income data for 2014 (US Department of Labor [2014]); status scores for 2015 (General Social Survey [2015]). I use income data from 2014 to make comparable calculations relative to the gross family income as a modest wage that uses data for 2014.
103 General Social Survey, 2015.
104 Ferro, 2016.
105 Gabler, 2016.

The occupations of privileged labor are caste-based, including division by gender and race. For example, according to self-reports of the biggest technology companies, men significantly outnumbered women (mostly white) in technology positions. Airbnb was the most diverse (52.5 percent male, 47.5 percent female) followed by eBay (58.1 percent male, 41.9 percent female), LinkedIn (61.9 percent male, 38.1 percent female), Hewlett-Packard (66.9 percent male, 33.1 percent female), Facebook (71.2 percent male, 28.8 percent female), Google (72.2 percent male, 27.8 percent female), Cisco (74.4 percent male, 26.6 percent female), Microsoft (75.7 percent male, 24.3 percent female), and Intel (76.2 percent male, 23.8 percent female).[106] Women represented an even lower percentage in technology leadership positions.

Racial diversity is even lower than gender diversity. Notice how the percentages drop dramatically as skin tone gets darker: LinkedIn (51.1 percent white, 40.1 percent Asian, 4.3 percent Hispanic, 2.1 percent black), Cisco (54.4 percent white, 36 percent Asian, 5 percent Hispanic, 3.4 percent black), Intel (55.9 percent white, 30.7 percent Asian, 8.2 percent Hispanic, 3.5 percent black), Facebook (57.1 percent white, 34.1 percent Asian, 3.9 percent Hispanic, 1.5 percent black), eBay (60.5 percent white, 25.2 percent Asian, 5.4 percent Hispanic, 7 percent black), Microsoft (60.7 percent white, 29 percent Asian, 5 percent Hispanic, 3.4 percent black), Google (60.9 percent white, 30.5 percent Asian, 4.4 percent Hispanic, 1.9 percent black), Airbnb (66.2 percent white, 19.6 percent Asian, 6.1 percent Hispanic, 2.8 percent black), Hewlett-Packard (69.7 percent white, 14.4 percent Asian, 7.7 percent Hispanic, 6.7 percent black).[107] People of color represented a sliver in technology leadership positions in 2015.

Note that salaries for women and minorities are consistently lower than for their white male counterparts, a condition found throughout the economy and across time.

2.4 Required Labor

Villeins were the required labor of 1086 England, comprising 40 percent of the population (see Table 5.3). They were the better-off serfs and most common of the unfree peasants, with more rights than bordars or cottars, who were the lowest serfs.[108] Some were prosperous. Villeins could own property but not land, to which they were tied and prohibited from leaving. Villeins were allowed to rent and farm roughly 45 percent of land in exchange for cash, produce, or

---

106 Jones and Trop, 2015.
107 Ibid.
108 Domesday Book; National Archives (UK).

labor to the landowner, typically consisting of three days each week and even more during harvest time.[109] By the twelfth century they began to pay rent with money instead of labor, which was still the norm. The arrangement that villeins had is not much different in postmodern times. The day dating from January 1 that Americans have to work to pay their annual taxes is called Tax Freedom Day. In 2016 Tax Freedom Day was on April 24 (which meant 114 days that year were devoted to working just to pay taxes). These tax payments are larger than food, clothing, and housing expenses combined. If annual federal borrowing were included, which represents future taxes, Tax Freedom Day would be 130 days after January 1.[110] By comparison, the villeins worked 150 days per year at most.[111]

Postmodern villeins, also known as semi-periphery workers, as a percentage of the population represent half what they did in feudal times—now roughly 20 to 25 percent of the population, corresponding to the second richest quintile. They hold 8.8 percent of wealth and have an income share of 22.9 percent of the total (see Table 5.3). Their average net worth in 2011 was $205,985.[112] In 2014 their income ranged from $68,290 at the upper income limit at the 60th percentile to $112,391 at the upper income limit of the 80th percentile.[113] The mean household income for this group was $87,935. A family of four needed a gross income of $60,608 to $98,722 with an average of $70,657 as a modest living wage, depending on the region (Figure 5.1). Therefore this group falls between 0.97 and 1.60 times a modest living wage (at the upper and lower income limits), with an average of 1.24 times (based on mean income). Therefore, they either carry some debt or accumulate modest savings at best.

Semi-periphery workers eat relatively safe food, mostly at home, purchased from midlevel supermarkets, and eat at better fast-food chains. They shop at midlevel retailers and big-box stores. Their children attend average public or parochial schools. They are likely to obtain a four-year college degree from a public institution. The privileged and required labor castes are consumers of symbolic democracy. They think they have political power or at least a voice, when in fact they have none.[114] Worse, privileged and required labor can easily be offshored or automated, or the skills of this group can become obsolete.

---

109 Ibid.
110 Greenberg, 2016.
111 Schor, 1992.
112 US Census Bureau D.
113 Income data for 2014 (US Department of Labor, 2014); status scores for 2015 (General Social Survey, 2015). I use income data from 2014 to make comparable calculations relative to the gross family income as a modest wage that uses data for 2014.
114 See Bartel, 2005; Gilens and Page, 2014.

Therefore, many will join the ranks of precarious labor when their skills are no longer in demand or when they fall on hard times.

2.5 Precarious Labor

In 1086 England, bordars also known as cottars or cottagers, comprised 32 percent of the population (Table 5.3). They were the poorest of subjugated serfs, generally the younger sons of villeins. Bordars had access to 5 percent of the land, typically small plots for subsistence.[115] They were ceremoniously 'bonded' to a lord in exchange for basic protections and access to land (bonded labor). Typically one became a serf because of debts, making this indentured servitude. During the twelfth century many slaves were given land and became bordars. By the Middle Ages, peasants obtained more freedom but also became more impoverished. This lowered the price of labor, making it cheaper for nobles to pay wages per task instead of extracting traditional labor services. This was the birth of wage-slavery; the only problem is that it happened over six hundred years before the "invention" of capitalism.

Postmodern bordars and cottars are the precarious labor caste, also known as periphery workers, surplus labor, or contingent labor. Their ranks have doubled since feudal times and today comprise 60 percent of the population. They are unemployed, underemployed, or employed in low-end supervisory positions, office work, retail sales, food preparation, and waiting tables. Their annual mean wages are significantly below the average of all occupations.[116] Their employment is precarious. They eat processed foods from convenience stores and fast-food chains, leading to childhood obesity, diabetes, heart attacks, and the like. They purchase home food from low-quality grocers and shop at low-end local or big-box stores. Their children attend decrepit public schools, from which many drop out. Most do not attend college. The few that do mostly enroll in community colleges.

The bottom 60 percent of households hold a measly 3 percent of wealth, with an income share of 25.6 percent (see Tables 5.1 and 5.2). In contrast, bordars, who comprised a smaller percentage of the population, were demonstrably better off, with access to 5 percent of the land. The highest rungs of precarious labor, the third quintile from the bottom, had a wealth share of 2.8 percent, with an average net worth of $68,839. The second quintile's wealth share was 0.5 percent, with an average net worth of $7,263. However, the bottom quintile's

---

115 Domesday Book; National Archives (UK).
116 US Department of Labor, 2014.

wealth share was -0.3 percent, with an average net worth of -$6,029 indicating virtually perpetual indebtedness.[117]

According to the Organisation for Economic Cooperation, secure positions with middle-income wages have been steadily replaced by low-wage jobs over the past thirty years.[118] In 2014 the income limit at the 60th percentile was $68,290.[119] At the lower limit, precarious labor earns between zero (many at the bottom have no income) or at best 0.17 (based on the upper income limit of $12,290 at the 10th decile) times the average modest family wage of $70,657.[120] At the upper income limit of $68,290 at the 60th percentile, precarious labor earns 0.97 times the average modest family wage of $70,657. On average, the mean household income of the third highest quintile was $54,103 (0.77 times the average modest family wage).[121] The mean household income for the second lowest quintile was $31,123 (0.44 times the average modest family wage), and for the lowest quintile it was $11,689 (0.17 times the average modest family wage).[122] This means that roughly 60 percent of households were either near poverty, in poverty, or in structural wage-debt (known in the past as debt slavery, debt bondage, or bonded labor). This is why Leicht and Fitzgerald call them "postindustrial peasants."[123] Everyone's life chances in the poorest 60 percent are fundamentally the same. A survey by the Federal Reserve Board is indicative. Neal Gabler writes:

> The Fed asked respondents how they would pay for a $400 emergency. The answer: *47 percent* of respondents said that either they would cover the expense by borrowing or selling something, or they would not be able to come up with the $400 at all. . . . A 2014 Bankrate survey, echoing the Fed's data, found that only 38 percent of Americans would cover a $1,000 emergency-room visit or $500 car repair with money they'd saved [that means 62 percent do not have $500 for an emergency]. Two reports . . . by the Pew Charitable Trusts found, respectively, that 55 percent of households didn't have enough liquid savings to replace a month's worth of lost income. . . . A similar study conducted by Annamaria Lusardi of George

---

117 See Table 5.1 for wealth shares; average net worth for 2011 from US Census Bureau D.
118 Buchheit, 2013.
119 Income data for 2014, US Census Bureau B; I use income data from 2014 to make comparable calculations relative to the gross family income as a modest wage that uses data for 2014.
120 US Census Bureau B.
121 Ibid.
122 Ibid.
123 Leicht and Fitzgerald, 2006.

Washington University, Peter Tufano of Oxford, and Daniel Schneider, then of Princeton, asked individuals whether they could 'come up with' $2,000 within 30 days for an unanticipated expense. They found that slightly more than one-quarter could not, and another 19 percent could do so only if they pawned possessions or took out payday loans. The conclusion: Nearly half of American adults are 'financially fragile' and 'living very close to the financial edge.' Yet another analysis, this one led by Jacob Hacker of Yale, measured the number of households that had lost a quarter or more of their 'available income' in a given year—income minus medical expenses and interest on debt—and found that in each year from 2001 to 2012, at least one in five had suffered such a loss and couldn't compensate by digging into savings.[124]

The status of precarious labor is consistent with its economic ranking. The status score for registered nurses was 66 (mean income $69,790), while police officers score 60 (mean income of $59,530), waiters score 28 (mean income $21,640), short order cooks score 28 (mean income $21,430), bartenders score 25 (mean income $22,620), and janitors score 16 (mean income $25,460).[125] Extensive studies confirm that socioeconomic inequality, even more than poverty, results in life expectancy for poor people that is nine years shorter than for rich people.[126] Health consequences from the hardships of extreme poverty—such as access to health care and poor diet—account for one-third of the disparity. The rest of the gap is due to the lack of control over one's life, resulting in stress and poor health. This is referred to as the "health gradient," a concept that has become accepted in public health circles outside of the United States.[127]

The precariat's life is a daily struggle with poverty, debt, and intermittent under- and unemployment. The new ranks of the poor are increasingly people who work, often full-time, but are paid poverty-level wages. In 2011, 28 percent of workers earned poverty-level wages.[128] These were people with high school degrees or less, non-marketable college degrees (such as in philosophy or art history), and contingent professionals, such as adjunct professors who rely on food stamps.

---

124 Gabler, 2016.
125 Income data for 2014, US Department of Labor, 2014; status scores for 2015, General Social Survey, 2015. I use income data from 2014 to make comparable calculations relative to the gross family income as a modest wage that uses data for 2014.
126 Marmot, 2005.
127 Ibid.
128 Mishel, et al., 2012.

The national poverty rate was 13.5 percent in 2015.[129] Poverty is experienced disproportionately by lower castes (e.g., for blacks it was 24.1 percent and for Hispanics it was 21.4 percent, compared to 11.6 percent for whites).[130] However, the Census Bureau acknowledges that the realistic poverty measure is twice the official rate, placing the actual national poverty rate at around 27 percent.[131] The official poverty threshold in 2015 for a family of four was $24,257.[132] Based on the twice the official rate suggestion, the poverty line would be $34,999.[133] Household income for 44.8 percent of Americans in 2015 was $49,999 or less, indicating that nearly half of Americans were at or near poverty.[134] This is supported by wage data from the Internal Revenue Service.[135] Major sectors of employment reserved for precarious labor fall below either measure of poverty. This includes 8,648,920 retail sales workers (the largest occupation in thirty-six states) earning an annual mean of $24,020; 12,277,720 in food preparation and serving-related occupations earning an annual mean of $21,980; 21,638,470 in office and administrative support occupations earning $35,530; and 8,934,050 in production occupations earning $35,490.[136]

As for political power, they have none, whereas their feudal counterparts had their third estate.[137]

2.6 Institutional Slaves

Max Weber wrote, "Those men whose fate is not determined by the chance of using goods or services for themselves on the market, e.g. slaves, are not, however, a 'class' in the technical sense of the term. They are, rather, a 'status group.'"[138] At the bottom of England's feudal system were slaves, constituting approximately 10 percent of the population (see Table 5.3).

Postmodern formal and informal slavery is as widespread as slavery in any epoch, and it is practiced in 167 out of 196 countries, affecting 48.8 million people.[139] Sweatshops and forced prostitution are examples of informal slavery through human trafficking and debt bondage. Typically, sweatshop workers

---

129 US Census Bureau B.
130 Ibid.
131 Buchheit, 2013.
132 US Census Bureau B. This poverty threshold yields a 13.5 percent poverty rate.
133 Ibid. The income limit at the 30th percentile that is around twice the poverty rate.
134 Ibid.
135 Buchheit, 2013.
136 US Department of Labor, 2014.
137 See, for example, Gilens and Page. 2014: 564; Hayes, 2012.
138 Quoted in Gerth and Mills, 1946: 183.
139 Global Slavery Index. Here slavery is defined as human trafficking, debt bondage, forced labor, forced or servile marriage, and commercial sexual exploitation.

are undocumented immigrants in debt bondage to repay their traffickers, who treat them as slaves. They work under abysmal conditions and are sometimes forced to live in the factory behind locked doors. This is why many die in factory fires: the doors are chained to prevent them from escaping, as in Hamlet, North Carolina, in 1991. In the case of undocumented immigrants, some have been promised various jobs in their destination country. However, many women are tricked and forced into prostitution or sex slavery. These women are sold from one gang to another, forcing them to repay new debts in a never-ending cycle.

In antiquity, many slaves were conquered enemy citizens who were sold for profit. Formal slavery continues in postmodern times based on conquest through a racialized criminal justice system. The difference between ancient and modern forms of institutional slavery is qualitative, in that there are no more chains or bounty hunters chasing runaways. These have been replaced with propaganda, debt collection agencies, and bail-bond bounty hunters, with prisons functioning as the new plantations. The postmodern institutional slave caste in the United States is roughly 2 to 3 percent of the population, about the same as before the Civil War. The overwhelming majority is derived from the lower rungs of the precariat, living under conditions little different than slaves on plantations. For example, a Justice Department report on events unfolding in Ferguson, Missouri, in 2014 found that the entire police department functioned mostly as plantation overlords:

> Conducting stops without reasonable suspicion and arrests without probable cause in violation of the Fourth Amendment; Interfering with the right to free expression in violation of the First Amendment.... Using unreasonable force in violation of the Fourth Amendment.... Focusing on revenue over public safety, leading to court practices that violate the 14th Amendment's due process and equal protection requirements. Court practices exacerbating the harm of Ferguson's unconstitutional police practices and imposing particular hardship upon Ferguson's most vulnerable residents, especially upon those living in or near poverty. Minor offenses can generate crippling debts, result in jail time because of an inability to pay and result in the loss of a driver's license, employment, or housing.... Ferguson's harmful court and police practices are due, at least in part, to intentional discrimination, as demonstrated by direct evidence of racial bias and stereotyping about African Americans by certain Ferguson police and municipal court officials.[140]

---

140 US Department of Justice, 2015.

Ferguson is not exceptional. Practices there represent the norm in many such communities.

Institutional slaves spend much of their lives under the supervision and control of coercive institutions or various government welfare agencies. There are 2.4 million people in state, federal, military, and US territorial prisons, jails, immigration detention facilities, 'civil commitment centers,' and juvenile correctional facilities.[141] In 2013 there were also 853,200 people on parole and 3,910,600 on probation for a total of 4,763,800.[142] That is approximately 7,163,800 people, 2.3 percent of the population, under some form of institutional supervision.[143]

Coercive institutions disproportionately affect lower castes. In 2008, 1 in 11 blacks (9.2 percent) and 1 in 27 Latinos (3.7 percent) were under correctional control.[144] The rate for whites was significantly lower at 1 in 45 (2.2 percent).[145] Blacks account for 36.5 percent of the imprisoned population, Latinos 22 percent, and whites 33.1 percent.[146] However, blacks make up only 13 percent of the population, Hispanics and Latinos 17 percent, and whites 78 percent. Black men also have a 1 in 3 lifetime likelihood of imprisonment, compared to 1 in 17 for white men.[147]

The incarcerated are also ripped from their children, spouses, parents, friends, and community, little different than during slavery in the 1800s. Many are transferred to prisons far away from their homes for financial gain, as discussed previously.[148] To say the least, they lack prestige. Their children move from one ghetto prison prep school to another as they bounce from one relative, foster home, or institution to another, under the supervision of the state—just like their parents. Prisoners and felons in the United States are stripped of their right to participate in the political process. Their economic participation is often limited to the informal economy (e.g., as drug dealers, prostitutes, and gangbangers). Their primary economic participation is as commodities for the prison industrial complex and welfare agencies. When they are under institutional control they eat industrial food and wear clothing provided by corporate vendors. They are given shopping opportunities for limited and overpriced

---

141 Wagner and Sakala, 2014.
142 US Department of Justice, 2014.
143 Based on the 2013 population of 316,497,531.
144 Moore, 2009.
145 Ibid.
146 Sentencing Project, 2012.
147 Ibid.
148 Case, 2009.

goods at the commissary, circumstances that function as an incentive system for them to accept prison jobs that pay cents per hour.

Postmodern slavery has been institutionalized as a profit-generating industry, making money not only for private prisons but for the many corporations that employ millions of prisoners. This is *insourcing* as opposed to *outsourcing*. However, it is UNICOR, a government agency, that sets condition and wage standards for working prisoners. Corporations pay prisoners an average of 23 cents to $1.15 per hour.[149] In comparison, the minimum wage is $7.25 per hour. Corporations also benefit from tax credits for employing prisoners. Companies using prison labor include Whole Foods, which purchases cheese and fish prepared by prisoners working for third parties at 74 cents per day.[150] Prisoners were thrown into solitary confinement for revealing that Victoria's Secret had hired them to replace "Made in Honduras" tags with "Made in U.S.A." In 1993, AT&T terminated thousands of unionized call center jobs and began using prison labor at $2 per day, which continues despite contravening company policy. BP hired mostly black prisoners to clean up its historic toxic spill in the Gulf Coast instead of hiring displaced local workers. The highest-paying prison job is sewing US flags on police uniforms, an irony that would not be lost on Debord or Baudrillard. Other corporations that have used or are using prison labor include Honda, JCPenney, Macy's, McDonald's, Microsoft, Nike, Nintendo, Pfizer, Saks Fifth Avenue, Starbucks, and Walmart.[151]

Undocumented immigrants are also captured as institutional slaves for private undocumented worker detention centers. In addition to charging taxpayers, these private detention centers profit from forced labor by people with even fewer rights and less recourse than the prison population. Immigrant detainees are given the option to work for $1 per day.[152]

Poor people are victims of institutional slavery too through the guise of welfare regulations.[153] The Personal Responsibility and Work Opportunity Reconciliation Act of 1996, signed by President Clinton, is an example. The act, commonly referred to as a welfare-to-work program, gutted social protections while forcing people out of assistance programs. Those who receive assistance are now required to work for cents per hour as a condition for receiving their benefits. This is no different than Victorian England, where the poor were once forced into poorhouses or workhouses and worked in exchange for room

---

149 Davidson, 2015.
150 Ibid.
151 Ibid.
152 Fault Lines, 2012.
153 See, for example, Abramovitz, 1996; Piven, 1993.

and board, resembling slave arrangements more than anything else. Today's caste-based debt bondage in return for subsistence represents a continuation of feudal social relations. According to the US Department of Health and Human Services, 110,489,000 Americans (35.4 percent of the population) received welfare assistance in 2016.[154] Many were in heavily regulated programs such as housing assistance (Temporary Assistance for Needy Families—TANF). The welfare industry is big business, with annual government expenditures of $131.9 billion. Welfare recipients in 2016 comprised 38.8 percent white, 39.8 percent black, and 15.7 percent Hispanic recipients.[155]

In the UK, the postmodern version of poorhouses evolved into Jobseeker's Allowance. The law forces recipients to work without pay for up to twelve weeks (with many working even longer), otherwise they lose the poverty income of £67 per week.[156] This has provided private welfare-to-work companies an abundance of virtually free labor. They place recipients in businesses, charities, and the public sector.[157] A sinister consequence of workfare laws is that this enormous pool of slave or bonded labor drives down wages and increases unemployment for everyone else, especially unionized workers.[158]

As during Victorian England and the United States over two hundred years ago, poverty continues to be criminalized. Local governments that are increasingly supplementing their budgets with revenues from traffic tickets and court fees provide a major example. These fees are often in the hundreds and sometimes thousands of dollars.[159] Those who cannot afford to pay are sentenced to jail time. Unfortunately, 44 percent of Americans would not be able to pay a $400 ticket.[160] The case of Gregory White in Louisiana is common.[161] He was arrested for stealing $39 worth of food when he was homeless. The court jailed him for 198 days for missing a few instalments in paying $339 in fines and court fees. The cost for jailing him was over $3,500. Jails are serving as modern-day debtors' prisons. However, imprisonment for debt when someone cannot afford to pay court fees or traffic tickets, unlike the well-to-do, violates their right to due process and equal protection under the Fourteenth Amendment.[162] Further, according to the 1993 Supreme Court ruling on *Bearden v. Georgia*, it is

---

154 National Low Income Housing Authority, 2016.
155 Ibid.
156 O'Reilly and Warren, 2011.
157 Ibid.
158 Greenhouse, 1997.
159 American Civil Liberties Union, n.d. B; Gittleson, 2018.
160 Gittleson, 2018.
161 American Civil Liberties Union, 2010.
162 American Civil Liberties Union, n.d. B.

illegal to imprison someone for debt unless it can be proven that they are able to pay but refuse to.[163] It was in 2018, not 1818, that the American Civil Liberties Union was perusing cases of imprisonment for court debts in fifteen states: Arkansas, California, Colorado, Georgia, Louisiana, Maine, Michigan, Mississippi, Nebraska, New Hampshire, Ohio, South Carolina, Tennessee, Texas, and Washington.[164]

3   Legitimizing Twenty-First-Century Serfdom

3.1   *Mr. Baptist Has Been Too Harsh on the Slavers*

The media continue to generate propaganda to normalize postmodern caste systems, even defending them as more humane than imaginary class systems. This includes international publications like the *Economist*.[165] It published a book review of *The Half Has Never Been Told: Slavery and the Making of American Capitalism*, by Edward E. Baptist, claiming "Mr Baptist has not written an objective history of slavery. Almost all the blacks in his book are victims, almost all the whites villains. This is not history; it is advocacy."[166] After a public outcry, the *Economist* issued an apology, clarifying that slavery was "evil" after all. The image industry has also been creating pro-slavery cultural content. Examples include Hollywood films such as *The Butler*, starring Forest Whitaker and Oprah Winfrey, which glorified the "dignity" of servitude, and *Field of Lost Shoes*, starring Jason Isaacs, which glorified South Virginian Military Institute cadets in a supposedly true story. They are presented as moral because they save a black baker from execution (although they don't free him) and then go on to fight the Yankee "aggressors." The latter film is an epic exaltation of the South that whitewashes slavery by pointing out that many whites in the South were "good" to the slaves.

Politicians too are hard at work altering history and therefore memory. They continue to invoke religion to justify slave-based caste systems. Pat Buchanan, for example, once claimed, "America has been the best country on earth for black folks. It was here that 600,000 black people, brought from Africa in slave ships, grew into a community of 40 million, were introduced to Christian salvation, and reached the greatest levels of freedom and prosperity blacks have

---

163   Gittleson, 2018.
164   American Civil Liberties Union, 2010.
165   *Economist*, 2014.
166   Ibid., online.

ever known."[167] Rev. Jesse Lee Peterson concurred, "Thank God for slavery, because if not, the blacks who are here would have been stuck in Africa." Wes Riddle, a GOP congressional candidate in Texas asked, "Are the descendants of slaves really worse off? Would Jesse Jackson be better off living in Uganda?"[168] Republican Jon Hubbard, an Arkansas state legislator, argued in a 2010 book that slavery was a blessing. John Celock writes in the *Huffington Post*, "Hubbard argued that blacks received a better quality of life as slaves in the U.S. than they did in Africa. ... Hubbard's comments ... led to a series of revelations about fellow Arkansas Republicans, including Rep. Loy Mauch (of Bismarck) writing a series of letters to the editor defending slavery and legislative candidate Charlie Fuqua writing in a 2012 book that he wanted to deport all Muslims and establish the death penalty for rebellious children."[169]

Oregon Republican congressional candidate Art Robinson owned a press that published a book arguing that "the negroes on a well-ordered estate, under kind masters, were probably a happier class of people than the laborers upon any estate in Europe."[170]

Michele Bachmann and Rick Santorum, presidential hopefuls in the 2016 race, signed a pledge asserting that slavery was beneficial to black children because a "child born into slavery in 1860 was more likely to be raised by his mother and father in a two-parent household than was an African American baby born after the election of the USA's first African American president."[171] Trent Franks, a congressman representing the Second Congressional District in Arizona, believes that blacks today would prefer slavery: "Far more of the African American community is being devastated by the policies of today than were being devastated by the policies of slavery."[172] Arkansas state legislator Loy Mauch asked in an article published by the *Democrat-Gazette*, "If slavery were so God-awful, why didn't Jesus or Paul condemn it, why was it in the Constitution and why wasn't there a war before 1861?"[173]

Since slavery turned out to be a windfall for blacks, it is natural to deny them undue compensation. David Horowitz, president of the David Horowitz Freedom Center, opposes reparations for slavery, saying, "If slave labor created wealth for Americans, then obviously it has created wealth for black

---

167 Howard, 2012.
168 Ibid.
169 Celock, 2012.
170 Howard, 2012.
171 Ibid.
172 Ibid.
173 Ibid.

Americans as well, including the descendants of slaves."[174] Of course, the statement ignores that almost all of that wealth is owned by a handful of whites—many of whom are descendants of slavers. Thom Tillis, a North Carolina Republican now serving in the US Senate, equated federal and state government welfare programs to slave reparations.[175] Thus one wonders: have the descendants of slaves really benefited from the nation's wealth, welfare programs, or are they double-dipping?

Such sentiments can be found in almost all postmodern societies. For example, Nigel Farage, founder of the UK Independence Party and member of the European Parliament, was interviewed for a documentary. One of his comments was that racial discrimination laws should be abolished because Britain is "color-blind." After public criticism, he denied having made this comment. However, the documentarians stated, "He was asked a direct question on whether there would be a law against discrimination on the grounds of race or color and he replied no."[176]

3.2 Teaching the Right Lessons

The educational indoctrination industry is also hard at work altering history and memory, replacing scientific facts with religious malarkey. Religion teaches faith without facts to legitimize obedience to hierarchical authority. In postmodern times, religious fictions, pseudo-facts, and 'corrected' history are introduced at a young age through the Trojan horse of school curricula and textbooks. In the United States, many textbooks promote the narrative that

> the Founding Fathers looked to Moses when trying to determine how to construct the fledgling American democracy. The McGraw-Hill United States Government textbook argues that the story of Moses and 'biblical idea of covenant' somehow 'influenced the formation of colonial governments and contributed to our constitutional structure.' Perfection Learning's Basic Principles of American Government suggests that Moses somehow gave the Founders the idea that 'A nation needs a written code of behavior.' Pearson Education's Magruder's American Government similarly claims, 'Moses was a lawgiver and a great leader. Like the founders of the United States, he helped establish a legal system to govern his people.' The intention of this Moses obsession is clear: To indoctrinate students into the idea that America is a Judeo-Christian nation based on

---

174   Ibid.
175   Strauss, 2014.
176   BBC, March 12, 2015.

the Bible. The problem is that's simply not true.... The Founders got their idea of a 'social contract' not from the Bible but from 'British political thought,' 'John Locke's thought in particular.'[177]

In Texas, the state's education board is replacing Thomas Jefferson, who favored separation of church and state, with the influence Moses and the "Jewish Ten Commandments" had on the constitution and "political and legal ideas."[178] An advisor to the board suggested that the Declaration of Independence proves that God "is at the heart of law, government and individual rights."

Attacks on science, such as denying or attempting to refute climate change and evolution, are being imbedded in curricula. Texas and Louisiana require that climate change denial be taught as a valid scientific position, while Utah and South Dakota deny climate change altogether.[179] Other states use a "teach the controversy" strategy, requiring that climate change be taught as a matter of debate rather than fact.[180] Many states have used vouchers to fund schools that teach creationism and assert that evolution is a "mistaken belief" and that the Bible "refutes the man-made idea of evolution."[181] Texas passed a law in 2007 intended to get schools to teach the Bible as history and literature. One district lists "biblical events side by side with historical developments from around the globe."[182] Many other schools teach that the Bible "proves" that the earth is only six thousand years old.[183] On the surreal side, according to a textbook used in Louisiana titled *Life Science* and published by Bob Jones University Press, scientists found dinosaur skulls that are dragons: "The large skull chambers could have contained special chemical-producing glands. When the animal forced the chemicals out of its mouth or nose, these substances may have combined and produced fire and smoke."[184]

In addition to attacks on science, there is an orchestrated effort to whitewash history and omit slavery, Indigenous genocide, social justice movements, and uprisings from school curricula and textbooks. Then there are good old-fashioned lists of banned books, lists created by school districts. In Colorado in 2014, for instance, the Jefferson County school board proposed a resolution that the curriculum for AP history "should promote citizenship, patriotism,

---

177 Marcotte, 2014.
178 McGreal, 2010.
179 Marcotte, 2013.
180 Ibid.
181 Ibid.
182 Ibid.
183 Ibid.
184 Ibid.

essentials and benefits of the free enterprise system, respect for authority and respect for individual rights. Materials should not encourage or condone civil disorder, social strife or disregard of the law. Instructional materials should present positive aspects of the United States and its heritage."[185] The proposed curriculum did not discuss D-Day or Founders such as Benjamin Franklin and James Madison. To make matters worse for lower-caste students, the College Board, which administers AP examinations, announced after the resolution that the Advanced Placement designation that carries college credit would not be applied if a school censors critical concepts from AP courses.[186] In response, at least one member of the the Texas State Board of Education wanted curricular changes that she said reflected the state's "statutory obligations to promote patriotism and to promote the free enterprise system. There seems to have been a move away from a patriotic ideology. There seems to be a denial that this was a nation founded under God. We had to go back and make some corrections."[187] The changes also imply that 1950s McCarthyism may have been defensible at the time and that economic prosperity requires "minimal government intrusion and taxation."

In addition to attributing the foundation of the United States to God, US history texts present a simulacrum account of how the nation was settled. The textbooks fail to note everyone who discovered America before Columbus (who never set foot in North America, north of the Caribbean). The story of Pocahontas is disconnected from facts, presented as a union between Native and settler. In reality, Pocahontas married a warrior (with whom she had a child), never loved John Smith, was kidnapped by the English, and was forced into captivity at age fifteen, after which she was shipped to England, where she married John Rolfe. In fact, American slavery predates Africans. Native Americans were among the first slaves (e.g., in Virginia).[188] Thanksgiving is also a simulacrum disconnected from fact. There was one meal shared by Wampanoag Indians and a Pilgrim settlement in 1621 as a symbol of peace. In 1636 Pequot Indians in Plymouth were blamed for a settler's murder, after which soldiers massacred four hundred men, women, and children.[189] Thanksgiving was invented the next day when William Newell, governor of the Massachusetts Bay Colony, proclaimed: "From that day forth, shall be a day of celebration and thanks giving for subduing the Pequots."[190] As for "redskins,"

---

185 Marcotte, 2014.
186 Brundin, 2014.
187 McGreal, 2010.
188 Coleman, 2013.
189 Schilling, 2014.
190 Ibid., online.

a football team's namesake, it refers to bounties for each Indian carcass. After the US Dakota Wars of 1862, the State of Minnesota offered a $200 reward "for every red-skin sent to Purgatory."[191]

US students are not taught that Hitler studied Bosque Redondo, an Indian reservation at Fort Sumner, New Mexico, to design Jewish concentration camps. Students are taught about the horrors perpetrated against the Jews by Nazis but not about the Native American or African holocaust perpetrated by European-Americans. They are told that the US government forced Japanese Americans into internment camps during World War II but that they were treated much better than those in the Nazi concentration camps, who were gassed. There is no discussion of the victims losing their jobs, property, and businesses like Europe's Jews did. Nor is there any mention of many being driven to suicide as a result.

Slavery is forgotten or redefined as something less sinister. In Texas, the curriculum was changed to focus on the "significant contributions" of pro-slavery Confederate leaders during the Civil War.[192] The slave trade was renamed "the Atlantic triangular trade," and Islamic fundamentalism was named as the cause of the Israeli-Palestinian conflict.[193] These changes were made in 2010. By 2015, Texas textbooks, in a section on immigration, referred to Africans transported to the Americas not as slaves but as "workers" for the plantations.[194] The text also referred to European immigrants as "indentured servants." The publisher of this propaganda was the for-profit mega-corporation McGraw-Hill Education. When parents ridiculed McGraw-Hill on social media, the company announced it would change the reference to slaves from "workers" to people who experienced "a forced migration."[195]

Historical memory of resistance is also altered through curricula. In the United States the civil rights movement has been rewritten to reflect the norms and values of elites, not facts. An amendment to Texas curricula describes the civil rights movement as creating "unrealistic expectations of equal outcomes" among minorities.[196] A Louisiana school funded by the state's voucher program uses a history textbook that offers this view of the 1960s: "Many young people turned to drugs and immoral lifestyles and these youths became known as hippies. They went without bathing, wore dirty, ragged, unconventional clothing, and deliberately broke all codes of politeness or manners. Rock music played

---

191   Ibid.
192   McGreal, 2010.
193   Ibid.
194   Fernandez and Hauser, 2015.
195   Ibid.
196   McGreal, 2010.

an important part in the hippie movement and had great influence over the hippies. Many of the rock musicians they followed belonged to Eastern religious cults or practiced Satan worship."[197] This is not a local or state problem but part of a concentrated effort to change the nation's curricula. Texas is one of the largest buyers of textbooks, allowing it to set textbook standards, since publishers produce textbooks tailored for the largest market rather than develop different books for smaller markets. Most states wind up using essentially the same textbooks produced for Texas.[198]

---

197   Marcotte, 2013.
198   McGreal, 2010.

Conclusion: Bakunin's Conundrum

Unions, which long ago became synonymous with the labor movement, accept the system that rapes labor rather than seeking to break from it.[1] In Foucault's terms, they share the same discourse ('imaginary' according to Castoriadis) as the system that birthed them. Instead of opposing the existing socioeconomic order, unions have become disciplining devices of labor in the service of elites (e.g., with no-strike clauses in every contract). Western socialist and communist parties have been co-opted through the political process that delimits the parameters of discourse. At most, in response to mass movements, governmental institutions may provide reformist policies that are illusory and always under attack. Rudolf Rocker, one of the exponents of classical anarchist theory is succinct:

> Political rights do not originate in parliaments, they are . . . forced upon parliaments from without. . . . even their enactment into law has for a long time been no guarantee of their security. Just as the employers always try to nullify every concession they had made to labour as soon as opportunity offered, as soon as any signs of weakness were observable in the workers' organisations, so governments also are always inclined to restrict or to abrogate completely rights and freedoms that have been achieved if they imagine that the people will put up no resistance. . . . Political rights do not exist because they have been legally set down on a piece of paper, but only when they have become the ingrown habit of a people, and when any attempt to impair them will meet with the violent resistance of the populace.[2]

For Baudrillard, the industrial system died some time ago. What remains is a simulacrum of it and an economy that no longer exists. Romanticizing a revolt by a nonexistent industrial proletarian class is utopian. As Baudrillard stated, "The working class is no longer the gold standard of revolts and contradictions. There is no longer a revolutionary subject of reference."[3] It is not so much that Marx has become irrelevant as that we ourselves have. We need to move beyond nineteenth-century thinkers and nihilist twentieth-century philosophers.

---

1   See Aronowitz, 1992; Brecher, 1997; and Mills, 1971 [1948].
2   Rocker, 1938: 111–12.
3   Quoted in Gilman-Opalsky, 2011: 39.

CONCLUSION   185

The postmodern spectacle is a slave system. Therefore, only a slave revolt might liberate the oppressed. Sadly, the slave revolts of ancient Rome taught us that Spartacus will always lose unless the members of the ruling caste are killed, enslaved, or jailed. This would require violence. History demonstrates that violence against elites can be effective in obtaining concrete demands.[4] It was violence through the Civil War that ended formal slavery in the United States—not political debate or peaceful social movements and protests. The civil rights movement was successful because of radical counter-ideology and violence (e.g., the ghetto revolts of the 1960s and 1970s) rather than in spite of them.[5]

Pablo Escobar, one of history's richest drug lords, managed to extract demands bordering on magical realism from the Colombian state oligarchy. Through a campaign of violence that included assassinations of elite judges, security personnel, and politicians, abductions of family members such as the former president's daughter (who was killed), and terrorizing the public with bombings, Escobar managed to negotiate his surrender to the government on the following conditions:

1) that popular extradition laws to the US would not be enacted;
2) that he be sentenced on only one count of smuggling;
3) that he serve his sentence in a prison constructed and staffed by him, including prison guards and inmates, without police or government officials coming closer than a few miles of the prison, including no overflights of the complex.

In exchange, he offered peace, through what became known as the "great lie"—referring to his symbolic (simulacrum) incarceration. One man was able to bring an entire ruling caste to its knees through violence.

People must engage in autonomous extra-institutional action to change social relations. However, revolts need to be more than spontaneous explosions that wither like the Arab Spring. In Castoriadis's terms, new relations require an autonomous imaginary that would have to become institutionalized as continuous praxis. But herein lays the problem. How will a new imaginary emerge and from whom? This is especially pertinent when all media, institutions, and public discourse are dominated by elites. How does a majority or at least

---

4 See, for example, Adamic, 2008 [1931]; Asimakopoulos, 2011; Brecher, 1997; Cobb, 2014; Graham and Gurr, 1969; Wicker, 1968; and Williams, 1962.
5 Asimakopoulos, 2011.

significant minority develop its own imaginary, let alone self-actualize and maintain it as continuous praxis? The problem is compounded if the masses are content in their slumber, as Debord argued. How will they overcome the power of elites and existing institutional arrangements? What is the role of violence in such social movements? Castoriadis acknowledges as much: "How would this tremendous explosion be able to go beyond the stage of a mere explosion without losing its creativity, how would this fantastic deployment of autonomous activity be able to institute lasting collective organizations that express it without drying it up or confiscating it, how would the contents that it was creating in abundance be able to find new forms—above all, *political* ones—that would permit them to rise to the level of full social-historical effectiveness?"[6]

For all these reasons, after the failure of the 1960s revolts, Debord and a number of postmodern thinkers concluded that the Marxist revolution would not come in the foreseeable future. This also meant no new imaginaries to challenge the social order. That constituted a major break with Marx and crisis theory predicting the inevitable end of capitalism. It rendered Marxian top-down revolutionary movements, which are another form of hierarchical organization, moot. Debord's response was counter-propaganda: delegitimizing acts through détournement that would serve to raise class consciousness as a base for future action. Unfortunately, political, economic, educational, and cultural institutions are thoroughly under the control of the postmodern spectacle. Elite-state means of total propaganda can never be matched by citizens. Therefore, détournement is nothing but feel-good street theater by society's marginal groups. The same can be said of other nonviolent tactics, such as Bey's Temporary Autonomous Zones and Occupy Wall Street protests.[7]

When postmodern serfs are happy to consume their "soma" (antidepressants and food stamps) in a comfortable slumber, not even thinking of opposition, what is the possibility of resistance?[8] Targeting corporations through institutional processes to shut them down or reform them is a fool's errand. Worse, the political process is meaningless, a pure simulation under the total control of elites.

Given these conditions, Bakunin may have been right in his conception of secret cells of revolutionaries dedicated to whatever action required. Given

---

6   Castoriadis, 1993: 274.
7   Bey, 2003.
8   Soma was a drug in Huxley's *Brave New World* (2004 [1958]) distributed by the government to the people. It eliminated pain, discomfort, embarrassment, sadness, or anger and induced bliss, arousal, and a feeling of well-being. Ironically, Soma today is the brand name for a muscle relaxer prescribed for back pain.

that a small number of elites are the puppet masters, it is they who should be targeted. There is no need for large social upheavals and protests only to obtain lip service. What if such revolutionary cells engaged in what nineteenth-century anarchists called "propaganda by the deed," including assassinations of elite politicians, judges, prosecutors, business executives, the wealthy and the families of these elites, and destruction of elite personal, corporate, and government property, demonstrated by Escobar's successful strategy? This would demoralize ruling elites. They would label this as terrorism. But resistance by the oppressed in a caste-war declared by elites is not terrorism but self-defense. True terrorism is perpetrated perpetually against the oppressed by hierarchical social orders. This leads us to the question of who these rebels might be and what they might do should they succeed. Would they establish a Maoist dystopia, as history has borne out, or step aside and let direct democracy come to life? Sadly, power corrupts, and rebels are ideologues, not philosopher-kings. Therefore, our options are nihilistic philosophy or pragmatic actions that may lead to utopia—or just as easily dystopia. Perhaps Baudrillard's pessimism was justified after all.

Bibliography

Abramovitz, Mimi. 1996. *Regulating the Lives of Women: Social Welfare Policy from Colonial Times to the Present*. Rev. ed. Boston: South End Press.

Abrams, Lindsay. July 14, 2014. Nestlé is bottling water straight from the heart of California's drought: The company is exporting a seriously limited resource with no oversight. *Salon*. Accessed on October 20, 2017. Retrieved from http://www.salon.com/2014/07/14/nestle_is_bottling_water_straight_from_the_heart_of_californias_drought/.

Adamic, Luis. 2008 [1931]. *Dynamite: The Story of Class Violence in America*. Oakland, CA: AK Press.

Ahmed, Saladdin. 2018. Panopticism and Totalitarian Space. *Theory in Action*, 11(1): 1–16. https://doi.org/10.3798/tia.1937-0237.1801.

Akard, Patrick J. 1992. Corporate Mobilization and Political Power: The Transformation of US Economic Policy in the 1970s. *American Sociological Review* 57, 597–615. https://doi.org/10.2307/2095915.

Alexander, Michelle. 2012. *The New Jim Crow: Mass Incarceration in the Age of Colorblindness Paperback*. New York: New Press.

Allen, Samantha. July 31, 2015. School's out: Death of a diploma mill: University of Phoenix going down in flames? *Daily Beast*. Accessed on November 26, 2017. Retrieved from http://www.thedailybeast.com/articles/2015/07/31/death-of-a-diploma-mill-university-of-phoenix-going-down-in-flames.html.

Allison, Bill, and Sarah Harkins. November 17, 2014. Fixed fortunes: Biggest corporate political interests spend billions, get trillions. Sunlight Foundation. Accessed on July 8, 2017. Retrieved from https://sunlightfoundation.com/2014/11/17/fixed-fortunes-biggest-corporate-political-interests-spend-billions-get-trillions/.

Alvaredo, Facundo, Lucas Chancel, Thomas Piketty, Emmanuel Saez, and Gabriel Zucman. February 2017. Global inequality dynamics: New findings from Wid. World. Working Paper 23119. Cambridge, MA: National Bureau of Economic Research. Accessed on April, 28, 2018. Retrieved from http://piketty.pse.ens.fr/files/ACPSZ2017NBERWP.pdf.

American Civil Liberties Union. October 2010. In for a penny: The rise of America's new debtors' prisons. American Civil Liberties Union. Accessed on May 8, 2018. Retrieved from https://www.aclu.org/files/assets/InForAPenny_web.pdf#page=6.

American Civil Liberties Union. n.d. A. Alternatives to immigration detention: Less costly and more humane than federal lock-up. Accessed on December 21, 2017. Retrieved from https://www.aclu.org/sites/default/files/assets/aclu_atd_fact_sheet_final_v.2.pdf.

American Civil Liberties Union. n.d. B. Ending modern-day debtors' prisons. Accessed on May 8, 2018. Retrieved from https://www.aclu.org/issues/criminal-law-reform/sentencing/ending-modern-day-debtors-prisons.

Aristotle. 1981. *The Politics*. New York: Penguin Classics.

ArkivDigital. Introduction to the Swedish estate inventories. Accessed on May 5, 2018. Retrieved from https://www.arkivdigital.net/swedish-genealogy/swedish-estate-inventories.

Aronowitz, Stanley. 1992. *False Promises: The Shaping of American Working Class Consciousness*. Durham: Duke University Press.

Aronowitz, Stanley, and William Difazio. 1994. *The Jobless Future: Sci-Tech and the Dogma of Work*. Minneapolis: University of Minnesota Press.

Asher, Saira. September 16, 2016. The moment hijabs dazzled the New York Fashion Week catwalk. BBC. Accessed on October 8, 2017. Retrieved from http://www.bbc.com/news/world-asia-37381770.

Asimakopoulos, John. 2009. Globally segmented labor markets. *Critical Sociology*, 35(2), 175–198. http://dx.doi.org/10.1177/0896920508099191.

Asimakopoulos, John. 2011. *Revolt! The Next Great Transformation from Kleptocracy Capitalism to Libertarian Socialism through Counter Ideology, Societal Education, and Direct Action*. Fair Lawn, NJ: Transformative Studies Institute.

Asimakopoulos, John. 2016. *Social Structures of Direct Democracy: On the Political Economy of Equality*. Chicago: Haymarket Books.

Asimakopoulos, John, and Richard Gilman-Opalsky. 2018. *Against Capital in the Twenty-First Century: A Reader of Radical Undercurrents*. Philadelphia: Temple University Press.

Associated Press. April 7, 2012. Five face charges in China over sale of youth's kidney. *New York Times*. Accessed on April 7, 2017. Retrieved from http://www.nytimes.com/2012/04/08/world/asia/5-face-trial-after-chinese-teenager-sells-kidney.html?_r=0.

Associated Press. November 6, 2014. GOP seizes on anger, demographics for success. *DailyMail.com*. Accessed on September 10, 2017. Retrieved from http://www.dailymail.co.uk/wires/ap/article-2823159/GOP-benefits-anger-demographics.html.

Attwood, Lynne. 2010. *Gender and Housing in Soviet Russia: Private Life in a Public Space*. Manchester: Manchester University Press. https://doi.org/10.7228/manchester/9780719081453.001.0001.

Banaji, Jairus. 2011. *Theory as History, Essays on Modes of Production and Exploitation*. Chicago: Haymarket Books.

Barbaro, Michael. November 27, 2009. Bloomberg Spent $102 Million to Win 3rd Term. *New York Times*. Accessed on August 20, 2018. Retrieved from https://www.nytimes.com/2009/11/28/nyregion/28spending.html.

Barstow, David, and Suhasini Raj. August 30, 2015. Caste quotas in India come under attack. *New York Times*. Accessed on April 25, 2018. Retrieved from http://www.nytimes.com/2015/08/31/world/asia/caste-quotas-in-india-come-under-attack.html?partner=rss&emc=rss.

Bartel, Larry. 2005. Economic inequality and political representation. Department of Politics and Woodrow Wilson School of Public and International Affairs, Princeton University. Accessed on September 6, 2013. Retrieved from http://citeseerx.ist.psu.edu/viewdoc/summary?doi=10.1.1.172.7597.

Baudrillard, Jean. 1994. *Simulacra and Simulation*. Ann Arbor: University of Michigan Press.

BBC. November 3, 2014. World America. Broadcast on PBS.

BBC. March 12, 2015. Nigel Farage would axe "much of" race discrimination law. Accessed on April 25, 2018. Retrieved from http://www.bbc.com/news/uk-31846453.

BBC. December 18, 2015. Stormtroopers in the White House for Star Wars screening. Accessed on April 25, 2018. Retrieved from http://www.bbc.com/news/world-us-canada-35141075.

BBC. June 18, 2017. UK wealth gap "widening over past decade" says report. Accessed on April 25, 2018. Retrieved from http://www.bbc.com/news/business-40318284.

BBC. December 10, 2017. In your face: China's all-seeing state. Accessed on April 25, 2018. Retrieved from http://www.bbc.com/news/av/world-asia-china-42248056/in-your-face-china-s-all-seeing-state.

Belluck, Pam. August 2, 2017. In breakthrough, scientists edit a dangerous mutation from genes in human embryos. *New York Times*. Accessed August 20, 2017. Retrieved from https://www.nytimes.com/2017/08/02/science/gene-editing-human-embryos.html.

Bengtsson, Erik, Anna Missiaia, Mats Olsson, and Patrick Svensson. 2017. The wealth of the richest: Inequality and the nobility in Sweden, 1750–1900. Lund Papers in Economic History: General Issues 161). Lund: Department of Economic History, Lund University. Accessed on April 28, 2018. Retrieved from http://portal.research.lu.se/portal/en/publications/the-wealth-of-the-richest(67a26ecb-7c02-4012-86b0-6042567af29b).html.

Bey, Hakim. 2003. *T.A.Z.: The Temporary Autonomous Zone, Ontological Anarchism, Poetic Terrorism*. Brooklyn, NY: Autonomedia.

Bilger, Micaiah. February 17, 2016. Chinese hospital may have killed tens of thousands to sell their organs for profit. *LifeNews.com*. Accessed August 20, 2018. Retrieved from http://www.lifenews.com/2016/02/17/chinese-hospital-may-have-killed-tens-of-thousands-to-to-sell-their-organs-for-profit/.

Bindel, Julie. April 19, 2017. An example of capitalism literally milking the poor. *Truthdig*. Accessed on June 11, 2018. Retrieved from https://www.truthdig.com/articles/an-example-of-capitalism-literally-milking-the-poor/.

Björklund, Anders, Jesper Roine, and Daniel Waldenström. June 2012. Intergenerational top income mobility in Sweden: Capitalist dynasties in the land of equal opportunity? *Journal of Public Economics*, 96, 474–484. Accessed on June 20, 2018. Retrieved from http://www.sciencedirect.com/science/article/pii/S0047272712000163. https://doi.org/10.1016/j.jpubeco.2012.02.003.

Black, Stephanie, producer and director. 2003. *Life and Debt*. New York: New Yorker Video.

Blau, Peter. 1992. *Exchange and Power in Social Life*. New Brunswick, NJ: Transaction Publishers.

Blumenthal, Paul. November 5, 2012. Forbes 400 contribute record amount to presidential campaigns, super PACs. *Huffington Post*. Accessed on June 20, 2018. Retrieved from http://www.huffingtonpost.com/2012/11/05/forbes-400-campaign-contributions_n_2047750.html.

Blumer, Herbert. 1986. *Symbolic Interactionism: Perspective and Method*. Berkeley: University of California Press.

Boring, Nicolas. January 13, 2017. France: Controversial labor law reform adopted. Global Legal Monitor, Library of Congress Law Library. Accessed March 12, 2017. Retrieved from http://www.loc.gov/law/foreign-news/article/france-controversial-labor-law-reform-adopted/.

Borodovsky, Lev. January 9, 2018. Total U.S. student debt approaches $1.5 trillion. *Daily Shot* newsletter. *Wall Street Journal*. Accessed on June 20, 2018. Retrieved from https://blogs.wsj.com/dailyshot/2018/01/09/the-daily-shot-u-s-student-debt-outstanding-approaches-1-5-trillion/.

Boske, Christa, Walter S. Gershon, Lillian Benavente-McEnery, and Jennifer Speights-Binet. 2019. The "Dead Ends": Reconsidering place for school leaders. *Theory in Action*, 12(1): 1–53. https://doi.org/10.3798/tia.1937-0237.1901.

Brandt, Loren, and Barbara Sands. 1992. Land concentration and income distribution in republican China. In Thomas G. Rawski and Lillian M. Li (eds.), *Chinese History in Economic Perspective*. Berkeley: University of California Press. Accessed on April 28, 2018. Retrieved from https://publishing.cdlib.org/ucpressebooks/view?docId=ft6489pon6&chunk.id=d0e23027&toc.depth=1&brand=ucpress.

Brecher, Jeremy. 1997. *Strike!* Cambridge, MA: South End Press.

Brundin, Jenny. October 3, 2014. After protests over history curriculum, school board tries to compromise. National Public Radio, Morning Edition. Accessed on June 20, 2018. Retrieved from http://www.npr.org/2014/10/03/353327302/school-board-wants-civil-disorder-deemphasized-students-walk-out.

Buchheit, Paul. May 30, 2013. Half of Americans below or near poverty line. *Salon.com*. Accessed on June 20, 2018. Retrieved from http://www.salon.com/2013/05/30/half_of_americans_living_below_or_near_poverty_line_partner/.

Burris, Val. 1992. Elite policy-planning networks in the United States. *Research in Politics and Society*, 4, 111–134.

Business Wire. July 27, 2015. Research and markets: Global cosmetics market 2015–2020: Market was $460 billion in 2014 and is estimated to reach $675 billion by 2020. Accessed on September 10, 2017. Retrieved from http://www.businesswire.com/news/home/20150727005524/en/Research-Markets-Global-Cosmetics-Market-2015-2020-Market.

Callinicos, Alex. 1990. *Against Postmodernism: A Marxist Critique*. New York: St. Martin's Press.

Calvert, Clay. 2016. Freedom of speech extended to corporations. In Paul Finkelman, *Encyclopedia of American Civil Liberties*, vol. 1. New York: Routledge.

Carney, Scott. 2013. *The Red Market: On the Trail of the World's Organ Brokers, Bone Thieves, Blood Farmers, and Child Traffickers*. William Morrow.

Case, Patricia. 2009. Using prisons to stimulate demographic change: Understanding one community's concerns. *Theory in Action*, 2(1): 110–121. https://doi.org/10.3798/tia.1937-0237.08031.

Casey, B. J., Leah H. Somerville, Ian H. Gotlib, Ozlem Ayduk, Nicholas T. Franklin, Mary K. Askren, ... Yuichi Shoda. 2011. Behavioral and neural correlates of delay of gratification 40 years later. *Proceedings of the National Academy of Sciences*, 108(36): 14998–15003. https://doi.org/10.1073/pnas.1108561108.

Castoriadis, Cornelius. 1984. Marx today: An interview. *Thesis Eleven*, 8(1), 124–132. https://doi.org/10.1177/072551368400800111.

Castoriadis, Cornelius. 1988. *Political and Social Writings*, vol. 1, *1946–1955*. Minneapolis: University of Minnesota Press.

Castoriadis, Cornelius. 1991. *Philosophy, Politics, Autonomy: Essays in Political Philosophy*. New York: Oxford University Press.

Castoriadis, Cornelius. 1993. *Political and Social Writings*, vol. 3, *1961–1979*. Minneapolis: University of Minnesota Press.

Castoriadis, Cornelius. 1997. *The Imaginary Institution of Society*. Translated by Kathleen Blamey. Cambridge: MIT Press.

Celock, John. October 10, 2012. Jon Hubbard, Arkansas legislator, defends pro-slavery comments. *Huffington Post*. Accessed on September 10, 2017. Retrieved from http://www.huffingtonpost.com/2012/10/10/jon-hubbard-arkansas-slavery_n_1954902.html.

Center for Responsive Politics. Average wealth of members of Congress. Accessed on September 12, 2017. Retrieved from http://www.opensecrets.org/pfds/.

Cesar, Mary-Lynn. February 13, 2016. Of love and money: The rise of the online dating industry. Nasdaq. Accessed on September 12, 2017. Retrieved from http://www.nasdaq.com/article/of-love-and-money-the-rise-of-the-online-dating-industry-cm579616.

Chicago Tribune. December 22, 2017. Judge bars only organizers from Mall of America protest in Minneapolis. Accessed on June 12, 2018. Retrieved from http://www.chicagotribune.com/news/nationworld/ct-mall-of-america-black-lives-matter-protest-20151222-story.html.

Chin, Josh, and Liza Lin. June 26, 2017. China's all-seeing surveillance state is reading its citizens' faces. *Wall Street Journal.* Accessed on June 12, 2018. Retrieved from https://www.wsj.com/articles/the-all-seeing-surveillance-state-feared-in-the-west-is-a-reality-in-china-1498493020.

Cho, David. August 28, 2009. Banks "too big to fail" have grown even bigger. *Washington Post.* Accessed on June 9, 2018. Retrieved from http://www.washingtonpost.com/wp-dyn/content/article/2009/08/27/AR2009082704193.html.

Chomsky, Noam. 1989. *Necessary Illusions: Thought Control in Democratic Societies.* Boston: South End Press.

Chomsky, Noam. 1994. *Manufacturing Consent: Noam Chomsky and the Media.* New York: Black Rose Books.

Chomsky, Noam. 2002. *Media Control: The Spectacular Achievements of Propaganda.* New York: Seven Stories Press.

Chozick, Amy, Nicholas Confessore, and Michael Barbaro. October 7, 2016. Leaked speech excerpts show a Hillary Clinton at ease with Wall Street. *New York Times.* Accessed on June 9, 2018. Retrieved from https://www.nytimes.com/2016/10/08/us/politics/hillary-clinton-speeches-wikileaks.html?mcubz=1.

Clark, Gregory. August 26, 2014. The American Dream is an illusion: Immigration and inequality. *Foreign Affairs.* Accessed on November 4, 2017. Retrieved from http://www.foreignaffairs.com/articles/141932/gregory-clark/the-american-dream-is-an-illusion.

Cobb, Charles E., Jr. 2014. *This Nonviolent Stuff'll Get You Killed: How Guns Made the Civil Rights Movement Possible.* New York: Basic Books.

Cohen, Tamara. November 10, 2010. Look who owns Britain: A third of the country still belongs to the aristocracy. *Daily Mail.* Accessed on November 8, 2017. Retrieved from http://www.dailymail.co.uk/news/article-1328270/A-Britain-STILL-belongs-aristocracy.html.

Coindesk. December 8, 2017. Accessed on November 1, 2017. Retrieved from http://www.coindesk.com/price/.

Coleman, Arica L. 2013. *That the Blood Stay Pure: African Americans, Native Americans, and the Predicament of Race and Identity in Virginia.* Bloomington: Indiana University Press.

Collins, Chuck, and Josh Hoxie. 2015. *Billionaire Bonanza: The Forbes 400 ... and the Rest of Us.* Washington, DC: Institute for Policy Studies.

Collins, Lauren. May 24, 2016. The French counterstrike against work e-mail. *New Yorker.* Accessed on February 2, 2018. Retrieved from http://www.newyorker.com/culture/cultural-comment/the-french-counterstrike-against-work-e-mail.

Collins, Randall. 2004. *Interaction Ritual Chains*. Princeton, NJ: Princeton University Press. https://doi.org/10.1515/9781400851744.
ConceiveAbilities. Surrogacy fees and costs. Accessed on November 8, 2017. Retrieved from https://www.conceiveabilities.com/parents/surrogacy-cost.
Conference Board. April 12, 2016. "International Comparisons of Hourly Compensation Costs in Manufacturing, 2015—China and India." Accessed on May 2, 2018. Retrieved from https://www.conference-board.org/ilcprogram/index.cfm?id=38270.
Cooley, Charles Horton. 1909. *Social Organization: A Study of the Larger Mind*. New York: Charles Scribner's Sons. https://doi.org/10.1037/14788-000.
Coser, Lewis A. 2003. *Masters of Sociological Thought: Ideas in Historical and Social Context*. Long Grove, IL: Waveland Press.
Cowen, Tyler. May 30, 2014. Sweden has lots of wealth inequality. *Marginal Revolution*. Accessed on November 8, 2017. Retrieved from http://marginalrevolution.com/marginalrevolution/2014/05/wealth-inequality-in-sweden.html.
Dabla-Norris, Era, Kalpana Kochhar, Nujin Suphaphiphat, Frantisek Ricka, and Evridiki Tsounta. June 2015. Causes and consequences of income inequality: A global perspective. International Monetary Fund. Accessed January 30, 2017. Retrieved from https://www.imf.org/external/pubs/ft/sdn/2015/sdn1513.pdf.
Dahrendorf, Ralf. 1959. *Class and Class Conflict in Industrial Society*. Stanford: Stanford University Press.
Davidson, Kelley. August 30, 2015. These 7 household names make a killing off of the prison-industrial complex. *U.S. Uncut*. Accessed on November 11, 2017. Retrieved from https://www.schwartzreport.net/7-household-names-make-killing-off-prison-industrial-complex/.
Davis, Gerald F. 2009. *Managed by the Market*. New York: Oxford University Press.
Debord, Guy. 1990. *Comments on the Society of the Spectacle*. Brooklyn, NY: Verso.
Debord, Guy. 2012. *The Society of the Spectacle*. New York: Zone Books.
DeGraw, David. August 11, 2011. Meet the global financial elites controlling $46 trillion in wealth. *The Gathering Spot*. Accessed on November 21, 2017. Retrieved from http://www.gatheringspot.net/news-article/general-discussion/meet-global-financial-elites-controlling-46-trillion-wealth.
Democracy Now. July 8, 2015. Matt Taibbi: Eric Holder back to Wall Street-tied law firm after years of refusing to jail bankers. Accessed on March 27, 2018. Retrieved from http://www.democracynow.org/2015/7/8/eric_holder_returns_to_wall_street.
Domesday Book Online. Accessed on April 28, 2018. Retrieved from http://www.domesdaybook.co.uk/.
Domhoff, G. William. 1975. *The Bohemian Grove and Other Retreats: A Study in Ruling-Class Cohesiveness*. New York: Harper Torchbooks.
Domhoff, G. William. 2010. *Who Rules America? Challenges to Corporate and Class Dominance*. 6th ed. Boston: McGraw Hill.

Downes, Siobhan. October 31, 2014. Hong Kong politician likens protesters to African-American slaves. *Sinosphere* (*New York Times* blog). Accessed on January 4, 2018. Retrieved from http://sinosphere.blogs.nytimes.com/2014/10/31/hong-kong-politician-likens-protesters-to-african-american-slaves/?partner=rss&emc=rss.

Draznin, Haley. January 16, 2014. New York to pay $17.9 million to 2004 Republican Convention protesters. CNN. Accessed on January 3, 2018. Retrieved from http://www.cnn.com/2014/01/15/politics/new-york-republican-convention-settlement.

Durkheim, Émile. 1984 [1893]. *The Division of Labor in Society*. New York: Free Press. https://doi.org/10.1007/978-1-349-17729-5

Dvorsky, George. July 17, 2014. 9 unexpected outcomes of human cloning. *Gizmodo*. Accessed on January 7, 2018. Retrieved from http://io9.gizmodo.com/9-unexpected-outcomes-of-human-cloning-1606556772.

Economist. September 4, 2014. Our withdrawn review "Blood Cotton." Accessed on January 29, 2017. Retrieved from http://www.economist.com/news/books/21615864-how-slaves-built-american-capitalism-blood-cotton.

Evans, Brad, and Henry Giroux. 2015. *Disposable Futures: The Seduction of Violence in the Age of Spectacle*. City Lights Open Media.

Fault Lines. April 10, 2012. Punishment and profits, immigration detention. *Fault Lines*. Al Jazeera America. Accessed on April 1, 2017. Retrieved from https://www.aljazeera.com/programmes/faultlines/2012/04/201241081117980874.html.

Fay, Bill. 2015. Hospice and end-of-life options and costs. Debt.org, Accessed on January 2, 2018. Retrieved from https://www.debt.org/medical/hospice-costs/.

Fentiman, Linda C. 2009. Marketing mothers' milk: The commodification of breastfeeding and the new markets for breast milk and infant formula. *Nevada Law Journal*, 10(29. Accessed on January 2, 2018. Retrieved from http://digitalcommons.pace.edu/lawfaculty/566/.

Ferdman, Roberto A. April 3, 2015. Missouri Republicans are trying to ban food stamp recipients from buying steak and seafood. *Wonkblog* (*Washington Post* blog). Accessed on July 2, 2017. Retrieved from https://www.washingtonpost.com/news/wonk/wp/2015/04/03/missouri-republicans-are-trying-to-ban-food-stamp-recipients-from-buying-steak-and-seafood/.

Ferguson, Charles, director. 2011. *Inside Job*. Culver City, CA: Columbia TriStar Home Entertainment.

Fernandez, Manny, and Christine Hauser. October 5, 2015. Texas mother teaches textbook company a lesson on accuracy. Accessed on July 12, 2017. Retrieved from https://www.nytimes.com/2015/10/06/us/publisher-promises-revisions-after-textbook-refers-to-african-slaves-as-workers.html?_r=0.

Ferro, Shane. March 1, 2016. Here's how much Silicon Valley tech workers make: Even the average employee at a big tech company is pulling down six figures. *Huffington Post*. Accessed on July 8, 2017. Retrieved from http://www.huffingtonpost.com/entry/silicon-valley-salaries_us_56d61ee6e4b0bf0dab33ce96.

Financial Security and Mobility Project. Pew Foundation. Accessed on July 28, 2017. Retrieved from http://www.pewtrusts.org/en/projects/financial-security-and-mobility.

Finger, Lutz. February 17, 2015. Do evil: The business of social media bots. *Forbes*. Accessed on June 1, 2017. Retrieved from http://www.forbes.com/sites/lutzfinger/2015/02/17/do-evil-the-business-of-social-media-bots/#3b454f111104.

Foer, Franklin. 2017. *World without Mind: The Existential Threat of Big Tech*. New York: Penguin Press.

Food and Water Watch. August 31, 2015. Water privatization: Facts and figures: Privatizing local water and sewer systems usually does far more harm than good for our communities. Accessed on April 2, 2018. Retrieved from http://www.foodandwaterwatch.org/insight/water-privatization-facts-and-figures.

Forsythe, Michael. November 5, 2017. Paradise Papers shine light on where the elite hide their money. *New York Times*. Accessed on July 5, 2017. Retrieved from https://www.nytimes.com/2017/11/05/world/paradise-papers.html.

Foucault, Michel. 1977. *Discipline and Punish: The Birth of the Prison*. New York: Random House Vintage Books.

Foucault, Michel. 1980. *Power/Knowledge: Selected Interviews and Other Writings 1972–1977*. New York: Random House Vintage Books.

Frank, André Gunder. 2006. "Meet Uncle Sam–without Clothes–parading around China and the World." *Critical Sociology*, 32(1), 17–44. https://doi.org/10.1163/156916306776150340.

Freeland, Chrystia. 2013. *Plutocrats: The Rise of the New Global Super-Rich and the Fall of Everyone Else*. New York: Penguin Books.

Friedman, Matt. October 6, 2010. President Obama arrives in Cresskill for fundraising dinner. NJ.com. Accessed on May 2, 2017. Retrieved from http://www.nj.com/news/index.ssf/2010/10/president_obama_arrives_in_cre.html.

Friedman, Howard Steven. 2012. *The Measure of a Nation: How to Regain America's Competitive Edge and Boost Our Global Standing*. Amherst, NY: Prometheus Books.

Frontline. 2004. "Is Wal-Mart good for America? *Frontline*. PBS.

Fukuyama, Francis. Summer 1989. The end of history? *National Interest*, no. 16, 3–18.

Gabler, Neal. May 2016. The secret shame of middle-class Americans: Nearly half of Americans would have trouble finding $400 to pay for an emergency. *Atlantic*. Accessed on May 3, 2017. Retrieved from http://www.theatlantic.com/magazine/archive/2016/05/my-secret-shame/476415/.

Gerth, Hans, and C. Wright Mills. 1946. *From Max Weber: Essays in Sociology*. New York: Oxford University Press.

Getlen, Larry. February 23, 2014. Corrupt "Kids for Cash" judge ruined more than 2,000 lives. *New York Post*. Accessed on March 5, 2017. Retrieved from http://nypost.com/2014/02/23/film-details-teens-struggles-in-state-detention-in-payoff-scandal/.

Gilens, Martin, and Benjamin I. Page. September 2014. Testing theories of American politics: Elites, interest groups, and average citizens. *Perspectives on Politics*, 12(3): 564–581. https://doi.org/10.1017/S1537592714001595.

Gilman-Opalsky, Richard. 2011. *Spectacular Capitalism: Guy Debord and the Practice of Radical Philosophy*. Brooklyn, NY: Minor Compositions.

Gilmore, Ruth Wilson. 2007. *Golden Gulag: Prisons, Surplus, Crisis and Opposition in Globalizing California*. Berkeley: University of California Press.

Gilson, Dave. April 18, 2011. Only little people pay taxes. *Mother Jones*. Accessed on March 2, 2018. Retrieved from http://www.motherjones.com/politics/2011/04/taxes-richest-americans-charts-graph.

Giroux, Henry A. 2014. *The Violence of Organized Forgetting: Thinking beyond America's Disimagination Machines*. San Francisco: City Lights.

Giroux, Henry. 2017. Poisoned city in the age of casino capitalism. *Theory in Action*, 10(1): 7–31.

Gittleson, Kim. April 30, 2018. Why does the US still have "debtors" prisons'? BBC. Accessed on May 8, 2018. Retrieved from http://www.bbc.com/news/av/world-us-canada-43916040/why-does-the-us-still-have-debtors-prisons.

Glassdoor. March 14, 2018. Senior counsel salaries in New York City, NY Area. Glassdoor. Accessed on July 9, 2018. Retrieved from https://www.glassdoor.com/Salaries/new-york-city-senior-counsel-salary-SRCH_IL.0,13_IM615_KO14,28.htm.

Glenza, Jessica. January 16, 2018. Why does it cost $32,093 just to give birth in America? Accessed May 28, 2018. Retrieved from https://www.theguardian.com/us-news/2018/jan/16/why-does-it-cost-32093-just-to-give-birth-in-america.

Global Slavery Index. What is the estimated prevalence of modern slavery country by country, and what is the absolute number by population? Global Slavery Index 2016. Accessed on June 28, 2018. Retrieved from http://www.globalslaveryindex.org/findings/.

Global Wealth Report 2014. 2014. Credit Suisse Research Institute. Accessed on September 9, 2017. Retrieved from https://publications.credit-suisse.com/tasks/render/file/?fileID=60931FDE-A2D2-F568-B041B58C5EA591A4.

Global Wealth Databook 2016. 2016. Credit Suisse Research Institute. Accessed on September 9, 2017. Retrieved from https://www.credit-suisse.com/media/assets/corporate/docs/about-us/research/publications/global-wealth-databook-2016.pdf.

Goffman, Erving. 1959. *The Presentation of Self in Everyday Life*. New York: Anchor Books.

Goffman, Erving. 1961. *Asylums: Essays on the Social Situation of Mental Patients and Other Inmates*. New York: Doubleday Anchor.

Gold, Howard R. n.d. Never mind the 1 percent. Let's talk about the 0.01 percent. Chicago Booth Review. Accessed September 8, 2018. Retrieved from http://review.chicagobooth.edu/economics/2017/article/never-mind-1-percent-lets-talk-about-001-percent.

Golden, Daniel. 2006. *The Price of Admission: How America's Ruling Class Buys Its Way into Elite Colleges—and Who Gets Left Outside the Gates.* New York: Crown Publishers.

Golden, Daniel. November 18, 2016. How did "less than stellar" high school student Jared Kushner get into Harvard? Accessed on March 5, 2017. *Guardian.* Retrieved from https://www.theguardian.com/commentisfree/2016/nov/18/jared-kushner-harvard-donald-trump-son-in-law.

Goldenberg, Suzanne. December 8, 2015. Greenpeace exposes sceptics hired to cast doubt on climate science. *Guardian.* Accessed on April 2, 2018. Retrieved from http://www.theguardian.com/environment/2015/dec/08/greenpeace-exposes-sceptics-cast-doubt-climate-science.

Gold Price. December 8, 2017. Accessed on March 10, 2018. Retrieved from http://goldprice.org/.

Gordon, M. David, Richard Edwards, and Michael Reich. 1982. *Segmented Work, Divided Workers: The Historical Transformation of Labor in the United States.* Cambridge University Press: Cambridge.

Gould, Elise, Tanyell Cooke, and Will Kimball. August 26, 2015. *What Families Need to Get By: EPI's 2015 Family Budget Calculator.* Issue Brief 403. Washington, DC: Economic Policy Institute. Accessed on April 28, 2018. Retrieved from http://www.epi.org/publication/what-families-need-to-get-by-epis-2015-family-budget-calculator/.

Graceland.com. 2017. Accessed on March 11, 2018. Retrieved from https://www.graceland.com/about-graceland.

Graeber, David. 2011. *Debt: The First 5,000 Years.* Brooklyn, NY: Melville House.

Graeber, David. March 18, 2014. The truth is out: money is just an IOU, and the banks are rolling in it. *Guardian.* Accessed on August 23, 2017. Retrieved from http://www.theguardian.com/commentisfree/2014/mar/18/truth-money-iou-bank-of-england-austerity.

Graham, Hugh Davis, and Ted Robert Gurr. 1969. *The History of Violence in America.* New York: Bantam Books.

Gramsci, Antonio. 1971. *Selections from the Prison Notebooks of Antonio Gramsci.* Edited and translated by Quintin Hoare and G. N. Smith. New York: International Publishers.

Gramsci, Antonio. 2000. *The Gramsci Reader: Selected Writings, 1916–1935.* Edited by David Forgacs. New York: New York University Press, 2000.

Green, Guerin Lee. March 17, 2014. Stunning revelation: Bill Gates has spent $2.3 billion on Common Core—#PARCC. *North Denver News.* Accessed on August 22, 2018. Retrieved from http://northdenvernews.com/stunning-revelation-bill-gates-has-spent-2-3-billion-on-common-core/.

Greenberg, Scott. April 6, 2016. Tax Freedom Day 2016 is April 24. Tax Foundation. Accessed on October 22, 2017. Retrieved from https://taxfoundation.org/tax-freedom-day-2016-april-24/.

Greenhouse, Steven. July 7, 1997. Wages of Workfare. *New York Times*. Accessed on September 23, 2017. Retrieved from http://www.nytimes.com/1997/07/07/nyregion/wages-of-workfare.html.

Greenwald, Glenn. 2014. *No Place to Hide: Edward Snowden, the NSA, and the U.S. Surveillance State*. London: Penguin Books.

Greenwald, Robert, producer and director. 2004. *Outfoxed: Rupert Murdoch's War on Journalism*. New York: Disinformation.

Greenwald, Robert, producer and director. 2005. *Wal-Mart: The High Cost of Low Price*. New York: Retail Project.

Greenwald, Robert, producer/director. 2012. *Koch Brothers Exposed*. New York: Disinformation.

Guilbeault, Douglas, and Samuel Woolley. November 1, 2016. How Twitter bots are shaping the election. *Atlantic*. Accessed on August 25, 2017. Retrieved from http://www.theatlantic.com/technology/archive/2016/11/election-bots/506072/.

Happiness Research Institute. 2015. *The Facebook Experiment: Does Social Media Affect the Quality of Our Lives?* Copenhagen: Happiness Research Institute.

Harrell, Antoinette. February 28, 2018. Blacks were enslaved well into the 1960s. *Vice*. Accessed on May 8, 2018. Retrieved from https://www.vice.com/en_us/article/437573/blacks-were-enslaved-well-into-the-1960s.

Harrison, Peter. 2017. *The Freedom of Things: An Ethnology of Control*. Fair Lawn, NJ: Transformative Studies Institute.

Harvey, David. 2005. *A Brief History of Neoliberalism*. New York: Oxford University Press.

Hayes, Thomas. 2012. Responsiveness in an era of inequality: The case of the U.S. Senate. *Political Research Quarterly*, October 11.

Heartfield, James. 2012. *British Workers and the US Civil War: How Karl Marx and the Lancashire Weavers Joined Abraham Lincoln's Fight against Slavery*. London: Reverspective.

Hess, Amanda. November 13, 2014. The golden egg: Couples want their egg donors to be smart, athletic, and good-looking. *Slate*. Accessed on December 20, 2017. Retrieved from http://www.slate.com/articles/technology/future_tense/2014/11/egg_donation_study_couples_want_donors_to_be_smart_athletic_good_looking.html.

Hilton, R.H. 1975. *The English Peasantry in the Late Middle Ages*. New York: Oxford University Press.

History Channel. October 2012. What's the earth worth? A&E Networks.

Hoback, Cullen. 2013. *Terms and Conditions May Apply*. Hyrax Films.

Holly, Robert. May 12, 2015. Agribusiness companies capitalize on tax breaks, grants, subsidies and loans. Midwest Center for Investigative Reporting. Accessed on July 19, 2017. Retrieved from http://investigatemidwest.org/2015/05/12/agribusiness-companies-capitalize-on-tax-breaks-grants-subsidies-and-loans/.

Homans, George Caspar. 1974. *Social Behavior: Its Elementary Forms*. Harcourt Brace.

Howard, Mark. October 12, 2012. Ten conservatives who have praised slavery. *Salon*. Accessed on December 20, 2017. Retrieved from http://www.salon.com/2012/10/12/ten_conservatives_who_have_praised_slavery.

Huxley, Aldous. 2004 [1958]. *Brave New World and Brave New World Revisited*. New York: HarperCollins.

IndexMundi. Accessed on April 28, 2018. Retrieved from https://www.indexmundi.com/facts/russia/income-distribution and https://www.indexmundi.com/facts/china/income-distribution.

Inman, Phillip, and Helena Smith. March 4, 2010. Greece should sell islands to keep bankruptcy at bay, say German MPs. *Guardian*. Accessed on July 19, 2017. Retrieved from http://www.theguardian.com/business/2010/mar/04/greece-sell-islands-german-mps.

International Monetary Fund. IMF members' quotas and voting power, and IMF board of governors. Accessed August 25, 2017. Retrieved from http://www.imf.org/external/np/sec/memdir/members.aspx.

Isaacnov, Mike. November 22, 2016. Facebook said to create censorship tool to get back into China. *New York Times*. Accessed on December 20, 2017. Retrieved from http://www.nytimes.com/2016/11/22/technology/facebook-censorship-tool-china.html?partner=rss&emc=rss&_r=0.

ISDA Market Survey. 2010. Notional amounts outstanding at year-end, semiannual data, all surveyed contracts, 1987–present. International Swaps and Derivatives Association (ISDA). Accessed on December 20, 2017. Retrieved from https://www.isda.org/a/6tiDE/isda-market-survey-results1987-june-2010.pdf.

It's Conceivable. June 2, 2011. Sperm bank fees. Accessed on February 5, 2018. Retrieved from http://itsconceivablenow.com/2011/06/02/sperm-bank-fees/.

Jacobs, Ken. April 15, 2015. Americans are spending $153 billion a year to subsidize McDonald's and Wal-Mart's low wage workers. *Washington Post*. Accessed on October 5, 2017. Retrieved from https://www.washingtonpost.com/posteverything/wp/2015/04/15/we-are-spending-153-billion-a-year-to-subsidize-mcdonalds-and-walmarts-low-wage-workers/.

Jilani, Zaid. March 5, 2015. Now they're saying it in public: Professor at Koch-funded university department calls for "Less Democracy". *AlterNet*. Accessed on November 20, 2017. Retrieved from http://www.alternet.org/education/now-theyre-saying-it-public-professor-koch-funded-university-department-calls-less.

Johnston, Chris. January 22, 2018. Amazon opens a supermarket with no checkouts. BBC. Accessed August 6, 2018. Retrieved from https://www.bbc.com/news/business-42769096.

Jones, Stacy, and Jaclyn Trop. July 30, 2015. See how the big tech companies compare on employee diversity. *New York Times*. Accessed on November 2, 2017. Retrieved from http://fortune.com/2015/07/30/tech-companies-diveristy/.

Justia. A. *Pembina Consolidated Silver Mining Co. v. Pennsylvania*, 125 U.S. 181 (1888). Accessed on November 18, 2017. Retrieved from https://supreme.justia.com/cases/federal/us/125/181/case.html.

Justia. B. *Diamond v. Chakrabarty*, 447 U.S. 303 (1980). Accessed on November 18, 2017. Retrieved from https://supreme.justia.com/cases/federal/us/447/303/case.html.

Kantor, Jodi. July 31, 2007. Primed for a second stint as First Daughter. *New York Times*. Accessed on November 22, 2017. Retrieved from http://www.nytimes.com/2007/07/31/us/politics/31chelsea.html?_r=0).

Kantor, Jodi, and David Streitfeldaug. August 15, 2015. Inside Amazon: Wrestling big ideas in a bruising workplace. *New York Times*. Accessed on November 30, 2017. Retrieved from http://www.nytimes.com/2015/08/16/technology/inside-amazon-wrestling-big-ideas-in-a-bruising-workplace.html?_r=1.

Kapur, Ajay, Niall Macleod, and Narendra Singh. March 5, 2006. Revisiting plutonomy: The rich getting richer. Citigroup. Accessed on September 5, 2018. Retrieved from https://delong.typepad.com/plutonomy-2.pdf.

Kiel, Paul, and Chris Arnold. September 15, 2014. Unseen toll: Wages of millions seized to pay past debts. ProPublica. Accessed on July 23, 2017. Retrieved from http://www.propublica.org/article/unseen-toll-wages-of-millions-seized-to-pay-past-debts.

Kimball, Alan. 2015. Russian peasants and village lands, 1861–1917. Kimball Files, University of Oregon. Accessed on April 28, 2018. Retrieved from http://pages.uoregon.edu/kimball/1861-1917.krx.lnd.htm#1870s For Land distribution.

Kirp, David L. September 4, 2013. The wrong kind of education reform: Three new books decimate the case for charter schools and vouchers. *Slate*. Accessed on June 21, 2018. Retrieved from http://www.slate.com/articles/news_and_politics/science/2013/09/charters_schools_and_vouchers_decimating_the_case_for_privatizing_public.html.

Kollmuss, Anja, Lambert Schneider, and Vladyslav Zhezherin. 2015. Has joint implementation reduced GHG emissions? Lessons learned for the design of carbon market mechanisms. Stockholm Environment Institute, Working Paper 2015–07. Accessed on February 8, 2017. Retrieved from https://www.sei.org/publications/has-joint-implementation-reduced-ghg-emissions-lessons-learned-for-the-design-of-carbon-market-mechanisms-brief/.

Kozol, Jonathan. 1991. *Savage Inequalities: Children in America's Schools*. New York: Broadway Books.

Kozol, Jonathan. 2005. *The Shame of the Nation: The Restoration of Apartheid Schooling in America*. New York: Three Rivers Press.

Krugman, Paul. February 23, 2015. Knowledge isn't power. *New York Times*. Accessed on February 21, 2018. Retrieved from http://www.nytimes.com/2015/02/23/opinion/paul-krugman-knowledge-isnt-power.html?ref=todayspaper&_r=1.

Labrecque, Jackie, and KATU News. Woman producing more than a gallon of breast milk a day helping hundreds of new moms. Newschannel 9/abc. July 19, 2017. Accessed on June 11, 2018. Retrieved from http://newschannel9.com/news/offbeat/woman-producing-more-than-a-gallon-of-breast-milk-a-day-helping-new-moms.

Laville, Sandra. July 18, 2012. Royal wedding protesters lose high court case. *Guardian*. Accessed on March 11, 2017. Retrieved from http://www.theguardian.com/uk/2012/jul/18/royal-wedding-protesters-lose-case.

Leicht, Kevin, and Scott Fitzgerald. 2006. *Postindustrial Peasants: The Illusion of Middle-Class Prosperity*. New York: Worth Publishers.

Leigh, David, and Richard Norton-Taylor. January 9, 2006. MPs leaked Bush plan to hit al-Jazeera. *Guardian*. Accessed on October 14, 2017. Retrieved from http://www.theguardian.com/media/2006/jan/09/Iraqandthemedia.politicsandiraq.

Leithner, Chris. April 22, 2010. H. L. Mencken on governments and politicians. *American Mercury*. Accessed on September 23, 2017. Retrieved from http://theamericanmercury.org/2010/04/h-l-mencken-on-governments-and-politicians/.

León, Clarissa A. July 21, 2014. These top 10 food companies control nearly everything we eat. *AlterNet*. Accessed on September 23, 2017. Retrieved from http://www.alternet.org/food/food-brands-climate-change.

Lerer, Lisa, and Jill Colvin. November 5, 2016. Trump says he's fine by himself; Clinton hangs with Beyoncé. Associated Press. Accessed on May 30, 2017. Retrieved from https://www.norwichbulletin.com/news/20161105/trump-says-hes-fine-by-himself-clinton-hangs-with-beyoncxe9.

Lexology. June 24 2016 Privatizations in Greece: Approval of HRADF Asset Development Plan and establishment of a "Hyper-Fund." Accessed on September 26, 2017. *Lexology*. Retrieved from http://www.lexology.com/library/detail.aspx?g=7eb4b1b3-9a2a-41cd-97b0-cf05fbfce564.

Li, Roland. Jun 6, 2017. San Francisco's home price hits new record: $1.5 million. *San Francisco Business Times*. Accessed on August 27, 2017. Retrieved from https://www.bizjournals.com/sanfrancisco/news/2017/06/06/san-francisco-record-home-condo-prices-sf-buying.html.

Lindert, Peter H., and Jeffrey G. Williamson. 2012. *American Incomes 1774–1860*. Cambridge, MA: National Bureau of Economic Research. Accessed on April 28, 2018. Retrieved from http://www.nber.org/papers/w18396.pdf.

Los Angeles Times. June 4, 2017. At $75,560, housing a prisoner in California now costs more than a year at Harvard. Accessed on May 28, 2018. Retrieved from http://www.latimes.com/local/lanow/la-me-prison-costs-20170604-htmlstory.html.

Luhby, Tami. December 31, 2015. Here's how much the richest Americans make. CNNMoney. Accessed on April 28, 2018. Retrieved from http://money.cnn.com/2015/12/31/news/economy/richest-americans/index.html.

Luscombe, Belinda. May 20, 2014. Inside the scarily lucrative business model of human trafficking. *Time.* Accessed on September 18, 2017. Retrieved from http://time.com/105360/inside-the-scarily-lucrative-business-model-of-human-trafficking/.

Luttrell, Gina. June 18, 2014. Top 10 anti-homeless measures used in the United States. *Blaze.* Accessed on April 28, 2018. Retrieved from http://www.theblaze.com/contributions/top-10-anti-homeless-measures-used-in-the-united-states/.

Lutz, Ashley. June 14, 2012. These 6 Corporations control 90 percent of the media in America. Businessinsider.com. Accessed on August 23, 2017. Retrieved from http://www.businessinsider.com/these-6-corporations-control-90-of-the-media-in-america-2012-6.

Maguire, Kevin, and Andy Lines. November 22, 2005. Bush plot to bomb his Arab ally: Madness of war memo. *Daily Mirror.* Accessed April 25, 2017. Retrieved from https://web.archive.org/web/20051128012515/http://www.mirror.co.uk/news/tm_objectid%3D16397937%26method%3Dfull%26siteid%3D94762%26headline%3Dexclusive--bush-plot-to-bomb-his-arab-ally-name_page.html.

Maheshwari, Sapna, and Alexandra Stevenson. September 15, 2017. Google and Facebook face criticism for ads targeting racist sentiments. *New York Times.* Accessed on May 4, 2018. Retrieved from https://www.nytimes.com/2017/09/15/business/facebook-advertising-anti-semitism.html?partner=rss&emc=rss.

Marcotte, Amanda. March 13, 2013. 11 heinous lies conservatives are teaching America's schoolchildren: The Right has a new plan to capture the country's youth vote: Take over public school curriculums. *Salon.* Accessed on April 12, 2018. Retrieved from http://www.salon.com/2013/03/13/11_heinous_lies_conservatives_are_teaching_americas_school_children_partner/.

Marcotte, Amanda. September 25, 2014. Conservative school board revolution: Column: Rewriting history presents a threat to the future of American public education. *USA Today.* Accessed on December 23, 2017. Retrieved from https://www.usatoday.com/story/opinion/2014/09/25/school-board-curriculum-conservative-history-column/16159795/.

Marlowe, Lara. July 13, 2013. French nobles give Bastille Day right royal "non": France's 6,000 aristocrats struggle to slow the erosion of their traditions. *Irish Times.* Accessed on May 4, 2018. Retrieved from http://www.irishtimes.com/news/world/europe/french-nobles-give-bastille-day-right-royal-non-1.1462071.

Marmot, Michael. 2005. *The Status Syndrome: How Social Standing Affects Our Health and Longevity.* New York: Holt Paperbacks.

Marx, Karl. 1973 [1848]. *The Communist Manifesto.* New York: International Publishers.

Marx, Karl. 1994 [1852]). *The Eighteenth Brumaire of Louis Bonaparte.* New York: International Publishers.

Marx, Karl. 1970 [1859]. *A Contribution to the Critique of Political Economy.* Moscow: Progress Publishers.

Marx, Karl. 1977 [1867]. *Capital*, vol. 1. New York: Vintage Books.
Marx, Karl. 1978 [1845–1846]. *The German Ideology*. Edited by R. C. Tucker. In *The Marx-Engels Reader*. Norton: New York.
Marx, Karl. 1981[1895]. *Capital*, vol. 3. New York: Vintage Books.
Massey, Douglas S., Jonathan Rothwell, and Thurston Domina. 2009. The changing bases of segregation in the United States. *ANNALS of the American Academy of Political and Social Science*, 626, 74–90. https://doi.org/10.1177/0002716209343558.
McCauley, Lauren. March 28, 2015. Students and parents rally against Cuomo's billionaire-backed education scheme. *Common Dreams*. Accessed on October 13, 2017. Retrieved from http://www.commondreams.org/news/2015/03/28/thousands-rally-against-cuomos-billionaire-backed-education-scheme.
McDonald, Lawrence G., and Patrick Robinson. 2009. *A Colossal Failure of Common Sense: The Inside Story of the Collapse of Lehman Brothers*. New York: Crown Business.
McGreal, Chris. May 16, 2010. Texas schools board rewrites US history with lessons promoting God and guns: US Christian conservatives drop references to slave trade and sideline Thomas Jefferson who backed church-state separation. *Guardian*. Accessed on March 15, 2017. Retrieved from https://www.theguardian.com/world/2010/may/16/texas-schools-rewrites-us-history.
McLaren, Peter. August 16, 2015. Chapman democracy activist offers a radical critique of capitalism (interview with Jonathan Winslow). *Orange Register*. Accessed on July 20, 2017. Retrieved from http://www.ocregister.com/articles/critical-677896-peda gogy-mclaren.html.
McMichael, Philip. 2008. *Development and Social Change*. Thousand Oaks, CA: Pine Forge Press.
McMillan, Tracie. March 3, 2016. The SNAP gap: Benefits aren't enough to keep many recipients fed. National Public Radio. Accessed August 28, 2017. Retrieved from http://www.npr.org/sections/thesalt/2016/03/03/468955099/the-snap-gap-benefits-arent-enough-to-keep-many-recipients-fed.
Memos, Christos. 2014. *Castoriadis and Critical Theory: Crisis, Critique and Radical Alternatives*. New York: Palgrave Macmillan. https://doi.org/10.1057/9781137034465.
Merton, Robert K. 1968. *Social Theory and Social Structure*. New York: Free Press.
Michaels, Matthew. March 21, 2018. Jeff Bezos made an average of $107 million per day last year. Business Insider. Accessed September 9, 2018. Retrieved from https://www.busi nessinsider.com/how-much-jeff-bezos-richest-billionaires-make-every-day-2018-3.
Milanovic, Branko, Peter H. Lindert, and Jeffrey G. Williamson. October 2007. Measuring ancient Inequality. NBER Working Paper 13550. National Bureau of Economic Research. Accessed on April 28, 2018. Retrieved from http://www.nber.org/papers/w13550.
Mills, C. Wright. 1971 [1948]. *The New Men of Power: America's labor Leaders*. New York: Augustus M. Kelley.

Mills, C. Wright. 2000a [1956]. *The Power Elite*. New York: Oxford University Press.

Mills, C. Wright. 2000b. *The Sociological Imagination*. New York: Oxford University Press.

Mishel, Lawrence, Josh Bivens, Elise Gould, and Heidi Shierholz. 2012. *The State of Working America*. 12th ed. Economic Policy Institute. Ithaca, NY: Cornell University Press.

Moore, Michael. January 30, 2016. 10 things they won't tell you about the Flint water tragedy. But I will. *Reader Supported News*. Accessed on May 5, 2018. Retrieved from http://readersupportednews.org/opinion2/277-75/34902-10-things-they-wont-tell-you-about-the-flint-water-tragedy-but-i-will.

Moore, Solomon. March 2, 2009. Prison spending outpaces all but Medicaid. *New York Times*. Accessed on June 2, 2017. Retrieved from http://www.nytimes.com/2009/03/03/us/03prison.html?_r=0.

Morris, Chris. January 20, 2015. Things are looking up in America's porn industry. CNBC. Accessed on August 2, 2017. Retrieved from http://www.nbcnews.com/business/business-news/things-are-looking-americas-porn-industry-n289431.

Morrisson, Christian, and Wayne Snyder. 2000. The income inequality of France in historical perspective. *European Review of Economic History*, 4, 59–83. https://doi.org/10.1017/S1361491600000149.

Moulier-Boutang, Yann. 1997. *De l'esclavage au salariat: Economie historique du salariat bride*. Paris: Presses Universitaires de France.

Moyers & Company. October 17, 2014. Keeping faith in democracy. PBS.

Müller, Andreas, and Marcel Grandi. April 2000. Weather derivatives: A risk management tool for weather-sensitive industries. *Geneva Papers on Risk and Insurance*, 25(2), 273–287. https://doi.org/10.1111/1468-0440.00065.

Myers, Virginia. Summer 2015. University Inc.: The pernicious effects of corporate influence. *On Campus* (American Federation of Teachers) 34(4), 4–9.

Nafziger, Steven, and Peter H. Lindert. September 2012. Russian inequality on the eve of revolution. Working Paper 18383. National Bureau of Economic Research. Accessed on April 28, 2018. Retrieved from http://www.nber.org/papers/w18383.

Nagourney, Adam. October 1, 2010. In California bid, Whitman spends record but struggles. *New York Times*. Accessed on November 24, 2017. Retrieved from http://www.nytimes.com/2010/10/02/us/politics/02calif.html.

National Archives (UK). The social order. World of Domesday. National Archives (UK). Accessed on August 20, 2017. Retrieved from http://www.nationalarchives.gov.uk/domesday/world-of-domesday/order.htm.

National Funeral Directors Association. October 1, 2015. NFDA releases results of 2015 member general price list survey. Accessed on July 5, 2017. Retrieved from http://www.nfda.org/news/media-center/nfda-news-releases/id/840/nfda-releases-results-of-2015-member-general-price-list-survey.

National Institutes of Health. November 1, 2016. Can genes be patented? Accessed on October 2, 2017. National Institutes of Health, National Library of Medicine. Retrieved from https://ghr.nlm.nih.gov/primer/testing/genepatents.

National Low Income Housing Authority. April 11, 2016. Finally, the truth about welfare. *Low Income and Urban Housing Blog*. Accessed June 4, 2018. Retrieved from http://blog.lowincome.org/2016/04/truth-about-welfare-foodstamps-how-many-blacks-vs-whites.html.

Neville, Sarah. June 15, 2015. Top firms' "poshness test" imposes class ceiling. ft.com. Accessed on March 17, 2017. Retrieved from http://www.ft.com/intl/cms/s/0/1177939c-10e6-11e5-9bf8-00144feabdco.html#axzz3d8AaHpVW.

New York Times. April 4, 2016. The Panama Papers: Here's what we know. Accessed on October 21, 2018. Retrieved from http://www.nytimes.com/2016/04/05/world/panama-papers-explainer.html.

NJTV News. September 13, 2017. Newark regains local control of public schools. Accessed on May 8, 2018. Retrieved from http://www.pbs.org/video/flanagan-newark-schools-1505312720/.

Norden, Lawrence, and Christopher Famighetti. 2015. America's voting machines at risk. Brennan Center for Justice at NYU School of Law. Accessed on June 29, 2018. Retrieved from https://www.brennancenter.org/publication/americas-voting-machines-risk.

Norton, Michael I., and Dan Ariely. 2011. Building a better America—one wealth quintile at a time. *Perspectives on Psychological Science*, 6(1) 9–12. https://doi.org/10.1177/1745691610393524.

Novokmet, Filip, Thomas Piketty, and Gabriel Zucman. November 9, 2017. From Soviets to oligarchs: Inequality and property in Russia, 1905–2016. VoxEU.org. Accessed July 18, 2017. Retrieved from https://voxeu.org/article/inequality-and-property-russia-1905-2016.

NPR. February 12, 2018. Trump administration wants to decide what food SNAP recipients will get. Accessed on March 20, 2018. Retrieved from https://www.npr.org/sections/thesalt/2018/02/12/585130274/trump-administration-wants-to-decide-what-food-snap-recipients-will-get.

Nutrition Digest. USDA defines food deserts. *Nutrition Digest* (American Nutrition Association), 38(2). Accessed August 28, 2017. Retrieved from http://americannutritionassociation.org/newsletter/usda-defines-food-deserts.

O'Brien, Jay, and William Roseberry. 1991. *Golden Ages, Dark Ages: Imagining the Past in Anthropology and History*. Berkeley: University of California Press.

O'Connor, Clare. April 15, 2014. Report: Walmart workers cost taxpayers $6.2 billion in public assistance. *Forbes*. Accessed on January 25, 2017. Retrieved from http://www.forbes.com/sites/clareoconnor/2014/04/15/report-walmart-workers-cost-taxpayers-6-2-billion-in-public-assistance/#59e93f027cd8.

OECD (Organisation for Economic Cooperation and Development). 2010. A family affair: Intergenerational social mobility across OECD countries. In *Economic Policy Reforms 2010: Going for Growth*. Accessed on September 8, 2017. Retrieved from http://www.keepeek.com/Digital-Asset-Management/oecd/economics/economic-policy-reforms-2010_growth-2010-en#page1. https://doi.org/10.1787/growth-2010-38-en.

OECD (Organisation for Economic Cooperation and Development). November 24, 2016. Income inequality remains high in the face of weak recovery. Accessed on April 28, 2018. Retrieved from http://www.oecd.org/social/inequality-and-poverty.htm.

O'Grady, Mary Anastasia. May 23, 2009. Don't monetize the debt: The president of the Dallas Fed on inflation risk and central bank independence. *Wall Street Journal*. Accessed on August 19, 2017. Retrieved from http://www.wsj.com/articles/SB124303024230548323.

O'Hara, Phillip Anthony. 2001. Recent changes to the IMF, WTO and FSP: An emerging global monetary-trade-production social structure of accumulation for long wave upswing? Paper presented at the conference of the Association for Social Economics, New Orleans, January 5, 2001.

Olivera, Oscar. 2004. *¡Cochabamba! Water War in Bolivia*. Cambridge, MA: South End Press.

Ollman, Bertell. n.d. Marx's use of "class." Dialectical Marxism: The Writings of Bertell Ollman, NYU Web, New York University. Accessed May 23, 2017. Retrieved from https://www.nyu.edu/projects/ollman/docs/class.php.

On Campus. Summer 2015. The power of Pearson threatens academic integrity. *On Campus* (American Federation of Teachers), 34(4), 12–13.

Open Secrets. Top industries, federal election data for Hillary Clinton, 2016 election cycle. Accessed on June 20, 2018. Retrieved from https://www.opensecrets.org/pres16/indus.php?cycle=2016&id=N00000019&type=f.

Oreskes, Naomi, and Erik M. Conway. 2010. *Merchants of Doubt: How a Handful of Scientists Obscured the Truth on Issues from Tobacco Smoke to Global Warming*. New York: Bloomsbury Press.

O'Reilly, Anne-Marie, and Warren Clark. November 2011. All work and no pay—the rise of workfare. *Red Pepper*. Accessed on September 28, 2017. Retrieved from http://www.redpepper.org.uk/all-work-and-no-pay/.

Orwell, George. 1992 [1949]. *Nineteen Eighty-Four*. New York: Alfred A. Knopf.

Orwell, George. 1993 [1945]. *Animal Farm*. New York: Alfred A. Knopf.

Oxfam International. January 2017. An economy for the 99 percent. Oxfam Briefing Paper, published by Oxfam GB for Oxfam International.

Palast, Greg. 2004. *The Best Democracy Money Can Buy*. New York: Plume.

Palast, Greg. 2012a. *Billionaires and Ballot Bandits: How to Steal an Election in 9 Easy Steps*. New York: Seven Stories Press.

Palast, Greg. June 26, 2012b. Robert Mundell, evil genius of the euro. *Guardian*. Accessed on January 28, 2017. Retrieved from http://www.theguardian.com/commentisfree/2012/jun/26/robert-mundell-evil-genius-euro.

Palmer, Griff, and Michael Cooper. December 14, 2012. How maps helped Republicans keep an edge in the House. *New York Times*. Accessed on September 23, 2017. Retrieved from https://www.nytimes.com/2012/12/15/us/politics/redistricting-helped-republicans-hold-onto-congress.html.

Panitch, Leo, and Sam Gindin. 2005. Finance and American empire. In Leo Panitch and Colin Leys (eds.), *The Empire Reloaded*, 46–81. New York: Monthly Review Press.

Paul, Katherine, and Ronnie Cummins. September 7, 2013. GMO and the corporate patenting of living organisms: Monsanto's patents on life. Centre for Research on Globalization. Accessed on October 22, 2017. Retrieved from http://www.globalresearch.ca/gmo-and-the-corporate-patenting-of-living-organisms-monsantos-patents-on-life/5324781.

PBS NewsHour. Broadcast June 4, 2014. Tiananmen Square massacre resonates in China despite enforced "amnesia." Accessed on February 21, 2017. Retrieved from https://www.pbs.org/newshour/show/tiananmen-square-resonates-china-despite-enforced-amnesia.

PBS NewsHour. Broadcast March 19, 2015. What's splitting a new generation of haves and have-nots. Accessed on August 14, 2017. Retrieved from http://www.pbs.org/newshour/bb/whats-splitting-new-generation-haves-nots/.

PBS. NewsHour. Broadcast September 5, 2017. How online graduate programs offer degrees at significant savings. Accessed on May 1, 2018. Retrieved from http://www.pbs.org/newshour/bb/online-graduate-programs-offer-degrees-significant-savings/.

PBS NewsHour Extra. June 15, 2017. Do you control your phone or does your phone control you? Accessed May 15, 2018. Retrieved from http://www.pbs.org/newshour/extra/daily-videos/do-you-control-your-phone-or-does-your-phone-control-you/.

Perelman, Michael. 2000. *The Invention of Capitalism: Classical Political Economy and the Secret History of Primitive Accumulation*. Durham: Duke University Press. https://doi.org/10.1215/9780822380696.

Perrone, Matthew. November 16, 2016. Drug prices don't budge even after pressure from Congress. Associated Press. Accessed on April 29, 2018. Retrieved from https://apnews.com/8bb39908692f418e85ee15fd9516bd9c.

Piketty, Thomas. 2014. *Capital in the Twenty-First Century*. Cambridge, MA: Belknap Press. https://doi.org/10.4159/9780674369542.

Piven, Frances Fox. 1993. *Regulating the Poor: The Functions of Public Welfare*. New York: Vintage.

Plato. 1970. *The Laws*. Translated by Trevor J. Saunders. Harmondsworth, England: Penguin Books.

Plato. 1991. *The Republic of Plato*. Translated by Allan Bloom. 2nd ed. New York: Basic Books.

Pleming, Sue. June 27, 2005. Halliburton's Iraq deals described as contract abuse. Reuters. Accessed on August 13, 2017. Retrieved from https://dearkitty1.wordpress.com/2006/12/28/usa-halliburtons-iraq-deals-contract-abuse/.

Pogrebin, Robin, and Scott Reyburn. May 18, 2017. A Basquiat sells for "mind-blowing" $110.5 million at auction. *New York Times*. Accessed on October 6, 2017. Retrieved from https://www.nytimes.com/2017/05/18/arts/jean-michel-basquiat-painting-is-sold-for-110-million-at-auction.html?_r=0.

Popken, Ben. August 23, 2016. Mylan CEO's pay rose over 600 percent as EpiPen price rose 400 percent. NBC News. Accessed on March 27, 2017. Retrieved from http://www.nbcnews.com/business/consumer/mylan-execs-gave-themselves-raises-they-hiked-epipen-prices-n636591.

Public Citizen. 2017. Trans-Pacific Partnership (TPP): Expanded corporate power, lower wages, unsafe food imports. Public Citizen. Accessed on June 20, 2018. Retrieved from https://www.citizen.org/our-work/globalization-and-trade/nafta-wto-other-trade-pacts/trans-pacific-partnership.

Putnam, Robert D. 2015. *Our Kids: The American Dream in Crisis*. New York: Simon & Schuster.

Rampell, Catherine. November 25, 2009. Your senator is (probably) a millionaire. *New York Times*. Accessed on September 16, 2017. Retrieved from http://economix.blogs.nytimes.com/2009/11/25/your-senator-is-probably-a-millionaire/?_r=0.

Reeves, Richard. V. 2017. *Dream Hoarders: How the American Upper Middle Class Is Leaving Everyone Else in the Dust, Why That Is a Problem, and What to Do about It*. Washington, D.C.: Brookings Institution Press.

Rifkin, Jeremy. 1996. *The End of Work: The Decline of the Global Labor Force and the Dawn of the Post-Market Era*. New York: G. P. Putnam's Sons.

Riley, Charles. February 14, 2014. Tom Perkins' big idea: The rich should get more votes. CNNMoney. Accessed on May 10, 2018. Retrieved from http://money.cnn.com/2014/02/14/investing/tom-perkins-vote/index.html?hpt=hp_t1.

Ritzer, George. 2008. *The McDonaldization of Society*. 5th ed. Thousand Oaks, CA: Pine Forge.

Rizzo, Jennifer. September 22, 2011. Defense cuts: The jobs numbers games. CNN. Accessed on June 2, 2018. Retrieved from http://security.blogs.cnn.com/2011/09/22/defense-cuts-the-jobs-numbers-game/.

Rocker, Rudolf. 1938. *Anarcho-Syndicalism*. London: Secker and Warburg.

Roden, Lee. February 16, 2017. Sweden's wealth inequality exposed by new research. *Local SE*. Accessed on March 29, 2017. Retrieved from https://www.thelocal.se/20170216/swedens-wealth-inequality-exposed-by-new-research.

Roine, Jesper, and Daniel Waldenström. 2015. Long-run trends in the distribution of income and wealth. In Anthony B. Atkinson and François Bourguignon (eds.),

Handbook of Income Distribution, vol. 2A Amsterdam: Elsevier. Accessed on April 28, 2018. Data retrieved from http://www.uueconomics.se/danielw/Handbook.htm.

Rosiek, Jerry, and Kathy Kinslow. 2016. *Resegregation as Curriculum: The Meaning of the New Racial Segregation in U.S. Public Schools*. New York: Routledge.

Ross, Stephen L., and John Yinger. 2002. *The Color of Credit: Mortgage Discrimination, Research Methodology, and Fair-Lending Enforcement*. Cambridge: MIT Press.

Rothkopf, David. 2009. *Superclass: The Global Power Elite and the World They Are Making*. New York: Farrar, Straus and Giroux.

Russi, Luigi. 2013. *Hungry Capital: The Financialization of Food*. Washington, D.C.: Zero Books.

Saez, Emmanuel, and Gabriel Zucman. May 2016. Wealth inequality in the United States since 1913: Evidence from capitalized income tax data. *Quarterly Journal of Economics*, 131(2), 519–578. Accessed on April 28, 2018. Retrieved from http://gabriel-zucman.eu/files/SaezZucman2016QJE.pdf.

Schaefer, Richard. 2017. *Sociology: A Brief Introduction*. Singapore: McGraw-Hill.

Schilling, Vincent. November 8, 2014. 8 things the history books don't tell us about Native people. *Everyday Feminism*. Accessed on September 23, 2017. Retrieved from http://everydayfeminism.com/2014/11/history-books-dont-tell-natives/.

Schor, Juliet B. 1992. *The Overworked American: The Unexpected Decline of Leisure*. New York: Basic Books.

Schultz, Ellen E., and Theo Francis. April 19, 2002. Companies profit on workers' deaths through "dead peasants" insurance. *Wall Street Journal*. Accessed on May 15, 2017. Retrieved from http://www.wsj.com/articles/SB1019165486226300040.

Scott, E. Robert, Carlos Salas, and Bruce Campbell. 2006. *Revisiting NAFTA: Still Not Working for North America's Workers*. Washington, DC: Economic Policy Institute.

Sentencing Project. May 2012. Trends in U.S. corrections. Accessed on February 20, 2017. Sentencing Project. Retrieved from http://sentencingproject.org/doc/publications/inc_Trends_in_Corrections_Fact_sheet.pdf.

Shimanaka, Kazutaka. August 6, 2009. Lactating ladies nurse customers at Kabukicho milk bar. *Tokyo Reporter*. Accessed on June 19, 2017. Retrieved from https://www.tokyoreporter.com/2009/08/06/lactating-ladies-nurse-customers-at-kabukicho-milk-bar/.

Shroud.com. 2017. Shroud exhibitions. Accessed on September 29, 2017. Retrieved from https://www.shroud.com/expos.htm.

Simmel, Georg. 1955. *Conflict and the Web of Group-Affiliations*. New York: Free Press.

Simmel, Georg. 2011. *The Philosophy of Money*. New York: Routledge.

Simpson, Peter. 2012. China covers up death of top official's son after he crashed Ferrari "while playing sex games with two semi-naked girls." *Daily Mail*. Accessed on July 25, 2017. Retrieved from http://www.dailymail.co.uk/news/article-2198246/Ling-Gu-death-Ferrari-crash-covered-Chinese-officials.html#ixzz3yYiNTkwU.

Smellie, Alice. June 2, 2012. From Hindu temple to Hollywood hairdo: How thousands of Indian women have their heads shaved to please the gods ... only for the hair to end up as £3,000 extensions. *Daily Mail.* Accessed on February 20, 2017. Retrieved from http://www.dailymail.co.uk/femail/article-2153691/From-Hindu-temple-Hollywood-hairdo-How-thousands-Indian-women-having-heads-shaved-gods-hair-end-3-000-extensions.html.

Smith, Aaron. April 28, 2010. Greek crisis fears deepen. CNNMoney.com. Accessed on February 2, 2017. Retrieved from http://money.cnn.com/2010/04/28/news/international/greek_bonds/.

Smith, Greg B. December 14, 2016. City puts up homeless families for $600 per night at Times Square hotels. *New York Daily News.* Accessed on March 25, 2017. Retrieved from http://www.nydailynews.com/news/politics/city-puts-homeless-600-night-hotels-times-square-article-1.2909862.

Sourcebook of Criminal Justice Statistics Online. No date. Table 6.28.2010: Number and rate (per 100,000 resident population in each group) of sentenced prisoners under jurisdiction of state and federal correctional authorities on December 31, by sex, United States, 1925–2010. Sourcebook of Criminal Justice Statistics. University at Albany, Hindelang Criminal Justice Research Center. Accessed on November 14, 2017. Retrieved from http://www.albany.edu/sourcebook/pdf/t6282010.pdf.

Spitznagel, Eric. October 22, 2013. Germs, male customers, and the online breast milk market. *Businessweek.com.* Accessed on February 26, 2017. Retrieved from http://www.businessweek.com/articles/2013-10-22/online-breast-milk-markets-faces-germs-and-hygiene-issues-in-new-pediatrics-study#p1.

Stilson, Jeff, director. 2010. *Good Hair.* Santa Monica, CA: Lionsgate.

Stirner, Max. 2004. *The Ego and His Own: The Case of the Individual against Authority.* Mineola, NY: Dover Publications.

Stockholm International Peace Research Institute. 2013. Military expenditure. Stockholm International Peace Research Institute. Accessed on February 6, 2017. Retrieved from http://www.sipri.org/yearbook/2013/03.

Strauss, Daniel. October 13, 2014. GOPer Tillis: Dems "redistributed" trillions on "de facto reparations." *Talking Points Memo.* Accessed on February 10, 2017. Retrieved from http://talkingpointsmemo.com/dc/thom-tillis-reparations-comments-north-carolina.

Taibbi, Matt. November 6, 2014a. The $9 billion witness: Meet JPMorgan Chase's worst nightmare. *Rolling Stone.* Accessed on November 23, 2018. Retrieved from http://www.rollingstone.com/politics/news/the-9-billion-witness-20141106.

Taibbi, Matt. 2014b. *The Divide: American Injustice in the Age of the Wealth Gap.* New York: Spiegel & Grau.

Tanner, Kristi. January 16, 2016. All Flint's children must be treated as exposed to lead. *Detroit Free Press.* Accessed on February 12, 2017. Retrieved from http://

www.freep.com/story/opinion/contributors/raw-data/2016/01/16/map-8657-flints-youngest-children-exposed-lead/78818888/.

Taylor, Bryan. October 26, 2013. Tiberius used quantitative easing to solve the financial crisis of 33 AD. *Business Insider*. Accessed on March 3, 2017. Retrieved from http://www.businessinsider.com/qe-in-the-financial-crisis-of-33-ad-2013-10?r=US&IR=T&IR=T.

Taylor, Harriet. August 30, 2016. How Apple managed to pay a 0.005 percent tax rate in 2014. CNBC. Accessed on January 27, 2017. Retrieved from http://www.cnbc.com/2016/08/30/how-apples-irish-subsidiaries-paid-a-0005-percent-tax-rate-in-2014.html.

Teffer, Peter. January 29, 2016. EU carbon credits drop below €6. *EU Observer*. Accessed on September 20, 2017. Retrieved from https://euobserver.com/environment/132045.

Third Coast Conspiracy. January 18, 2016. Democracy, disposability, and the Flint water crisis. *Third Coast Conspiracy*. Accessed October 3, 2017. Retrieved from https://thirdcoastconspiracy.wordpress.com/2016/01/18/democracy-disposability-and-the-flint-water-crisis/.

Thomas, William Isaac. 1923. *The Unadjusted Girl: With Cases and Standpoint for Behavior Analysis*. Boston: Little, Brown.

Tuttle, Brad. January 7, 2016. More retailers accused of misleading customers with fake price schemes. *Time*. Accessed on January 20, 2017. Retrieved from http://time.com/money/4171081/macys-jc-penney-lawsuit-original-prices/.

Twenge, Jean M. September 2017. Have smartphones destroyed a generation? *Atlantic*. Accessed on March 20, 2018. Retrieved from https://www.theatlantic.com/magazine/archive/2017/09/has-the-smartphone-destroyed-a-generation/534198/.

Urquhart, Michael. April 1984. The employment shift to services: Where did it come from? *Monthly Labor Review*, 107(4), 15–22. Accessed on May 30, 2017. Retrieved from http://www.bls.gov/opub/mlr/1984/04/art2full.pdf.

U.S. Census Bureau A. Historical income tables: Income inequality. Table H-2, Share of aggregate income received by each fifth and top 5 percent of households; Table H-4, Gini ratios for households, by race and Hispanic origin of householder. Accessed on May 15, 2018. Retrieved from https://www.census.gov/data/tables/time-series/demo/income-poverty/historical-income-inequality.html.

U.S. Census Bureau B. Income and poverty in the United States: 2015. Poverty thresholds for 2015 by size of family and related children under 18 years; Table A-1, Households by total money income, race, and Hispanic origin of householder: 1967 to 2015; Table A-2, Selected measures of household income dispersion: 1967 to 2015. Accessed on May 10, 2018. Retrieved from https://www.census.gov/data/tables/2016/demo/income-poverty/p60-256.html.

U.S. Census Bureau C. Foreign Trade in Goods with China. Accessed June 28, 2018. Retrieved from https://www.census.gov/foreign-trade/balance/c5700.html.

U.S. Census Bureau D. n.d. Where is the wealth? Median household net worth by quintile. Accessed on February 21, 2017. Retrieved from https://www.census.gov/content/dam/Census/newsroom/releases/2014/cb14-156_net_worth_graphic.pdf.

U.S. Department of Agriculture. August 2014. Expenditures on children by families. Accessed on November 9, 2017. Retrieved from https://www.fns.usda.gov/resource/2013-expenditures-children-families.

U.S. Department of Defense. April 2013. Fiscal year 2014 budget request. Accessed on October 30, 2017. Retrieved from http://comptroller.defense.gov/Portals/45/Documents/defbudget/fy2014/FY2014_Budget_Request_Overview_Book.pdf.

U.S. Department of Defense. January 27, 2017. About the Department of Defense. Accessed on February 8, 2017. Retrieved from https://web.archive.org/web/20170202011529/https://www.defense.gov/About.

U.S. Department of Justice. December 2014. Correctional Populations in the United States, 2013. Accessed on October 1, 2017. Retrieved from http://www.bjs.gov/content/pub/pdf/cpus13.pdf.

U.S. Department of Justice. March 4, 2015. Justice Department announces findings of two civil rights investigations in Ferguson, Missouri. Accessed on November 2, 2017. Retrieved from http://www.justice.gov/opa/pr/justice-department-announces-findings-two-civil-rights-investigations-ferguson-missouri.

U.S. Department of Labor. Bureau of Labor Statistics. N.d. Labor force statistics from the current population survey. Accessed on March 18, 2018. Retrieved from http://data.bls.gov/timeseries/LNS11300000.

U.S. Department of Labor. Bureau of Labor Statistics. May 2014. May 2014 national occupational employment and wage estimates, United States. Accessed on February 23, 2018. Retrieved from https://www.bls.gov/oes/2014/may/oes_nat.htm#00-0000.

U.S. Senate Committee on Governmental Affairs. 1978a. *Voting Rights in Major Corporations*. Washington, DC: US Government Printing Office.

U.S. Senate Committee on Governmental Affairs. 1978b. *Interlocking Directorates among the Major US Corporations*. Washington, DC: US Government Printing Office.

United States Elections Project. 2017. Accessed on February 20, 2018. Retrieved from http://www.electproject.org/.

Van Buren, Peter. July 9, 2014. Chelsea Clinton makes $900,000 for doing almost nothing. *Shadow Proof*. Accessed on January 20, 2017. Retrieved from https://shadowproof.com/2014/07/09/chelsea-clinton-makes-900000-for-doing-almost-nothing/.

Varoufakis, Yanis. August 26, 2018. Greece was never bailed out—it remains locked in an EU debtor's prison. *Guardian*. Accessed August 27, 2018. Available at: https://www.theguardian.com/commentisfree/2018/aug/26/greece-was-never-bailed-out--it-remains-a-debtors-prison-and-the-eu-still-holds-the-keys?CMP=share_btn_fb.

Veblen, Thorstein. 2012 [1899]. *The Theory of the Leisure Class*. USA: Renaissance Classics.

Wachowski, Larry, and Andy Wachowski. 2002. *The Matrix: The Shooting Script*. New York: Newmarket Press.

Wagner, Peter, and Leah Sakala. March 12, 2014. Mass incarceration: The whole pie. Prison Policy Initiative. Accessed on November 20, 2017. Retrieved from http://www.prisonpolicy.org/reports/pie.html.

Ward, Susannah, director. 2013. *Secrets of the Manor House*. PBS.

Webb, Gary. 1998. *Dark Alliance: The CIA, the Contras, and the Crack Cocaine Explosion*. New York: Seven Stories Press.

Weber, Max. 1992 [1930]. *The Protestant Ethic and the Spirit of Capitalism*. New York: Routledge.

Weinstein, Deena, and Michael Weinstein. 1993. *Postmoder(ized) Simmel*. New York: Routledge.

Whitehouse, Sheldon. 2017. *Captured: The Corporate Infiltration of American Democracy*. New York: New Press.

Wicker, Tom. 1968. *Report of the National Advisory Commission on Civil Disorders*. New York: Bantam.

Williams, Robert F. 1962. *Negros with Guns*. New York: Marzani & Munsell.

Wing, Nick. December 5, 2012. Sheldon Adelson vows to "double" donations to GOP after huge 2012 election failure. *Huffington Post*. Accessed on January 9, 2018. Retrieved from http://www.huffingtonpost.com/2012/12/05/sheldon-adelson-gop_n_2244070.html.

Wise, Timothy A., and Marie Brill. October 2012. Fueling the food crisis: The cost to developing countries of US corn ethanol expansion. ActionAid International USA.

Wolf, Naomi. December 29, 2012 Revealed: How the FBI coordinated the crackdown on Occupy. *Guardian*. Accessed on January 5, 2017. Retrieved from http://www.theguardian.com/commentisfree/2012/dec/29/fbi-coordinated-crackdown-occupy.

Wolff, Edward N. December, 2014. Household wealth trends in the United States, 1962–2013: What happened over the great recession? Working Paper 20733. Cambridge, MA: National Bureau of Economic Research.

Wolff, Richard D. 2012. *Democracy at Work: A Cure for Capitalism*. Chicago: Haymarket Books.

World Bank. Voting powers. Accessed August 25, 2017. Retrieved from http://www.worldbank.org/en/about/leadership/votingpowers.

World Wealth and Income Database. Accessed on April 28, 2018. Retrieved from http://wid.world/data/.

Yagoub, Mimi. February 5, 2014. Narco-aesthetics: How Colombia's drug trade constructed female "beauty". *Colombia Reports*. Accessed on September 28, 2017. Retrieved from http://colombiareports.com/narco-aesthetics-colombias-drug-trade-constructed-female-beauty/.

Zepezauer, Mark. 2004. *Take the Rich off Welfare*. Cambridge, MA: South End Press.
Zerzan, John. 1999. *Elements of Refusal*. Columbia, MO: Columbia Alternative Library.
Zucman, Gabriel. 2015. *The Hidden Wealth of Nations: The Scourge of Tax Havens*. Chicago: University of Chicago Press. https://doi.org/10.7208/chicago/9780226245560.001.0001.

Index

academic papers, bogus 55
achieved status 3, 96, 138
Ackman, Bill 110
addiction to smart phones, tablets, etc. 48–49
Adelson, Stuart 63
adjunct college teachers. *See* college teachers: adjunct
advertising 34, 44, 48, 49, 50, 51
    détournement 23n57
African Americans 14, 97, 98–99, 139, 177–79
    Ebonics 40
    Flint, Michigan 66–67, 125
    hair industry 114–15
    housing assistance 176
    housing segregation 38
    incarceration 98, 111, 174
    New Orleans 70–71, 125
    poverty rate 172
    technology industry 167. *See also* civil rights movement
agriculture/agribusiness 121–22, 145
    employment 94
    Middle Ages 97
    subsidies 84, 145
    tenant farmers 98
Airbnb 167
air traffic controllers' strikes 86, 136
Alexander, Michelle 98–99
alienation 3, 4, 35, 36, 37, 65, 111
Al Jazeera 72
American Indians. *See* Native Americans
anarchist theory 14, 184
ancient Greece (Athens) 18–19, 31, 56, 95, 96, 143, 157
ancient Rome 84, 104
    law 2
    slave revolts 185
Anderson, Cami 57
Animal Farm (Orwell) 65, 90
Apple Computer 42, 51, 145
architecture 48
aristocrats and aristocracy 75–76, 81, 97, 143–44, 162
    ancient Greece 95

Aristotle view 64
    Britain 97, 152, 158
    France 75, 97, 158–59
    Russia 75
Aristotle 19, 46, 56, 64, 100
ascribed status 3, 76, 87, 97, 138, 139–43
Asian Americans in high-tech industry 167
Association for Molecular Pathology v. Myriad Genetics, Inc. 109
Athens 126. *See also* ancient Greece (Athens)
attorneys. *See* lawyers
audience (spectatorship). *See* spectatorship
audience segmentation 33–37, 47, 48
authority, legitimate and illegitimate, xii 10, 32
automation 36, 41, 61
autonomy 18, 20, 31, 185–86
    crowds and 35

Bachmann, Michele 178
Bakunin, Mikhail 2, 186
bankruptcy 57, 97, 107
banks and banking 68, 84, 91, 102, 132–33
    Bank of England 100
    U.S. history 101. *See also* Federal Reserve; World Bank
banned books. *See* censorship
Baptist, Edward: *Half Has Never Been Told* 177
Barthes, Roland 15, 26
base and superstructure (Marxist theory) 2, 104
Basquiat, Jean-Michel 119
Baudrillard, Jean 15, 25, 26–29, 30, 33, 51, 99–100, 184
    on China 80
    on cloning 116
    hyper-commodification 108
    on medium as message 51–52
    view of value 100
Bearden v. Georgia 176–77
beauty industry 115
Benson, Bob 55
Bentham, Jeremy 21

Bey, Hakim 9, 23, 186
Bible 180
Big Brother (Orwell entity) 61
Bill and Melinda Gates Foundation 57
billionaires 46, 52, 57, 63, 140, 146, 161
    annual incomes 160
biofuels 121–22
birth, medicalization of 117
Bitcoins 101
black Americans. *See* African Americans
Blau, Peter 5–6, 7–8, 9–10, 34, 79
blood trade 115
Bloomberg, Michael R. 63, 160, 161
Blumer, Herbert 6, 7
Bolivia 123
book-banning. *See* censorship
bordars (cottars) 93, 95, 152, 167, 169
bots (algorithms) 48
bourgeoisie (middle class) 75, 92
    Dahrendorf view 75
    debt 106–7
    lower 93, 152
    Marx views 92, 93, 94
    petite 92, 93
    Sweden 75, 152, 154
    upper (haute) 75–76
Brattin, Rick 45
Brave New World (Huxley) 51, 186n8
Brave New World Revisited (Huxley) 40, 69
breast milk monetization 112–13
Bresch, Heather 110
Bretton Woods Accord 131–32
Britain 72
    breast milk monetization 112
    caste 141
    "color-blindness" of 179
    hair monetization 114
    as hegemon 105
    income inequality 147, 150, 154
    wealth inequality 147–48, 154, 156
    welfare 176. *See also* East India Company; England
broadcasting 129, 141–42. *See also* television
Buchanan, Pat 177–78
Buffet, Warren 160, 161
Bush, George W. 72
Butler, Judith 16

California 63, 66, 111, 122, 145
call centers 128, 175

Callinicos, Alex 15
Cambodia 113
campaign financing. *See* elections: campaign financing
Capital (Marx) 73, 91–92, 94, 103
"capital" and "capitalism" (words) 103, 104
carbon trading 124
Carnegie, Andrew 161
caste, x, xi 2, 30, 33–34, 73, 74–75, 80–82, 87, 96, 157–77
    African Americans 97–99, 139
    ascribed status and 87
    boundary-blurring 97–98
    education and 40–44
    food and 45
    hardening of 79, 81
    India 33, 37–38, 39, 137, 138
    law and 67
    social and spatial isolation 39–40
    Soviet Union 89, 90
    United States 80, 97–99, 139–42, 159–62, 165–67, 170–77
    Weber 13, 14, 17, 31. *See also* ruling caste
Castoriadis, Cornelius 15, 17–21, 25, 30, 61–62, 73, 80, 142
    "bureaucratic capitalism" 88
    Debord and 23
    "imaginary" 18, 19–20, 184, 185
    on labor interdependence 83
    on monetary reward 85–86
    on revolt 186
    views of caste 13, 17, 74
Catholic Church 119
Celock, John 178
censorship 52, 72, 180–81
Cha, Laura 62
charter schools 57–58, 144
Cheney, Dick 120
children: death penalty for 178
    labor 77
    Marxist view 86
    monetization 117
    Plato view 147
    play (simulacrum) 49, 129
China 31, 62, 81, 131, 137, 157
    Baudrillard on 80
    carbon trading 124
    collective memory 53
    "cyber wall" 52
    Disney resorts 25, 28

eighteenth century 152, 156
Hollywood film industry 127
income inequality 151, 156–57
online dating 118
organ trade 115
Panama Papers and 145
rich people 90
Song dynasty 103
surveillance 71
Tiananmen Square massacre, 1989 53, 62, 81
trade 135
wealth inequality 88–89, 149, 156
choice, illusion of 52
Chomsky, Noam 52
Christianity 119, 177–78, 179–80
Ciavarella, Mark, Jr. 111
Cisco Systems 52, 167
cities, emergency management of. *See* emergency management of cities
Citigroup 66
Citizens United v. Federal Election Commission 59, 63
City University of New York 56
civil rights movement 182, 185
Civil War (United States) 76
Clark, Gregory 87
class, x 30, 89, 90–99
  education and 42
  mobility, xi 10
  Weber 11–12, 13. *See also* bourgeoisie; social mobility; working classes
"class" (word) 91
class conflict 30
Clemente, Frank 55
climate change 83
  denial 50, 55, 180
Clinton, Bill 47, 63, 141, 142, 175
Clinton, Chelsea 141–42
Clinton, Hillary 47, 48, 63, 64, 142
cloning 109, 116
closed circuit TV cameras 71
Coca-Cola 121, 127
Cold War 111
COLI. *See* corporate-owned life insurance (COLI)
college education 42–43, 55–58, 139–40, 141, 162
college teachers 85, 140
  adjunct 58, 61, 87, 171

Collins, Randall 7
Colombia 117, 185
commodification 108–37
Common Core program 58, 144
commons, enclosure of 57, 77, 78, 82, 129
community colleges 43
Comte, Auguste 5
conflict of interest 55
conflict theory 14
conformity and nonconformity 5, 8, 9
Congress, U.S. *See* U.S. Congress
"conscious collective" (Durkheim), 6
conspicuous consumption 26, 97, 117, 128
Conspicuous Consumption (Veblen) 128
consumer alienation 35
consumer debt 57, 59, 101, 106–7, 170. *See also* student loans
consumption 36, 127, 128–29, 137
  Baudrillard views 26
  caste and 44–45
  culture and 10–11
  debt and 107. *See also* conspicuous consumption
Cooley, Charles Horton 6
corn 121–22
corporate charters 104–5
corporate control of food 120–22
corporate-owned life insurance (COLI) 118
corporate personhood 58–59
corporate taxes 144–45
corporations, high-tech. *See* high-tech corporations
corruption, judiciary. *See* judiciary corruption
cosmetics industry 115
cosmetic surgery 117–18
cottars. *See* bordars (cottars)
courts 176. *See also* judiciary corruption; U.S. Supreme Court
Cowen, Tyler 75
creation myths 18
  creationism 180
creditor-debtor relations 91, 126
credit default swaps 102
criminalization of poverty 176
criminal justice 110–12, 173–77. *See also* prison
crises 20–21
  permanent 69. *See also* financial crises
critical pedagogy 29
critical theory 14–29

crowds 35, 44
Cuba 62, 81
cultural segmentation. *See* sociocultural segmentation
culture 4–5, 40, 51
    capitalist 25, 127
    inequality and 9
currency 100–101, 131n111, 135
customer service 36, 128
Cyprus: fertility industry 116

Dahrendorf, Ralf 13, 32, 75, 90–91, 93, 96, 103
Dalit 37–38
dating, online. *See* online dating
death, monetization of 118–20
death penalty for children 178
Debord, Guy 17, 23–28, 30, 31, 47, 61–62, 75, 79, 80, 186
    détournement 23, 186
    on law 67
    on leisure 129
    Marxism and 15, 23
    on money 108
    on social isolation 36–37
    on spectacular government 53
    on state-economy integration 159
    on terrorism 70
    on unification of time 127–28
    view of architecture 48
    view of production and consumption of images 51
    view of spectacular socialism 88
    views of capitalism 2, 24, 79
debt 74, 101, 106
    monetization 108
    money as 101. *See also* consumer debt; creditor-debtor relations; international debt
defense industry 69
"definition of the situation" (Thomas) 6
deflation (economics) 60, 100
dehumanization 39
delayed gratification. *See* gratification, instant versus delayed
Deleuze, Gilles 16
democracy, direct. *See* direct democracy
democracy, representative. *See* representative democracy
democracy, symbolic/simulated 61–66, 80, 81, 168, 186

demonstrations and protests. *See* protests and demonstrations
demos. *See* masses (people)
depressions 60, 84
Derrida, Jacques 15, 16
determinism 2, 20
détournement 9, 23
Detroit 66–67, 166
DeVos, Betsy 57
Diamond v. Chakrabarty 109
dictatorship 24, 40
digital currency. *See* electronic currency
digital technology 48. *See also* electronic currency; internet
Diller, Barry 142
direct democracy 18–19, 31, 95, 143, 157
Discipline and Punish (Foucault) 21
discouraged workers 60
Disney. *See* Walt Disney Company
Disneyland 27
Disposable Futures (Evans and Giroux) 70
distribution of wealth. *See* wealth distribution
dollar 123, 131n111, 135, 136
drinking water contamination: Flint, Michigan 45–46, 125
drug crime sentencing 67
Durkheim, Émile 6

Earnest, Josh 52
East India Company 85, 105
economic institutions 58–61. *See also* banks and banking
economic stagnation 76–77, 89
education 19, 29, 86, 179–83
    caste and 40–44, 161, 163, 165, 169, 171
    commodification 117. *See also* college education; public education
egalitarian orders. *See* horizontal orders
elections 46–47, 61, 81
    campaign financing 63
    Georgia, xi
    Rousseau on 65
    U.S. 65
    U.S. presidential 48, 63, 64, 66. *See also* voting
Electoral College 66
electronic currency 100–101, 104
elites 3, 26, 63–64, 159–64
    democracy and 65–66
    education 42, 55

financial collapse of 2008   68
financial regulation   60
income   144
intra-elite conflict   31, 75, 76
Middle Ages   92
politicians   61
as recommended target   187
Soviet Union   90
spatial isolation   39, 40
Sweden   75. *See also* nobility
email   128
emergency management of cities   66–67, 125–26
emergency rooms. *See* hospital emergency rooms
emissions trading ("cap and trade"). *See* carbon trading
employment   60–61, 94
   agricultural   94
   caste-based   44–46, 90
enclosure of commons. *See* commons, enclosure of
Engels, Friedrich   2, 73, 92
England: Bank of England   100
   Middle Ages   87, 95, 97, 152, 157, 162, 167–68, 169, 172
   spinning jenny   105
   workhouses   175–76
entertainment   40
   as propaganda   51–52
   violence in   70
environment, pollution of. *See* pollution
environment as commodity   82, 122, 124
EpiPens   110
equality   5, 29, 155
   Gini coefficient   147n41
   simulacrums/illusions of   80, 139
   See also inequality
Escobar, Pablo   117, 185
ethanol   121–22
euro (currency)   133
European Union (EU)   62, 85, 131
   Apple Computer and   145
   emissions trading   124
   Greece and   126
   IMF and   132, 133
   stagnation   77
Evans, Brad   70
evictions from public space   130

evolution (biology)   180
exchange theory. *See* social exchange theory

Facebook   37, 51, 52, 166
falseness and fakery   23, 50, 108, 179. *See also* fraud; simulacra and simulation
family   4, 5, 17
   aristocracy   158
   caste and   140, 141–42, 143
   death and   119
   Debord view   36–37
   homeless families   130
   income   164, 166, 168, 170, 172
   prison and   111–12
   social isolation and   36, 111–12
Farage, Nigel   179
farming. *See* agriculture/agribusiness
fast-food industry   14, 42, 44, 142, 146, 168, 169. *See also* McDonald's
FBI   72, 81
fear, xii   49, 61, 69, 81. *See also* terrorism
Federal Reserve   60, 68, 100–101, 102
   "Volcker shock"   136
Fentimen, Linda   112
Ferguson, Missouri   173–74
fertility tourism industry   116
feudalism   75, 76, 77, 92, 93, 97, 104, 143
   England   164
   China   152, 156
   Russia   94, 153, 156
   twenty-first century   139
   wealth inequality   152–53
fiat money   100
films   40, 51, 52, 70, 71, 72, 127, 177
finance   67–68, 101–2, 131–34
   regulation   59–60. *See also* banks and banking; money
financial crises   84
   collapse of 2008   60, 67–68, 85, 101–2, 108. *See also* depressions
financial instruments   67, 101
   environment and   123–24
   food and   121
First Amendment: corporations and   59
Flint, Michigan   45–46, 66–67, 125–26
Florida State University   55
food: caste and   44–45, 160, 163, 165, 168, 169
   commodification   120–22
   prison labor and   175. *See also* agriculture; fast-food industry

food deserts 44–45
food stamps 45, 145, 171
foreign direct investment (FDI) 133, 135
for-profit colleges and universities 43
fossil fuels and fossil fuels industry 55, 83
 See also oil spills
Foucault, Michel 9, 21–23, 24, 30, 99, 184
Fourteenth Amendment 58
Fox Broadcasting 53
fracking 122
France 135
 history 95–96
 income inequality 150, 157
 wealth inequality 148, 154, 156
 See also French Revolution
Franks, Trent 178
fraud: academic papers 55
 financial industry 67–68
 Victoria's Secret 175
 weapons contractors 120
free trade agreements (FTAs) 85, 134–35
French Revolution 75, 95–96
Friedman, Howard 87
Fukuyama, Francis 28
funeral costs 119
Fuqua, Charlie 178

Gabler, Neal 170–71
Gates, Bill 58, 160, 161
Gates Foundation. See Bill and Melinda Gates Foundation
Geithner, Tim 64
gender inequity in high-tech industry 167
gene editing and genetic engineering 116, 121
gene patenting 109
General Electric (GE) 84, 109, 120, 144
genetically modified crops 121
GEO group 112
Georgia, x 176–77
Georgia Tech 43
Germany 126, 135. See also Nazi Germany
gerrymandering 47
ghettos 37–38, 41, 42
 revolts 81
Gilman-Opalsky, Richard 80–81, 88
Gindin, Sam 136
Gini coefficient 147–51, 154
Giroux, Henry 70, 125–26

Goffman, Erving 16, 35, 48
Golden, Daniel 139–40
Goldman Sachs 64
Goldsmith, Peter, Baron 72
Google 51, 129, 167
Graeber, David 1, 74–75, 91, 101, 102, 104–5, 106n91, 107, 108
 view of war financing 106n91, 120
Gramsci, Antonio 4, 94
gratification, instant versus delayed 49
Great Britain. See Britain
Greece 62
 international debt 126–27, 133
 See also ancient Greece (Athens)
greenhouse gas emissions trading. See carbon trading
Greenwald, Glenn 71
groups, social. See social groups

Habermas, Jürgen 15, 37
hair monetization 113–15
The Half Has Never Been Told: Slavery and the Making of American Capitalism (Baptist) 177
Halliburton 120
Happer, William 55
Harrell, Antoinette 98
Harvard University 140
health care. See medical care
"health gradient," 171
hegemons (dominant nations) 130–31
hegemony, cultural 4
heirs. See inheritance
Helmsley, Leona 143–44
heteronymy 18, 20, 31
Hewlett-Packard 167
hierarchical orders and relations 3, 4, 5, 14, 30, 31
 accumulation in 104
 Castoriadis view 17–18
 formation of 79
 Marxist movements 186
 memory control and 53
 propaganda and 47
higher education. See college education
high-tech corporations 37, 167
hippies in history textbooks 182–83
Hispanics. See Latinos

historical materialism   20, 94
history   22–23, 30, 31, 73–79
    altering/erasure of   53, 179, 182
    banks and banking   101
    Baudrillard views   28–29
    capitalism   102–7
    ceasing of   25, 28, 73
    class   94–99
    slavery   177–79
    study and teaching   179–82
Hitler, Adolf   49–50, 182
hoi polloi. *See* masses (people)
Holder, Eric   68
Hollywood film industry   177
Homans, George Caspar   8, 10
homelessness   130
homeownership   38–39, 165
Hong Kong   28, 62
horizontal orders   3–5, 31
Horowitz, David   178–79
hospice care   119
hospital emergency rooms   110
house values   60
housing assistance   176
housing inequality: segregation   37–39
    Soviet Union   90
Hubbard, Jon   178
human body, monetization of   110–19
human organ trade. *See* organ trade
Hume, David   78
hunger   78
Husserl, Edmund   16
Huxley, Aldous   54, 56, 69
    Brave New World   51, 186n8
    Brave New World Revisited   40, 69

ICE. *See* U.S. Immigration and Customs Enforcement (ICE)
ideological (professional) class   92, 93
The Imaginary Institution of Society (Castoriadis)   1
IMF. *See* International Monetary Fund (IMF)
immigrants: detention   112, 174, 175
    undocumented   112, 172–73, 175
imprisonment for debt   176–77
income and caste privilege   142
income inequality   85–88, 90, 147, 150–51, 154–57, 159, 160, 163

income tax   144
indentured servitude   74, 169
India: caste   33, 37–38, 39, 137, 138
    blood and organ trade   115
    hair monetization   114
    surrogate pregnancy   116
    wages   135
Indians, American. *See* Native Americans
industrialization   41, 87, 94, 105
Industrial Revolution   19, 27
industry-funded think tanks   51
inequality   4, 9, 10–11, 13, 63, 138, 146–77
    China   88–89
    education   40–44
    health   171
    high-tech industry   167
    inheritance and   143
    sentencing   67
    tax policy   144
    wealth and debt   59, 63, 82, 88–89, 159–60, 169–70. *See also* caste; class; housing segregation; income inequality
infertility clinics   116
inflation   60, 77, 84, 100, 132, 136
inheritance   141, 143, 146, 160, 161, 163
An Inquiry into the Nature and Causes of the Wealth of Nations (Smith)   103
instant gratification. *See* gratification, instant versus delayed
institutions   4, 10
    economic   58–61
    educational   55–58
    legal   67–68
    political   61–67
    protective   68–72
    symbolic   54
Intel   167
interactionism. *See* symbolic interactionism
international calling centers   128
international debt   126–27, 132, 133
International Monetary Fund (IMF)   85, 126, 129, 131–33
internet, xi   37, 48, 128, 129
    censorship   52
    crypto-currency   101
    porn   118
    surveillance   71. *See also* Google
interracial marriage   39

Iraq   72, 120
Ireland   145
isolation, social. *See* social isolation
Ivy League colleges   40, 42, 139–40, 141

Japan   76, 113, 134
Japanese American internment   182
Jesus Christ, monetization of   119
Jim Crow   98–99
jobs. *See* employment; unemployment
J.P. Morgan   102
JPMorgan Chase   68
judiciary corruption   111, 173

Kant, Immanuel   18
Keynes, John Maynard   84
King Louis XIV. *See* Louis XIV
King Louis XVI. *See* Louis XVI
kings and queens. *See* monarchs and monarchy
Koch brothers   46, 55, 58, 65, 83, 160
Kristeva, Julia   16
Krugman, Paul   140–41
Kushner, Jared   140

labor, child. *See* children: labor
labor, precarious. *See* precarious labor (surplus labor)
labor, privileged. *See* privileged labor
labor, prison. *See* prison labor
labor, "semi-periphery." *See* "semi-periphery workers"
labor interdependence   83
labor laws   128, 133, 154
labor market segmentation   131, 136–37
labor theory of value   99
labor unions. *See* unions
Lacan, Jacques   15–16, 18
land grabs   122, 125
landownership   152–53
    Britain   97, 152, 158, 159, 164
    landowners as a class   92, 93
    Middle Ages   97, 15, 164, 167–68
    villeins and   167–68
language   5, 16, 21, 40
    propaganda   49. *See also* linguistics
La Rochefoucauld, Pierre-Louis de   158, 159
Latinos: homeownership   38
    housing assistance   176
    incarceration   11, 174

poverty rate   17
technology industry   167
law and laws   2, 18, 49, 130
    anti-homeless   130
    Britain   176, 179
    Debord views   26, 67
    electoral   98
    enclosure   77
    France   154
    lobbying and   84
    Mundell views   133
    sentencing   111
    welfare   175, 176. *See also* labor laws
law enforcement   68–69, 71–72
    reality TV   70
    surveillance   71. *See also* police
lawyers   67, 86, 142, 165, 166
    corporate   68, 84, 125, 134
lead poisoning   45–46
Lefebvre, Henri   26
legal institutions   67–68. *See also* U.S. Supreme Court
legislation. *See* law and laws
Lehman Brothers   39, 101
Leung Chun-ying   62
Levi-Strauss, Claude   15
life expectancy   171
lifestyles   12, 14, 159, 160, 182
linguistics   5, 15–16
LinkedIn   166, 167
loans, student. *See* student loans
lobbying   63, 84, 110
Locke, John   77
"looking-glass self" (Cooley)   6
Louis XIV   161
Louis XVI   95–96, 158
Louisiana   98, 125, 176, 180, 182–83
lumpenproletariat   91, 92, 93
Luscombe, Belinda   118

Madoff, Bernie   59
Manning, Chelsea   71
marginal analysis (economics)   83
marketplaces   77, 129
markets   3, 7
    history   77
    "invisible hand"/self-regulation (supposed)   83, 84, 85, 89
    segmentation   34
Markowitz, Gerald   45–46

INDEX   225

marriage   3, 5
   caste and   39, 40, 75, 76, 97
Marx, Karl, x   2, 14, 84, 186
   Baudrillard and   26
   Capital   73, 91–92, 94, 103
   "capital" (word)   104
   Castoriadis and   17, 20
   class consciousness   11
   Dahrendorf on   96
   Debord and   23, 73
   labor theory of value   99
   "primitive accumulation"   78
   view of hegemons   130–31
   view of production   94
   views of capital   105–6
   views of class   91–96
   views of private property   96
Marxism   14, 15, 23, 76, 186
   Castoriadis   17, 20, 86
   class conflict   30
   Debord   23
   production   80. *See also* base and superstructure (Marxist theory)
masses (people)   33
   ancient Rome   90–91
   anger of   69
   Arthur Young view   77
   as a class   95
   entertainment   40
   forced bondage of   106
   Helmsley view   144
   Hillary Clinton and   47
   Huxley view   49–50
   isolation   36–37
   low voter participation   54
   public education   41
   in spectacular socialism   89
   See also peasants
The Matrix (film)   1, 102
Mauch, Loy   178
McDonald, Lawrence D.   39
McDonald's   41, 51, 107n95, 146, 175
McDonnell Douglas   120
McGraw-Hill   182
Mead, George Herbert   6–7, 15, 16
media   4, 40, 48, 51–53, 81, 177, 185. *See also* broadcasting; Hollywood film industry; internet; social media
medical care   109–10, 117, 119
Mencken, H. L.   56–57

mercantilism   103, 132
meritocracy   139, 141
Merton, Robert   54n90
Mexico   122, 132, 134, 135
Michigan   45–46, 66–67, 125–26
Microsoft   51, 167, 175
Middle Ages   74, 103
   England   157, 167–68, 169
middle class. *See* bourgeoisie (middle class)
Milburn, Alan   141
military services   68–69, 81
military spending   69, 120
Mills, C. Wright   16, 161–62
Mischel, Walter   49
Mnuchin, Steven   64
monarchs and monarchy   8, 63, 75, 76, 77, 97, 104, 161
   corporate charters and chartered monopolies   85, 104–5
   England   95, 97, 157, 158, 159
   France   95–96, 97, 158, 161
   historical erasure and   53
monetization. *See* commodification
money   9, 85–86, 100–102, 104
   Aristotle view of   100
   Debord on   108
   monetary policy   60, 84, 100–102, 131n111. *See also* currency
monopolies   85, 89
   information distribution   51
   violence   101
Monsanto   121, 122
Moore, Michael   125
Morris, Charles W.   15
mortgage practices, fraudulent   67–68, 101–2
movies. *See* films
Mundell, Robert   133
Muslims, deportation of   178
Mylan   110

NAFTA. *See* North American Free Trade Agreement (NAFTA)
National Security Agency   71
Native Americans   122, 181–82
Nazi Germany   39, 49–50, 182
NBC   141–42
neoliberalism   1–2, 81, 84, 85, 106, 125, 131–33, 136
nepotism   140, 141–42
Nestlé   118, 121, 122–23

Newark, New Jersey   38, 57
New Orleans   125
news media   40
New York City   63, 71, 166
New York State   57
New York Stock Exchange   59
Nietzsche, Friedrich   27
Nineteen Eighty-Four (Orwell)   47, 49, 51, 53, 54n92, 61, 69
nobility   76, 152–53, 157, 162–64
    England   95, 97, 152, 162
    France   95–96, 97, 158–59
    Sweden   75, 152, 154, 159
noblesse oblige   144
norms   4–5, 8, 9, 10, 21
North American Free Trade Agreement (NAFTA)   85, 134, 135, 136

Obama, Barack   63
obedience, xi, xiii   10, 47, 58, 61, 179
Occupy Wall Street (OWS)   71–72, 186
oil spills   109, 175
oligarchy   54, 65, 157, 159, 185
Ollman, Bertell   93
online dating   118
online education   42–43
online groups and communities. *See* virtual groups and communities
online retail   36, 41, 108
organ trade   115
Orwell, George: *Animal Farm*   65, 90
    Nineteen Eighty-Four   47, 49, 51, 53, 54n92, 61, 69

paideia   19
Panama Papers   145
Panitch, Leo   136
Panopticon   21
Paradise Papers   145
parking industry   130
patenting of genes. *See* gene patenting
patenting of seeds. *See* seed patenting
Patriot Act   49
Paulson, Hank   64
Pearson   42, 58, 179
peasants   74, 77, 152–54, 167
    Marx view   92
    postindustrial   170

Russia   94, 153
social mobility   97
Sweden   154. *See also* serfs
Pembina Consolidated Silver Mining v. Pennsylvania   58–59
Perelman, Michael   77–78
peripheral labor. *See* precarious labor (surplus labor)
Perkins, Tom   65
personal debt. *See* consumer debt
Peterson, Jesse Lee   178
pharmaceutical industry   110
phenomenology   16, 28
philanthropy   144, 161
Piketty, Thomas   82, 103–4, 141, 143, 155
plastic surgery. *See* cosmetic surgery
Plato   19, 62, 143
plea bargaining   67
Pocahontas   181–82
police   14, 24, 68, 69, 70, 71–72
    Ferguson, Missouri   173
    status and income   171
policing. *See* law enforcement
political campaign funding. *See* campaign funding
political institutions   61–67
political segmentation   46–47
pollution   83, 124
poor people   41–42, 77–78, 125, 169–77
    arrests   67
    consumption   44–45
    environment   83
    higher education   43, 57
    ignored by senators   65
    monetization   111
    noblesse oblige and   144
    Sweden   155
    voting   46. *See also* peasants
porn industry   118
post-structuralism and postmodernism   14–29
poverty   170, 171–72
    criminalization   176
    need for   82
    propaganda and   49. *See also* poor people
power relations   4, 9, 10, 31–32
    in architecture   48
    Foucault   21

INDEX

Weber 12–13
precarious labor (surplus labor) 77, 169–72
preemptive arrests 72
Presley, Elvis 119
price and prices 82
    breast milk 113
    carbon credits 124
    childbirth 117
    fertility industry 116
    food 121, 122
    McDonnell Douglas nuts 120
    prescription drugs 110
prison and prisoners 21, 81, 110–12, 173, 174
    African Americans 98, 111, 174
    China 115
    Latinos 174
    See also imprisonment for debt
prison labor 112, 175
private property, xii 81–82, 88, 96, 129
    China 89, 90. *See also* landownership
privatization 52, 129, 133
    China and Russia 88
    by emergency managers 66
    food production 122
    Greece 126
    mass transit 44
    media 52
    New Orleans 125
    schools and curricula 57, 58
    social welfare 144
    water 123
    See also commons, enclosure of
privileged labor 164–67
proletarians, x 80, 92, 93, 94, 96, 184
propaganda 34
    entertainment as 51–52
    in higher education 55
    neoliberalism as 81
    targeting rich people 44
    "total propaganda" 47–53
prostitutes and prostitution 42, 117, 172, 173, 174
protective institutions 68–72
protests and demonstrations 62
    against quota systems 138–39
    suppression of 81. *See also* China: Tiananmen Square massacre
Proudhon, Pierre-Joseph 20

pseudo-community (Debord) 36
public education 19, 41–42
    colleges and universities 56
    Mencken on 56–57
    privatization 57
public opinion, simulation of 37
punishment 5, 21–22
Putin, Vladimir 62, 145
Putnam, Robert 41

queens and kings. *See* monarchs and monarchy
quota systems 138

racial diversity in high-tech industry 167
racism in housing 38–39
Reagan, Ronald 52, 53, 111, 136
Reddit, xi
Reeves, Richard 42
religion 49, 177–78, 179–80, 182. *See also* Christianity
representative democracy 19, 61, 64, 65, 66, 80, 96, 138
required labor (caste) 167–69
retail 44, 82, 129, 172
    prison labor in 175. *See also* online retail
revolt and revolts 94, 184, 185, 186
    Castoriadis on 186
    fear of 81
    medieval England 95
    slaves 185
    suppression of 81
    U.S. ghettos 35, 38, 81, 185
revolution 20, 23, 73, 184, 186–87
    China 80
    Debord view 23
    Huxley view 40. *See also* French Revolution; Russian Revolution
Ricardo, David 99
rich people 75–76, 146, 154–56, 159–64
    ancient Athens 143
    congressional representation 65
    consumption 44
    education 42, 43
    life expectancy 171
    nepotism 140, 142
    spatial isolation 39, 40
    Sweden 75

Riddle, Wes   178
right to die   119
rituals, social. *See* social rituals
Ritzer, George   35–36, 107n95
Robinson, Patrick   39
Rodbertus, Johann Karl   78
Rockefeller, John D.   161
Rocker, Rudolf   184
rock music in history textbooks   182–83
roles, social. *See* social roles
Roman Catholic Church. *See* Catholic Church
Roman Empire. *See* ancient Rome
Rosner, David   45–46
Rousseau, Jean-Jacques   65
ruling caste   79, 82, 87, 93, 106, 119, 159–62
   clergy as   157
   violence against   185
"ruling class" (term)   93
Russia   31, 62, 74, 131
   capitalism   88
   carbon trading   124
   caste   75
   feudalism   94
   income inequality   151, 155, 156–57
   nineteenth-century landownership   153
   Panama Papers and   145
   wealth inequality   149, 155–56
Russian Revolution   89, 90, 94

sanctions   4–5
Santa Clara v. Southern Pacific   58–59
Santorum, Rick   178
Sartre, Jean-Paul   15, 27
Saussure, Ferdinand de   15
Schaeffler, Frank   126
Schlarman, Josef   126
scholarly papers, bogus. *See* academic papers, bogus
schools   41–43
   propaganda education   50
   textbooks   179–83
   voucher programs   57, 180, 182
Schütz, Alfred   16–17
Schwarzenegger, Arnold   52, 71
science, attacks on   180
scripted interactions in coffeeshops   35
Securities and Exchange Commission (SEC)   59–60
seed patenting   121

segmentation, labor market. *See* labor market segmentation
segmentation, political. *See* political segmentation
segmentation, sociocultural. *See* sociocultural segmentation
segmentation, spatial. *See* spatial segmentation
segregation in housing. *See* housing segregation
semiotics   15, 27
"semi-periphery workers"   168–69
sentencing   67, 111
serfs   76, 77, 95, 128, 143, 164, 167–68, 169. *See also* bordars (cottars); villeins
sewer privatization   123, 126–27
sex workers and sex work. *See* prostitutes and prostitution
shopping centers   44
Shkreli, Martin   110
Shroud of Turin   119
signaling (economics)   42
sign-values   26–27
Simmel, Georg   9, 10, 16, 34
simulacra and simulation   27, 28, 33, 100
   carbon credits   124
   college education   42–43, 56
   community   36
   currency   101, 135
   democracy   61–66, 80, 81, 168, 186
   corporate personhood   58
   equality and justice   80
   food   45
   history   73, 181
   humans   109, 116
   incarceration   185
   industrial system   184
   in media   52
   plants and animals   109
   play   129
   postmodern labor markets   61
   protests   62
   public opinion   37
   Shroud of Turin   119
   in social mobility   88
   in stock market regulation   59
   in "total propaganda"   48, 52
   violent spectacle   70
slavery   2, 74, 76, 93, 97, 98, 110, 172–77, 185

ancient Greece   157
  in films   177
  hunger as replacement for   78
  slaves as capital   103–4
Smith, Adam   20, 59, 91, 99, 103
smoking   50
SNAP. *See* food stamps
Snowden, Edward   71
"social action" (Weber)   8
social approval   8–9
social class. *See* class
social control   21–22, 23–23, 26, 31
social exchange theory   7–8
social groups   4, 10
  classes as   93
  Middle Ages   97
  primary groups.   6
  Simmel view   34n5. *See also* audiences; caste; crowds; virtual groups and communities
social integration   4, 8, 19
socialism and communism, spectacular. *See* spectacular socialism and communism
social isolation   36–37
social media, x   37, 40, 48, 51, 64
social mobility   10, 79, 87–88, 96, 97, 138
  in spectacular socialism   89–90
social norms. *See* norms
"social order" (Weber)   11–12
The Social Organization (Cooley)   6
social performance   35–36
social rituals, xi   7, 64
social roles   3–4, 7
social segmentation. *See* sociocultural segmentation
social status. *See* status
Social Structures of Direct Democracy (Asimakopoulos)   29
social values   4, 9, 10
social welfare programs. *See* welfare
sociocultural segmentation   37–40
Soon, Willie   55
Soviet Union   24, 31, 53, 62, 80, 81, 157
  production   89
  stagnation   77
space and time. *See* time and space
spatial segmentation   37–39
spectacle, xiii   17, 29–30, 33–37, 41, 47–48, 50, 79–86, 99

Baudrillard   28, 29
Debord   9, 23–26, 29, 31, 47, 53, 67, 79, 131
Hillary Clinton and   64
value and   99–100
of violence   70
spectacular socialism and communism   17, 62, 80, 88–90
spectatorship   31, 35, 36, 49, 62, 128–29
sports   40
sperm donation   116
spinning jenny   105
sports   40
stagnation (economics). *See* economic stagnation
"Stanford marshmallow test"   49
Starbucks   35–36, 175
Star Wars franchise   52
State University of New York (SUNY)   57
status   3, 12, 161, 166, 171
  consistency   11
  leisure and   128
  mobility   87
  Weber   11, 13, 14, 94. *See also* achieved status; ascribed status
Stirner, Max   9
stock market and stock ownership   59, 102, 144
structuralism   15–16, 21
student loans   43, 57, 107
suicide   37, 119, 137, 182
SUNY. *See* State University of New York (SUNY)
Supplemental Nutrition Assistance Program (SNAP). *See* food stamps
Supreme Court, U.S. *See* U.S. Supreme Court
surgery: organ trade and   115
  See also cosmetic surgery
surplus labor. *See* precarious labor (surplus labor)
surveillance   21–22, 71
sweatshop workers   172–73
Sweden   75
  eighteenth century   152, 154
  income inequality   151, 155, 157
  nobility   75, 152, 154, 159
  pre-industrial   87
  wealth inequality   149, 152, 154, 155, 156
symbolic institutions   54, 67. *See also* simulacra and simulation

symbolic interactionism   5–7, 11, 16, 24, 30
Syngenta   121, 122
SYRIZA   62

taxation   124, 143–46
  colonial   74
  corporate   84
  debtor nations   133
  deductions   118
  evasion   132, 143–44, 145
  Greece   127
  of inheritance   143
  international trade and   134
  Mundell view   133
  offshore havens   84, 132, 145
  prison labor and   175
  Tax Freedom Day   168
technology   48–49
  capitalism and   105–6
  caste and   33
  digital communications   128
  evolution of   30. *See also* automation; high-tech corporations; internet
teachers, college. *See* college teachers
Teffer, Peter   124
telecommunications companies   51
television   53, 64, 70, 141–42
Temple, William   77, 78
tenure (colleges and universities)   58, 61
terrorism   70–71, 187
Texas: public education policy and textbooks   180, 181, 182, 183
textbooks   179–83
texting   49, 128
Thanksgiving, invention of   181
Thessaloniki   126–27
think tanks   51, 55, 162
Thomas, William Isaac   6n7
"three strikes laws"   111
Tiananmen Square massacre, 1989. *See* China: Tiananmen Square massacre
Tillis, Thom   179
time and space   127–28
tobacco industry   50
Townsend, Joseph   78
trade   85, 132–33, 134–35
Trans-Pacific Partnership (TPP)   134
Trump, Donald   48, 52, 64, 140, 161

TV. *See* television
Twitter, x   48, 64
two-party system   61

undocumented worker detention centers   112, 175
unemployment   60–61
UNICOR   175
unions   58, 175, 176, 184
United Kingdom. *See* Britain
United Nations: carbon trading   124
United States, xi–xii   84
  "Americanization of finance"   133–34
  banking history   101
  breast milk monetization   112–13
  caste/inequality   60, 139–42, 146–48, 150, 153, 159–62
  Civil War   76
  cosmetic surgery   117
  criminal justice   110–12, 173–77
  financial collapse of 2008   60, 67–68, 101–2
  hair monetization   114
  health care   110
  higher education   42–43, 55–58, 139–40, 141
  history (study and teaching)   179–82
  ideological conformity in   52
  IMF role   132
  immigration detention   112
  income inequality   150, 156–57
  as international hegemon   131
  landownership   153
  military spending   120
  monetary policy   60, 100–102, 136
  nobility   162–64
  pollution   83
  poor people   41–45, 57, 65, 83, 111, 125, 169–77
  prescription drug prices   110
  presidential elections   48, 63, 64
  privileged labor   164–67
  racial caste   98–99
  Reconstruction   98
  ruling caste   159–62
  semi-periphery workers   168–69
  sex industry   118
  slavery   2, 76, 93, 97, 98, 185

social immobility   96
wages and benefits   117, 134
wealth inequality   148, 156
welfare   45, 145–46. *See also* African Americans; Federal Reserve; U.S. Congress; U.S. Constitution; U.S. Supreme Court
universities and colleges. *See* college education
upper middle class   42
U.S. Congress   45, 134
   drug price hearings   110
   elections and candidates   47, 178
   millionaires in   64
   public opinion   54. *See also* U.S. Senate
U.S. Constitution   49, 139
U.S. Federal Reserve. *See* Federal Reserve
U.S. Immigration and Customs Enforcement (ICE)   112
U.S. Senate   66, 179
   Judiciary Committee   68
USSR. *See* Soviet Union
U.S. Supreme Court   58–59, 63, 64, 109, 176–77

Valeant Pharmaceutical   110
Varoufakis, Yanis   127
Veblen, Thorstein   12, 26, 100, 128
Victoria's Secret   175
video games   49
villeins   167–68
violence: against elites, xiii   185, 186, 187
   by elites/state   24, 31, 68, 100, 101, 111
   normalization of   70
   See also war and wars
virtual currency. *See* electronic currency
virtual groups and communities   4, 34, 37
voting   46–47, 54, 65
   ancient Athens   18–19. *See also* elections

wages and wage labor   74, 78, 137
   debtor nations   133
   Greece   127
   international comparisons   134
   stratification of wages   85–86
   United States   117, 138
   wage garnishing   107
   Walmart   44, 84, 118, 129, 145–46, 175

Walt Disney Company   25, 28, 118
   See also Disneyland
war and wars   69, 106n91, 120, 182
water, commodification of   122–23
water contamination. *See* drinking water contamination
wealth distribution   52–53, 82, 147–49, 159–60, 162–64
   caste and   143
   China   88–89
   inheritance and   143, 146
The Wealth of Nations (Smith). *See An Inquiry into the Nature and Causes of the Wealth of Nations* (Smith)
wealthy people. *See* rich people
Weber, Max   8, 11–14, 30, 31, 32, 94, 100
   on class struggle origin   91
   influence on Castoriadis   17
   "iron cage"   21, 107n95
   on slave caste   172
   verstehen   16
   view of caste   74, 75
welfare   45, 145–46, 175–76, 179
whistle-blowers   48–49, 59, 71
White, Gregory   176
Whitman, Meg   63
Whole Foods   175
Wolf, Naomi   71–72
Wolff, Richard   46
workfare   175, 176
work hours   77
working classes: Baudrillard view   184
   college and   40, 87
   Marx view   95
   UK   141
   Volcker shock and   136
   William Temple view   78
workplace surveillance   22
World Bank   85, 123, 131–33
World Trade Organization (WTO)   85, 134, 135, 136
World War II   182

Yagoub, Mimi   117
Young, Arthur   77

Zerzan, John   9
Zuckerberg, Mark   160, 161

www.ingramcontent.com/pod-product-compliance
Lightning Source LLC
Chambersburg PA
CBHW071339080526
44587CB00017B/2889